Making

the Biblical History and Roots of

Alcoholics Anonymous

Dick B.'s Reference Titles on Alcoholics Anonymous History
Paradise Research Publications, Inc., Publisher;
Good Book Publishing Company, Distributor P.O. Box 837, Kihei, HI
96753-0837
Phone/Fax: (808) 874 4876; Email: dickb@dickb.com; URL:
http://www.dickb.com/index.shtml
**Publisher's December 1, 2005 List of Titles by Author Dick B.; All
list prices: Effective December 1, 2005**

Anne Smith's Journal, 1933-1939, 3rd ed.; 1998; 6 x 9; 180 pp.; $16.95
*By the Power of God: A Guide to Early A.A. Groups & Forming Similar
        Groups Today*; 2000, 6 x 9; 260 pp., $16.95
Cured!: Proven Help for Alcoholics and Addicts; 2003, 6 x 9; 182 pp.,
        $17.95
Dr. Bob and His Library, 3rd ed.; 1998; 6 x 9; 156 pp.; $15.95
God and Alcoholism: Our Growing Opportunity in the 21st Century;
        2002; 6 x 9; 190 pp.; $17.95
*Good Morning!: Quiet Time, Morning Watch, Meditation, and Early
        A.A.*; 2d ed.; 1998; 6 x 9; 154 pp.; $16.95
Henrietta B. Seiberling: Ohio's Lady with a Cause, Rev. ed.; 2004; 46
        pp.; 8 ½ x 11; spiral bound, $15.95
*Making Known The Biblical History and Roots of Alcoholics
        Anonymous: An Eleven-Year Research, Writing, Publishing and
        Fact Dissemination Project*, 2001, 160 pp., spiral bound, $24.95
New Light on Alcoholism: God, Sam Shoemaker, and A.A.; 2d ed.; 1999;
        6 x 9; 672 pp.; $24.95
The Akron Genesis of Alcoholics Anonymous, 2d ed.; 1998; 6 x 9; 400
        pp.; $17.95
The Books Early AAs Read for Spiritual Growth, 7th ed.; 1998; 6 x 9;
        126 pp.; $15.95
The First Nationwide A.A. History Conference - Comments of Dick B.,
        2003, 8 ½ x 11, 79 pp., spiral bound, $17.95
The Golden Text of A.A.: God, the Pioneers, and Real Spirituality; 1999;
        6 x 9; 76 pp.; $14.95
The Good Book and The Big Book: A.A.'s Roots in the Bible; 2d ed.;
        1997; 6 x 9; 264 pp.; $17.95
*The James Club: The Original A.A. Program's Absolute Essentials, 3rd
        ed.,* 2005; 6 x 9; $17.95
The Oxford Group & Alcoholics Anonymous, 2d ed.; 1998; 6 x 9; 432
        pp.; $17.95
That Amazing Grace (Clarence & Grace S.); 1996; 6 x 9; 160 pp.; $16.95

Turning Point: A History of Early A.A.'s Spiritual Roots and Successes; 1997; 6 x 9; 776 pp.; $29.95

Twelve Steps for You: Let Our Creator, A.A. History, and the Big Book Be Your Guide; 2003; 6 x 9; 90 pp. $17.95

Utilizing Early A.A.'s Spiritual Roots for Recovery Today; Rev. ed.; 1999; 6 x 9; 106 pp., $14.95

When Early AA s Were Cured and Why; 2003; 8 ½ x 11; spiral bound; 114 pp.; $17.95

Why Early A.A. Succeeded: The Good Book in Alcoholics Anonymous Yesterday and Today (a Bible Study Primer), 2001; 6 x 9; 340 pp., $17.95

Available through other distributors

Hope: The Story of Geraldine O. Delaney, 2d ed. NJ: Alina Lodge

Our Faith Community A.A. Legacy (Dick B., ed and compiler). FL: Came to Believe Publications

Courage to Change (with Bill Pittman). MN: Hazelden

Women Pioneers of AA (Dick B., contributor). MN: Hazelden

Making Known
the Biblical History and Roots of
Alcoholics Anonymous

A Sixteen-Year Research, Writing, Publishing, and Fact Dissemination Project

Dick B.

Paradise Research Publications, Inc.
Kihei, Maui, Hawaii

Paradise Research Publications, Inc.
P.O. Box 837, Kihei, HI 96753-0837
Ph/fax: 808 874 4876
URL: http://www.dickb.com/index.shtml;
Email: dickb@dickb.com

This Paradise Research Publications Edition is published by arrangement with Good Book Publishing Company, P.O. Box 837, Kihei, HI 96753-0837

Cover Design: Terry Dunford (American Creations of Maui)

The publication of this volume does not imply affiliation with nor approval or endorsement from Alcoholics Anonymous World Services, Inc.

ISBN: 1-885803-97-4

This particular edition is dedicated to Ray G., archivist at Dr. Bob's home. The picture on the cover page of this edition is a picture of Dr. Bob's home in Akron, Ohio, and was graciously provided to us by Ray.

To Bob J., who has made so much of this possible in his many acts of kindness and generosity, all directed to the end that others may receive our biblical history if they wish to, and then check it out for themselves, and to the further end of believing, recovering, and being delivered–just as so many A.A. pioneers themselves were able to do by relying on the Word and what it taught them about the power of our Creator, Yahweh..

Also to Bonnie and Ozzie Lepper, Managers of the Wilson House in East Dorset, Vermont, who put their faith in my work in 1995, extended to me the privilege of delivering annual Heritage History Seminars each year at the Wilson House, and then acquired the Griffith House (where Bill Wilson was raised by his grandfather) for the purpose of establishing a complete, accessible, library of A.A. and temperance history. Thanks also for their receiving, cataloguing, and shelving much of the historical materials described here and donated several benefactors to the Griffith House Library, adjacent to the Wilson House. As this Third Edition was going to print, Ozzie Lepper passed on; but he lived to see the placement of these materials in Griffith Library and the Grand Opening of that Library in 2005.

In specific remembrance of Anne Ripley Smith, wife of A.A. co-founder Dr. Bob. For Anne saw the importance of studying the Bible as the main "Source Book" and doing it daily. She also saw the particular importance of the Book of Acts and commended it as a starting point for Bible study. Here are two compelling segments from that very book of Acts:

And the brethren immediately sent away Paul and Silas by night unto Berea: who coming *thither* went into the synagogue of the Jews. These were more noble than those in Thessalonica, in that they received the word with all readiness of mind, and searched the scriptures daily, whether those things were so. Therefore many of them believed; also of honourable women which were Greeks, and of men, not a few (Acts 17:10-12).

Having therefore obtained help of God, I [Paul] continue unto this day witnessing both to small and great, saying none other things than those which the prophets and Moses did say should come. That Christ should suffer, *and* that he should be the first that should rise from the dead, and would shew light unto the people, and to the Gentiles (Acts 16:22-23).

Anne said:

We can't give away what we haven't got. We must have a genuine contact with God in our present experience. Not an experience of the past, but an experience in the present–actual, genuine. When we have that, witnessing to it is natural, just as we want to share a beautiful sunset (Dick B., *Anne Smith's Journal, 1933-1939*, 3rd ed., p. 134).

Contents

ix

Foreword

Sixteen years ago, I started reading and traveling and researching. The impetus was a horde of undocumented, badly distorted details about the origins of A.A. in the Bible. I'd never heard about any of this despite attendance at thousands of meetings, conferences, and Big Book and Step studies. So I started with the scanty material in Conference Approved literature and in the two or three history books that had already been written. Then I quickly found what one of my ardent supporters–a learned Roman Catholic priest–called a "lacuna." That means **gap**–hole–missing dimension, etc. And the sad fact, sixteen years ago, was that there were books galore on alcoholism, addictions, treatment, mental health matters, psychology and all the rest. But there was not one adequate rendition of the facts about A.A.'s spiritual roots. Yet A.A. was styling itself as a "spiritual" program. And, before that, as a "religious" program. So what had become of "religion" in a fellowship that had only recently begun talking incessantly about, and in psychobabble about, "any god," "not-god," "not-god-ness," "higher power" "spiritual but not religious," and all the other self-made religion that has been creeping into the declining "recovery" scene. A scene which today can only boast of a 5% recovery rate compared to the 75 to 93% rate in the formative years when AAs rightly claimed they had a cure!

The counterfeit idolatry could and can be seen even in the religious arena. You talk to a clergyman today, and he sometimes talks about everything but God–he frequently speaks of a higher power, etc. Even Rev. Sam Shoemaker, the Episcopal priest who became known as the co-founder began using the phrase "higher power" in his later writings.Same thing with your physician, psychologist, counselor, probation officer, professor, and all the rest. What had become of God? Of the Bible? Of Jesus Christ? Of the gift of the Holy Spirit? Why the counterfeit terms? What had become of "recovered?" Of cure? All the things that dominated the language of every single A.A. "founder" from even the New Thought people to William James, Carl Jung, Frank Buchman, Sam Shoemaker, Bob, Bill, Anne, Henrietta, T. Henry, Bill D., and Clarence S. Yet today, if you mention God or the Bible or Jesus Christ in an A.A. meeting, you have about a seventy-five percent chance of being verbally trounced. Ask any honest AA who attends meetings regularly.

Anyway, I won't cover all the places I've gone, the people I've interviewed, the books I've read, the correspondence and calls and emails I've exchanged, the archival material I've been able to copy, the books and manuscripts I've bought, and the key people in the Oxford Group, Shoemaker circle, early A.A., and history community I've gotten to know quite well.

The bottom line is that I had assembled, at last count, in excess of 24,000 plus books, papers, audios, videos, magazines, articles and just about everything that had anything to do with A.A.'s roots. This meant materials on the Bible, Quiet Time, William James, Carl Jung, William D. Silkworth, Rev. Sam Shoemaker, the Oxford Group, the Oxford Group mentors, Anne Smith, Dr. Bob, Henrietta Seiberling, T. Henry and Clarace Williams, religious books AAs read, and talks and writings by A.A. old-timers such as Geraldine Delaney, Clarence Snyder, Dr. Bob's kids, Bill Wilson's secretary, A.A.'s archivists, and so on.

I've now published twenty-six titles, an equal number of video tapes, audio talks, several sets of seminar tapes and talks, 120 plus articles on the internet, a new series of audio talks, and on and on. But I wanted my own resource materials available to believers and doubters alike. Available where these materials can be seen, copied, reproduced, placed on the internet and all kinds of media, taken to A.A. meetings and conferences, etc. That required and requires money.

So far, several generous benefactors have made it possible for a large chunk of my research books and papers to be placed in the Griffith House Library at Bill Wilson's birthplace in Vermont. Several others enabled equally large chunks to go to Calvary Episcopal Church in Pittsburgh. Another made it possible to place a smaller, but growing chunk in Dr. Bob's church in Akron. Still others have assembled traveling resource libraries which they can take around the A.A. world. Two or three others have collected and set up smaller libraries in Delaware, Pennsylvania, Massachusetts, and California. Here on Maui, we still have a core library which we are using and making available for articles, community television, online items, and visits. We want to see more happen. We believe this entire inventory will tell you what we have, its value, how it can be used, and where you can help. We hope you will acquire a collection, donate to a collection, own one, and present one to A.A. archives and other places where they can be researched and enjoyed.

The Plans and Projects to Disseminate our History

First, of course, came sixteen years of research to find a spiritual history that had almost become lost as to details and, where extant, was so distorted and filled with gaps that it has left the recovery movement in the dark for years as to early A.A.'s use of the Bible and reliance on Yahweh, the Creator of the heavens and the earth–our "Heavenly Father" as Dr. Bob called Him.

Next, the writing and **publishing of 25 historical titles** (not including this one) by Dick B.

Next, establishing our websites (http://www.dickb.com/index.shtml) (http://www.dickb-blog.com) (http://freedomranchmaui.org) This has become a surprisingly large part of our outreach. Now, the main site (dickb.com) has more than 415,000 visits and links to hundreds and hundreds of other websites, rings, directories, and search engines. All established since its 1995 inception. It can be found at the very top of most search engines and is the premier complete A.A. history site on the net. Add to this our audio talks, images, and articles at http://www.dickb-blog,com.

Next, we have provided free talks and presentations at dozens of conferences, panels, and seminars all over the United States, including Dick's address at Archives 2000, the A.A. International Convention in Minneapolis. Dick's Archives 2000 talk is online and in writing.

Next writing and posting free a series of articles on websites and in newspapers such as Anonymousone.com, aabibliography and history, aa-history.com, Sponsor to Sponsor, Recovery Life, NICD, silkworth.net, sober city, Bible Study Notes, Mental Health Matters, Living the Solution, and Recovering Times.

Next, filming more than 15 video segments for VCR's and television stations across the United States, already running on three Hawaiian community television outlets..

Next, came the inventory in this volume. More books and articles are still pouring into Maui. But our objective is to provide this resource for AAs, 12 Step people, the religious, treatment people, non-profit and government agencies, scholars, historians, archivists, and collectors–all to the end of making our history known. Benefactors have now enabled distribution of most of the 23, 900 historical items to the places indicated..

If there is one group of questions that dominates all others, it is this: **Whatever happened in A.A. to Almighty God, our Creator, whose name is Yahweh**? What ever happened to His Son Jesus Christ, the gift of the Holy Spirit, the great truths of the best selling book of all time–the Good Book? What happened? And how can we get people to restore the power of God and a knowledge of the Bible to the recovery scene. To know about it! To utilize it if they so choose. Prior to 1935, nothing had worked effectively–not Prohibition, Temperance, pledges, anti-saloon leagues, mental institutions, probation, parole, correctional institutions, treatment centers, therapy, wars. Yet our Creator was waiting to be called, just as He is today, and can, if sought, respond with forgiveness, healing, deliverance, and guidance.

As stated, most of our collection is now at Griffith House Library, at the birthplace of A.A. Founder Bill Wilson in Vermont. We could use tax deductible donations to provide more items there. Some of our collection is now at St. Paul's Church in Akron, the birthplace of A.A. We could use tax deductible contributions to add to that church library at Dr. Bob's Church. A unique and complete collection, called "The Shoemaker Collection" is now situated in the Shoemaker Room at Calvary Episcopal Church in Pittsburgh. A very substantial collection known as the "Co-founders Collection"–including all of "Dr. Bob's Library" which consists of six shelves—has just been placed in the Griffith Library. We could use help in expanding donations to The Wilson House, in starting other traveling collections, and in placing more materials on TV, at conferences, on tapes, and particularly online. Your contribution to enable this to happen should be made payable to St. Paul's Church in Akron and mailed to Dick B., PO Box 837, Kihei, HI 96753-0837. Any amount is welcome.

Making Known the Biblical History and Roots of Alcoholics Anonymous

A Sifteen-Year Research, Writing, Publishing, and Fact Dissemination Project

Dick B.

This master inventory of papers, letters, audio and video cassette tapes, pictures, books, pamphlets, and articles has been prepared in love and as a service to those who have so long sought and wanted unhindered access to the history of the spiritual development of Alcoholics Anonymous. Some of the important topics upon which items in this inventory shed light include:

- Dr. Bob's youthful experiences in St. Johnsbury, Vermont and Christian Endeavor.
- The unusual introduction of New Thought ideas from Mary Baker Eddy to William James to Emmet Fox.
- The life-changing practices of Frank Buchman's A First Century Christian Fellowship (also known as The Oxford Group, and later as Moral Re-Armament)
- Rowland Hazard's encounter with Dr. Carl Jung.
- Rev. Sam Shoemaker's special work and influence on Bill Wilson.
- Anne Smith's role as the "Mother of A.A." and her spiritual journal
- The Quiet Time practices, Bible study, prayer, guidance, and devotional explorations in Akron.
- The Christian and other religious literature A.A. pioneers read.
- The Big Book's publication in 1939.

- The astonishing achievements in the pioneer A.A. fellowships from 1935 to the early 1940's.
- The resultant documented 75 to 93% success rate among "medically incurable alcoholics" who really tried for deliverance and truly placed their reliance for help on our Creator, whom Bill Wilson called God Almighty, our Maker, Father of Light, and God of our fathers; and Dr. Bob simply called our God of love and Heavenly Father.
- The extensive contributions of Clarence H. Snyder to the growth of early A.A.

Summary of Items in our Original Inventory

Pages of Historical Papers, Letters, Articles, and other items:

Video Cassette Tapes (estimate)

Audio Cassette Tapes (estimate)

Framed Pictures and Photographs (estimate)

Historical Books, Booklets, Articles

Total Number of Items in Our Original Inventory

Note: Thanks to continuing and recent acquisitions, the historical materials were increased from Dick B.'s own original 9,590 pages of research materials to 18,390. And from his original 943 books, pamphlets, and articles to 4,179. This has enabled us to plan for placing appropriate and selected books, tapes, pictures, and other items in several libraries and centers by allocating to each some duplicates and also some special items of interest to the particular library or center or to its likely audiences.

Allocated in Appropriate Groupings to the Following Centers:

- The Griffith House Library, Bill Wilson's birthplace,

East Dorset, Vermont
- The St. Paul's Episcopal Church (Dr. Bob's Church) A.A. History Library, Akron, Ohio
- Calvary Episcopal Church in Pittsburgh, Pennsylvania (Shoemaker's second church)
- One or two additional centers located in Delaware, Hawaii, and California

Our Vision

We are planning for, attempting to fund, and desirous of placing allocated portions of our inventory in the following libraries and centers with the indicated, anticipated audiences:

The Maui Historical Resource & Recovery Center

This was a core collection to be used for continuing research, programs, teaching conferences, and internet resource dissemination for alcoholics, addicts, families, youth, and visitors.

The Griffith House Library in East Dorset, Vermont

The Library itself is now located in the home where Bill Wilson was raised by his grandfather and is adjacent to the Wilson House where Bill was born and is near the cemetery where Bill and Lois Wilson are buried. Thousands visit these sites each year. Many stay at the non-profit inn at The Wilson House. Others attend A.A. and 12 Step meetings, Big Book Studies, Seminars, and Quiet Time meetings there. And still others celebrate there events such as Bill Wilson's birthday. Although there are presently many books in the library, we intend to place in the library and archives whatever additional books and historical materials (and they are many in number) are needed to assure that this library contains the complete spiritual history and roots of Alcoholics Anonymous and 12 Step programs in the Bible, Quiet Time, the teachings of Rev. Sam Shoemaker, the life-changing program of the Oxford Group, Anne Smith's Journal, and the large amount of Christian and other religious materials early AAs and their families read.

The Samuel M. Shoemaker Collection in Pittsburgh

Reverend Sam Shoemaker was called by Bill Wilson a co-founder of A.A. and the well-spring of its spiritual ideas. Sam concluded his long and illustrious career as rector of Pittsburgh's Calvary Episcopal Church. Sam challenged Pittsburgh leaders to make the city as famous for God as it was for steel. And the community has continued to meet the challenge through various organizations such as The Pittsburgh Experiment, the Pittsburgh Leadership Foundation, and a host of churches and charitable agencies. Many in Pittsburgh and particularly former Penn State Professor Karen Plavan, Ph.D., have worked with me for years to see Sam's works lodged in his own former church. The center there contains a premium collection of alcoholism, alcoholism history, 12 Step spiritual history, and treatment items open to 12 Step people; the religious, medical, therapy, and treatment communities; concerned non-profit agencies; businesses; government agencies; and the general public. All as influenced by Shoemaker. The library will be free, accessible, and open for study and reading, and be a foundation for future conferences and meetings on alcoholism, addiction, and other life-controlling problems of concern to Pittsburgh.

The A.A. History Library at St. Paul's Episcopal Church, Akron, Ohio

For sixteen years, St. Paul's Episcopal Church in Akron, its rector The Rev. Dr. Richard McCandless, and his secretary Marcheta Scott have supported my work, by receiving contributions, keeping account of benefactions, and facilitating research, travel, libraries, publishing, and media dissemination. All to the end that people will understand the Biblical roots of Alcoholics Anonymous–the unique Society born in Akron, Ohio. The original A.A. Christian Fellowship that took its basic ideas from the Bible. Akron pioneers encouraged Bible study, prayer, and reading of Christian literature. They insisted on surrender to Jesus Christ as Lord and Saviour. Their group was called a "Christian Fellowship" by Dr. Bob and many others. It often seemed much like an "old fashioned prayer meeting" and a fellowship like those in the Book of Acts. Yet Akron has been a dry spot when people wanted to see the history. For a long time, there was nothing. Then in later times, there was an intentional exclusion of most of the relevant religious history. More recently, some of it has appeared in Akron but under lock and key, unable to be copied or studied, and bearing little fruit for the visitors. Of late, the Seiberling Gate Lodge where Henrietta Seiberling hosted the six hour meeting of Bill Wilson and Dr. Bob, has become a new and open Akron resource of limited size. The St. Paul's collection is one of the most important repositories in the world when it comes to the history of A.A.'s biblical roots. Now, the church has established a library for the collection.

Additional Libraries and Centers

When first written, we stated, we still had three basic parts of our original collection: (1) The complete "Dr. Bob's Library." (2) A complete "Shoemaker Collection." (3) My own small core collection still being used as a resource for writing and for the internet postings. Now, the first has become "The Co-Founders Collection" and has, almost in its entirety, been placed at Griffith Library. The second has become "The Shoemaker Collection" and is located in Shoemaker's second church—Calvary Episcopal Church in Pittsburgh in the Shoemaker Room. The core collection, though small, remains in Maui where it is used for my ongoing research and writing.

Internet, Television, Radio, and Media Interactions

Plans are already in the making to link Maui, The Wilson House, and other locations to make available world-wide the materials available at these libraries and centers.

Overview of the Master Inventory

Part 1
Historical Research Papers, Letters, Pictures, and Tapes

The collections of Dick B., George Vondermuhll, Danny Whitmore, Dennis Cassidy, plus special, rare items.

Part 2

Books and Materials on, about, or by, A.A.

A.A. conference-approved literature, materials on or about A.A. (both for and against A.A.).

Part 3
Historical Books, Articles, and Pamphlets on
the Spiritual Origins and Principles of Alcoholics Anonymous

Items on the Bible, Quiet Time, Sam Shoemaker, the Oxford Group, early Christian mentors, Dr. Bob and Anne Smith, and the Christian and religious literature the pioneers read.

Part 4
Materials on Abstinence, Temperance, Prohibition,
the Washingtonian Movement, the Anti-Saloon League, and the
WCTU

Temperance Movement, Anti-Saloon League, Washingtonians, Prohibition, WCTU, Government

Part 5
Books and Articles about Alcoholism, Alcoholics, Addicts.

Items on alcoholics, alcoholism, histories about alcohol, works of scholars, manuals, medicine, and treatment modes

Part 6
Historian, Archivist, A.A., and other Donor Collection Sources

Where, how, and from whom our collections have been obtained over the past ten years.

Part 7

Sylmar, California
40 Binders (4"each) of Historical Materials, approximately 8,800 Items
2,171 Books, Pamphlets, and Articles
3 Large Boxes of Audio Cassette Tapes
2 Large Boxes of Pictures and Photograph

Part 1
Historical Research Papers, Letters, Pictures, and Tapes

Manuscripts, Correspondence, and Papers in Dick B.'s Personal Files

For more than sixteen years, Dick has gathered, purchased, or been given materials from the sources, among others, that are specified above. These materials, for the most part, have not been published. They are the heart of the evidentiary matter poured into Dick's twenty-six published titles on A.A. history. These are the items to which scholars can look for further research ideas, for documentation of statements, for leads, for criticism, for information, and for their own publishing work. The materials have not been copyrighted by Dick B. and are presented for the benefit and use of those pursuing accurate information about early A.A.'s roots in the Bible and its other spiritual sources and ideas

Materials Gathered from Archives

Stepping Stones Archives, Bedford Hills, New York [Stepping Stones is the former home of Bill and Lois Wilson and is managed by a foundation.] (Total Number of Pages: 323)

History of the Alcoholic/ The Alcoholic Foundation (6 pages);

August 11, 1938, 5 loose pages and 1 polaroid picture

Main Events. Alcoholics Anonymous (79 pages)

Handwritten outline and promotional data on proposed
Big Book (8 pages)

The original story group of names in Bill's hand and with
comments (4 pages)

Typewritten Outline of 25 proposed chapters of the Big
Book, plus a typewritten copy of Bill's original
"Chapter # 1 There Is a Solution" [second chapter
in actual Big Book that was printed] (13 pages)

Bill's own History from 1934 to 1941 [with intro called
W.G. Wilson Recollections] (34 pages)

Plus copies of Lois Wilson's Oxford Group Notes, Bill's
statement of faith in God, Bill's letter to Leonard
Strong stating he had religion, S. Shoemaker to
Bill (1935), Letter to Ruth Hock, notes from
Lois's diary about Oxford Group people she and
Bill had met. List of attendance at February 8th
Rockefeller dinner, and other letters. (20 pages)

Early A.A letters, diaries, memos of Bill and Lois Wilson (30
pages).

John Henry Fitzhugh Mayo story [became "Our Southern
Friend"] - 143 numbered lines

Lois Wilson's 1937 diary, Bill's handwritten letter to Sam
Shoemaker, Letter to McGhee Baxter in 1940
containing Bill's Oxford Group objections

Dick B.'s notes of what he found and what he copied at
his archive visits

Loose manuscript papers by Bill W.

Bill Wilson's Original Story and other papers (208 pages)

The Original Story in Bill's own hand [lines numbered 1
through 1180] (35 pages)

W. G. Wilson's Recollections [manila folder containing
"Bedford" Manuscript] (139 pages)

Bill's letter to Lois [2 copies] (6 pages)

Carl Jung to Bill Wilson, 1961 (1 page)

Miscellaneous letters from Bill's mother, Bob, Bill (10

pages)

Wilson to Carl Jung, 1961 (4 pages)

Notes on the original stories and data to be included in
Big Book (4 pages)

Miscellaneous letters and notes (9 pages)

A.A. Archives at General Service Office, New York (Total number of
pages: 112)

Transcripts of tapes of A.A. Pioneers (14 pages)

Bill Wilson interviews of Wally Gillam and Wally and
Annabel Gillam [Wally's story became "Fired
Again"]

Wilson interview of J. D. Holmes

Wilson interview of Dorothy Snyder Murphy [Clarence
Snyder's story became "Home Brewmeister"]

Interviews of Henrietta Dotson, Earl Treat, William Van
Horn [Bill Dotson's story became "Alcoholic
Anonymous Number Three" in the 3rd edition;
Earl Treat's story became "He Sold Himself
Short;" and William Van Horn's story became "A
Ward of the Probate Court"]

Peebles interview of Alex Marcona

Duplicates of Gillam and Holmes interviews

General Service Visit Records, and other letters and articles (14
pages)

Policy Statements, etc.

Letter of support from A.A.'s second archivist Frank
Mauser

Clippings and letters of retirement and then the death of
Frank Mauser

AA Grapevine issue, 1947 (6 pages)

3

Letter from Barry Leach, Ph.D. re spiral bound copy of Alcoholics Anonymous with corrections including those by Hank Parkhurst, dated April 10, 1979 [Parkhurst's story became "The Unbeliever"] (1 page)

Copies of Box 459 Newsletter from GSO, dated August/September, 1978 on "Conference Approved" and what that expression means, plus two letters from Al-Anon's archivist (8 pages)

Dick B.'s Notes of transcripts of T. Henry and Clarace Williams, Al L., Abby Golrick and other oldtimers previously mentioned above (31 pages)

Notes of talks with, and suggestions of, Frank Mauser, request of GSO for records, comments of Nell Wing about the large number of papers she took from Episcopal Archives in Texas, ltr to Larry Nelson (14 pages)

Dick B.'s penciled notes of what was found on first visit to GSO: letters of Wilson, Nell Wing memos, time lines, books in GSO library, Ruth Hock letter (24 pages)

Founders Day Archives and Founders Day Archivist's notes and records. (Total Number of Pages: 89)

Notes from Dr. Bob's Home; Mel B.'s drafts on Oxford Group & Frank Buchman, 2 pages on Golden Anniversary of A.A.'s founding, and Ciccolini's "Duet of Jesus Christ and Sister Ignatia" (54 pages)

David Adams's pictures of Sue Windows, Akron historical places, Dr. Bob's Home, Frank Buchman's birthplace and library; reproduction of "final draft of Chapter Five" as it appeared in 1938 from the AA Intergroup Office in Akron; copy of 8 page statement of Henrietta Dotson about her husband Bill who was AA # 3 (35 pages)

The Archives of the Episcopal Church USA, Austin, Texas (Total Number of Pages: 309)

Official Indices of the Archives (15 pages)

Entire body of Shoemaker records (out of fifty-eight boxes) copied at and taken from the archives, and including list of Oxford Group people and Metropolitan Team; Oxford Group reading list; letters to and from Eleanor Forde, Rowland Hazard, Philip Marshall Brown, F. Shepard Cornell; invitations to Oxford Group events; reports on OG events; Russell Firestone correspondence; correspondence of Sam with Bill Wilson; correspondence with Woolverton and A.A. over archival material taken from the church archives; correspondence with Oxford Group leaders and clergy; correspondence with Nell Wing; and extensive correspondence over Roman Catholic editing of AA Comes of Age and Twelve Steps and Twelve Traditions. Also over Bill's interest in LSD and spiritualism (294 pages)

Calvary Episcopal Church (Total Number of Pages: 301)

New York City. Church of which Sam was rector (132 pages)

The Calvary Evangel for May, 1930, plus numerous Oxford Group invitations and announcements (30 pages)

Folder: List of Shoemaker sermons; Summary of Shoemaker personal journal entries re Bill Wilson; notes of Dick B. visit to Calvary Church; Shoemaker's January 1935 letter to Bill Wilson; Numerous issues of Calvary Evangel for 1930's; articles and photos on Calvary Rescue Mission; Dick's Notes on visit to NYU to locate work of Thomas H. Uzzell, who edited the Big Book for Wilson (28 pages)

Letter from Ray Mews concerning untruth of "anointing with oil" story about early surrenders (5 pages)

Picture from October, 1928, showing Shoemaker's procession from Calvary Church to Madison Square [a procession in which Bill W. and Parks Shipley later participated] (1 page)

Various copies from Evangel and other notes from Sinclair Hart [SMS] (8 pages)

Priority Mail Folder containing numerous pamphlets about Calvary Episcopal Church in New York, Rowland Hazard's participation in church activities, and Shoemaker's annotated notes and Scripture references on "Finding God," December 12, 1937; the two eviction letters of 1941 in which Buchman and the Oxford Group were ordered out of Calvary (60 pages)

Pittsburgh, PA. Church of which Sam was rector after leaving New York City (169 pages)

Materials and letters from Wm. Anderson re Pittsburgh Edition of Dick B. book (4 pages)

Pamphlet on Dick B.'s talks in Pittsburgh and work with Rev. Dave Else on Shoemaker (119 pages)

Pamphlet, Common Crisis Roots Recovery from Rev. Dave Else (7 pages)

Ramada Folder with notes on Dick B.'s interview of "golf club crowd" and other work with, and talks for the Pittsburgh Leadership Foundation, Bishop Duncan, Fr. Geisler, and rector of Calvary (35 pages)

Blue Pittsburgh Experiment folder with Dick B. research notes (4 pages)

Hartford Seminary Archives, Hartford, Connecticut (Total Number of pages: 21)

Dick B.'s Notes on acquisitions from archives (1 page)

Folder: Notices regarding Frank Buchman; houseparties; letters from and to seminary officials; and loose articles (18 pages)

Hartford Seminary Catalog (2 pages)

Princeton University Archives (Total Number of Pages 60)

Dick B.'s Notes on Seeley G. Mudd Manuscript Library Contents [Shoemaker] (2 pages)

Dr. David Sack's Article of June, 1933, titled: "Sam Shoemaker and the "Happy Ethical Pagans" (58 pages)

Materials Gathered on or about A.A. "Founders"

Bill Wilson Materials (Total Number of Pages: 325)

Folder Number One: Copies of correspondence to and from Bill re the Oxford Group, Roman Catholics, the Sixth Step, Shoemaker, and Father Dowling; Letter from Wilson to Jack Alexander of 1941; Photo of Thomas Thetcher tombstone (the subject of the Doggeral in Bill's Story; Pamphlet by Charles J. Sigler titled: "Good Fruit of Bad Fruit?: The Pragmatic Roots of A.A. in Williams James." (27 pages)

Folder Number Two: Bill's materials on the Rockefeller Dinner and guests; Correspondence from Bill to Clarence Snyder; from Bill's Secretary Nell Wing to Dorothy Snyder (in duplicate), and from Bill's lady friend Helen Wynn to Dorothy Snyder on Bill's own stationary (12 pages)

Catalog: "The Bill Wilson Public Talks" (37 pages)

Folder Number Three: Bill's two articles in tribute to Rev. Sam Shoemaker and Rev. W. Irving Harris and his wife Julia Harris concerning their great contributions to A.A.'s "spiritual edifice." Article from *Time Magazine* of 1999 titled: "The Healer Bill W." Photo inscribed to Lois Wilson by Father Ed Dowling and depicting Bill and Father Dowling at dinner (6 pages)

A Few Yarns, transcript of a 1954 chat with Bill W., 1954 (13 pages)

Bill Wilson & The Vitamin B-3 Therapy, 1965-1971 by Bishop of Books (105 pages)

Bill Wilson's "White Light" Experience as described in various publications (10 pages)

Folder Number Four: Dick B.'s Notes on Sam Shoemaker's personal journal entries re Bill Wilson between 1934 and 1936; A.A. Tradition Pamphlet; Bill's letters re Oxford Group; Obits on Bill; Time article on Bill of 1971; Sam and Bill Program on The Mountain Top in which Dick B. was keynote speaker; Wilson on Emotional Sobriety; News article of March 26, 1943 in which Bill and Dr. Bob spoke of A.A. as religious and Bible study was urged; email on influences on Bill; transcript of Bill's 1954 Texas speech on "How the Big Book Was Put Together," Photo of Sam Shoemaker's personal journal specifically referring to Bill Wilson; Brooklyn pamphlet on how A.A. began; photo of Bill and Lois Wilson; article on Bill W.'s death and on Sam Shoemaker's "How to Find God;" part of Bill's letter on Anne Smith's death soliciting gratitude letters about Anne; Excerpts from Nell Wing's book and Pass It on re where A.A. came from; Extract of Bill's editing of original manuscript for Chapter 5 [personal notes in his hand] (110 pages);

Article by Bill W.: "Basic Concepts of Alcoholics Anonymous," May, 1944 (5 pages)

Dr. Robert H. Smith (Dr. Bob) Materials (Total Number of Pages: 200)

Folder Number One: Inscription from Bill to Bob in book given to Bob Xmas, 1956; memo re acquisition of Dr. Bob's Home; copy of Los Angeles talk by Bob and Bill in March, 1943 (in duplicate); Letter to Dr. Bob listing authors of each of the stories in the First Edition; Dr. Bob Obit (6 pages)

Folder Number Two: Pages from Co-Founder Pamphlet on Dr. Bob and the Bible (58 pages)

Folder Number Three: Pages from Dr. Bob and the Good Oldtimers on Sermon on the Mount as underlying philosophy of A.A., plus spiritual materials read , prayer, quiet time (30 pages)

Folder Number Four: Nell Wing's notes written on Dr. Bob manuscript (50 pages)

Folder Number Five: Photo of the Smiths, the Wilsons, Burwell, Ruth Hock, and two others taken in 1941 in New York; Article in remembrance of Dr. Bob; Materials written to and received from oldtimer Larry Bauer re James 5:16, Clarence Snyder and the early days; Larry Bauer's roster of Cleveland meetings in 1942; pictures of Dr. Bob's signature and remarks in part of his library that he loaned out and recommended and requested return of; Extract from Rufus Moseley book Perfect Everything owned by Dr. Bob (55 pages)

Folder Number Six: Wesley Parish letter re Dr. Bob's Home (1 page)

Anne Ripley Smith (Dr. Bob's Wife) Materials (Total Number of Pages: 250)

Tribute to Anne Smith (3 pages)

Anne Smith's Spiritual Journal [obtained by Dick B. from A.A. GSO Archives through archivist Frank Mauser and letter of Sue Smith Windows to Trustees' Archives Committee] (65 pages)

Folder Number One: Copies of pages from Anne's address book containing the names and addresses of several pioneers such as Bob Evans, Ernie Gerig, J.D. Holmes, Roland Jones, Bill Van Horn, Earl Treat, Bob Oviatt, and Tom Lucas (9 pages)

Folder Number Two Copies of the personal collection of Dr. Bob's and Anne's daughter-in-law Betty Smith (wife of Robert Smith) containing the letters about and tributes to Anne Ripley Smith and her A.A. role at the time of her death and at the request of Bill W. (70 pages)

Folder Number Three: Copies of the items at the back of the copy of Anne Smith's Journal located at Stepping Stones and including Soul Surgery, Shoemaker's "What if I had but one Sermon to Preach," Shoemaker's Three Levels of Life and a note in Anne's hand (30 pages)

Folder Number Four: Dick B.'s notes on interview of Betty Smith about her mother-in-law Anne Smith; two pages from Smitty's copy of Anne's Journal; copy of letter sent by Anne to John Seiberling; letter of appreciation from Anne Smith in her hand; and Anne Smith obit (8 pages)

Folder Number Five: Exact copy of Anne Smith's Journal transmitted from GSO to Dick B. and containing the page numbers of GSO archives (65 pages)

Henrietta Seiberling Materials (Total Number of Pages: 185)

John F. Seiberling Letter re the early books his mother read (1 page)

Dick B. Notes on phone interviews with John and Dorothy Seiberling on their mother (1 page)

Children of the Mayflower pamphlet as tribute to Henrietta, 1985 (7 pages)

Dick B.'s Letters to Seiberlings re their mother (6 pages)

Dick B.'s Outline of Henrietta Biography, notes to John Seiberling, and Willard Hunter notes on tape of Henrietta by Willard (10 pages)

Biography of Henrietta Buckler Seiberling written by Dick B. and approved by John Seiberling (11 pages)

Extensive personal notes of Dick B.'s interview of John Seiberling at his office at Akron University during a Founders Day celebration in Akron (13 pages)

Red Folder: Copies of personal notes in Henrietta's Bible obtained from Dorothy Seiberling, Henrietta's daughter; Signed statement of Dorothy Seiberling to Richard G. Burns in 1991; notes on interview of Dorothy by Dick B. at Dorothy's Town House in Manhattan; Transcript of Remarks of Henrietta B. Seiberling while John was a member of Congress. Letters from Dick B. to Dorothy and to Mary Seiberling Huhn, Henrietta's other daughter (40 pages)

Mary Seiberling Huhn Folder detailing her mother's reading with Dick B. correspondence and notes on phone interview (9 pages)

Page 344 from Dick B.'s first manuscript on "Henrietta Seiberling's Spiritual Infusion" (1 page)

Pamphlet from John Seiberling on his work in bringing USSR reps to US (8 pages)

John Seiberling Folder Number One: Primarily from John to Dick re Henrietta (35 pages)

John Seiberling Folder Number Two: Obits and other items; Ohio Women's Hall of Fame; Mrs. F.A. Seiberling; 1934 news articles; John Seiberling's search for indications of Sam Shoemaker's presence in Akron in 1934; other letters to Dick B.; tape transcript of Henrietta's "Origins of Alcoholics Anonymous" (43 pages)

T. Henry and Clarace Williams Materials (Total Number of Pages: 135)

Folder Number One: Correspondence of Dick B. and Dorothy Williams Culver—T. Henry's daughter (55 pages)

Letters from T. Henry and Clarace to Bill Wilson in 1935 and 1937 re program (5 pages)

Benjamin Forbes Pamphlet on T. Henry and Clarace, 1976 (17 pages)

Culver to Burns envelope (1 page)

Transcript of interview of Dorothy Culver (daughter of T. Henry) by T. Willard Hunter (40 pages)

Folder Number Two: Tributes to T. Henry and Clarace Williams (17 pages)

Rev. Samuel M. Shoemaker, Jr. Materials (Total Number of Pages: 217)

Letter from Rev. Sinclair Hart re Cleve Hicks, Vic Kitchen, and houseparties (1 page)

Extract "Lord, Teach Us To Pray," by Dr. Samuel M. Shoemaker (6 pages)

Addiction and Spirituality Pamphlet, 1992 (4 pages)

Photos and negatives of Sam Shoemaker (3 pages)

Manila Envelope: The Philadelphian Society with letters from Howard and Margaret Blake on the demise of the Christian organization at Princeton University (125 pages)

James D. Newton letters re Sam (2 pages)

Folder Number One: Picture of Sam as tribute from Bill Wilson; plus Dick B. notes of interview with Nickie Shoemaker Haggart on her father; plus notes of Dick B. on contents of Sam's personal journal relating to Bill Wilson (12 pages)

Folder Number Two: Exact typewritten summary of Shoemaker Journals from 1933 to 1935 as examined by Dick B. and Ken Burns in the home of Nickie Shoemaker Haggart (8 pages)

Folder Number Three: Copy of Sam Shoemaker's First Radio Talk in 1935 "Good Morning"; Oxford Group reading list; photostats of Sam's personal journals re Bill Wilson and Sam's spiritual experience and other Wilson/Shoemaker/OG friends; and 3 photos of Dick B., Shoemaker's daughters, and Willard Hunter (40 pages)

Folder Number Four: Copy of Billy Duvall letter re Bill's Conversion at Rescue Mission; Memos re Shoemaker and Ohio OG work; article on Shoemaker and Wilson; article on Rescue Mission; Sam's letter to Bill; news articles; and Bruce Washburn memos on Sam's address to the 1960 A.A. International Convention at Long Beach (16 pages)

Materials Gathered Concerning A.A.'s Spiritual Sources

Dr. Frank N. D. Buchman [Founder of the Oxford Group] (Total Number of Pages 217)

Inventory of Frank Buchman's Library, Lehigh County, PA (38 pages)

Lehigh County Historical Society Letter and news items re "Bible House Party (8 pages)

Blue-type: Christian Counter-attack (3 pages)

Frank Buchman Folder: Early letters (20 pages)

Miscellaneous Buchman papers from Hartford Seminary and incl. Billy Sunday letters (16 pages)

Schwenkfelder Church Folder (35 pages)

Early letters re Frank Buchman: Rev. Purkies and Bob Barstow (3 pages)

Early memo of Lt. Col D. Forrester on "willingness" idea (4 pages)

Library of Congress Inventory of Buchman, Ray Purdy, Moral Re-Armament items (13 pages)

Akron Beacon Journal Folder of Key Events in 1933 involving Dr. Buchman, the Oxford Group, Henrietta Seiberling,

Anne Smith, their two lady friends, Rev. Tunks, Harvey and Russell Firestone (77 pages)

Other Oxford Group Materials. (Total Number of Pages: 361)

Letters and data to Dick B. from OG writer Dr. Robin Mowat of Oxford (19 pages)

"A.A. Roots in the Oxford Group" by Willard Hunter with M.D.B. (incomplete article, 6 pages)

Letter to Dick B. from OG Leader Richard Hadden and article on Peter Howard (2 pages)

Invitations to Houseparties in 1928 at Northhampton and Annapolis (9 pages)

Invitations to Houseparties at Salem, Mass and at Briarcliff Lodge, with program and Bible-study agenda (10 pages)

Dick B. notes on George Vondermuhll, Jr. interview (5 pages)

Miscellaneous papers from 1931-33 houseparties and Parks Shipley article (7 pages)

Letter from Elmer Keith in Switzerland to Baylor, dated December 28, 1929, regarding Dr. Carl Jung, Dr. Frank Buchman and his fellowship, on an experience of God, sharing, and "power" from above (6 pages)

Oxford Group Housparties at Ashville, N.C. and Boston (8 pages)

Philip Hart memo (1 page)

People to People Therapy by John W. Drakeford (34 pages)

Extract from *The Eight Points of The Oxford Group* by C. Irving Benson (12 pages)

Book-Cadillac Invitation to Oxford Group (4 pages)

How to Listen [pamphlet from Akron A.A. Group] (2 pages)

Copy of Oxford Group *America Awake* Poster (1 page)

Miscellaneous papers on the Oxford Group and various OG houseparties (32 pages)

The Guidance of God by Eleanor Napier Forde (30 pages)

Oxford Group Movement: Is It of God Or Is It an Anglo-Catholic Movement? (11 pages)

Charles H. Haines Folder (8 pages)

James Houck, Sr. Folder (35 pages)

Michael Hutchinson Folder (42 pages)

Mary Lean Folder (*For a Change* Magazine and 7 pages)

The Role of Moral Re-Armament in the Self Help Movement by Willard Hunter (14 pages)

Articles on Garth D. Lean and by Willard Hunter (4 pages)

Folder of Dick B. Correspondence with Oxford Group Leaders throughout the world (59 pages)

Moral Re-Armament (MRA) Materials (Total Number of Pages: 576)

James Houck: "Going the Distance" article on Houck, A.A., MRA (1 page)

Charles Huston Haines (obit) early Buchman associate at Princeton, last of "3 troubadours" (1 page)

Caux: illustrated pamphlet, given Dick B. by Kenneth Belden (51 pages)

Folder Number One: Letter from Executive Director of MRA; Breakthroughs pamphlet of MRA; Democracy pamphlet; two pictures of The Minute Man and Minute Maids; Several "For a Change, " MRA, and MRA Pictorial magazines; What is MRA pamphlet; Caux Conference Center pamphlet; Caux Scholars Program pamphlet; MRA (Winter, 1961) "March to Victory;" Music score; Pictures; "Crowning Experience; " "Turning the Tide;" "New World News" (296 pages)

Folder Number Two: Dick B. Correspondence with Richard W. B. Ruffin, James Houck; Mary Lean; The Oxford Group Connection; Memoriam for and correspondence re J. Terence Blair; Correspondence with Sydney Cook, Michael Henderson; New Yorker Article of James Houck; Dick B. Article in For a Change; several copies of Breakthroughs and For A Change; Data on MRA and Oxford Group Offices throughout the world; Mitchell Klein charges and his subsequent apology to Dick B. and Richard Ruffin (227 pages)

James Draper and Eleanor Napier Forde Newton Materials (Total Number of Pages: 88)

St. Paul's Episcopal Church in Akron: Dr. Bob's last church, the church of the Firestones, and the church of Dr. Walter Tunks–the church which built its new edifice on the Firestone estate with Jim Newton as head of the fund-raising committee (13 pages)

Jim Newton and the Boy Scouts of America (22 pages)

Napkin (1 page)

Rough chronology [1905 to 1925] (4 pages)

St. Paul's Episcopal Church [Akron] pamphlet (13 pages)

Loose pages: "The New Witness" and Miss Eleanor Napier Forde [Newton] "The New Womanhood" (2 pages)

Notes from Jim Newton's own diary in 1931 corroborating the details in Sam Shoemaker's personal journals concerning the trip from Akron to Denver and back on the train, in which Russell Firestone was led to Christ by Sam and miraculously recovered from alcoholism (3 pages)

More notes and chronology (14 pages)

Clippings from Ellie Forde Newton's 100th birthday in Florida (5 pages)

M.R.A. magazine page honoring Ellie Newton (1 page)

Senator Connie Mack and Uncommon Friends Foundation (4 pages)

Miscellaneous papers (6 pages)

Sue Smith Windows Materials [Sue is the daughter of Dr. Bob and Anne Smith] (Total Number of Pages: 27)

Folder: Sue's list of her portion of the books owned and circulated by Dr. Bob (13 pages)

Notes of interview and Polaroid picture of Sue and Dick B. (2 pages)

The Love That Waits for You (2 pages)

Ed R. Andy, Sue Windows, and Larry Bauer: Notes and pictures on these oldtimers (10 pages)

Bob and Betty Smith Materials [Bob is the son of Dr. Bob and Anne Smith, and Betty was Smitty's wife. She recently died] (Total Number of Pages: 39)

Loose papers (2 pages)

The Art of Selfishness by David Seabury [extract from this book of Dr. Bob's] (2 pages)

Teach Us to Pray by Cora & Charles Fillmore [extract from a Dr. Bob book] (5 pages)

Handles of Power by Lewis Dunnington [extract from Dr. Bob book] (3 pages)

Quiet Talks with the Master by Eva Bell Werber [extract from Dr. Bob book] (2 pages)

The Psychology of Christian Personality by Ernest M. Ligon, Ph.D. [Extract, Dr. Bob book] (1 page)

The New Testament [James Moffatt Version, used by Dr. Bob, Extract] (2 pages)

Modern Man in Search of a Soul by C.G. Jung [a book given Dr. Bob by Bill, notes] (5 pages)

Founders Foundation [which owns Dr. Bob's Home] (1 page)

List in manila envelope (1 page)

A.A.'s Quiet Time Days by Dick B. (1 page)

Dr. R.H. Smith [notes and letters] (4 pages)

How to Find Health Through Prayer by Glenn Clark [Extract

from a Dr. Bob book] (4 pages)

Miscellaneous letters, notes, lists (6 pages)

Bible and Alcoholics Anonymous Ideas and Materials (Total Number of Pages: 125)

Notes on God as they understood Him (2 pages)
AA/Oxford Group/Wilson/Cult? (1 page)

"The Hidden Gospel of the 12 Steps" which appeared in Christianity Today [2 sets] (12 pages)

God as they understood Him [two copies each] (4 pages)

Early A.A. Bible ideas [University of Newcastle] (4 pages)

12 Steps and Their Bible Comparisons (1 page)

Music by Billie Lunn (3 pages)

Female concept of God (1 page)

God Delights in You (3 pages)

The Twelve Steps of Wholeness (1 page)

French Lick notes (9 pages)

The Bible and The Twelve Steps Pamphlet (8 pages)

Moral Re-Armament criticism by Rev. John N. Malony (32 pages)

Aspaxadrene ad (1 page)

The Well and The Shadows extract from Wm. Anderson (3 pages)

The New Book of Revelations by Charles W. Ferguson (13 pages)

20

"God" in the first 164 pages of the Big Book (8 pages)

Prayer (1 page)

Why We Were Chosen pamphlet (2 pages)

How to Listen to God pamphlet (4 pages)

Red Letter Edition (self-pronouncing) picture of King School Bible of Dr. Bob (4 pages)

Alcoholics Anonymous Comes of Age extract (4 pages)

"There It Is" (1 page)

Apologetics (2 pages)

A.A. Changing? [The Kingdom Within] (3 pages)

Quiet Time Materials (Total Number of Pages: 3)

Rowland Hazard Materials [Rowland Hazard was treated by Dr. Carl Jung for alcoholism; was told he needed a conversion experience; joined the Oxford Group; recovered; carried specific details about the Oxford Group to Edwin Throckmorton Thacher ("Ebby") who, in turn, carried the Oxford Group message to Bill Wilson. Hazard became a friend of Bill Wilson's, became active in Sam Shoemaker's church, and continued to be active with both Wilson and Shoemaker] (Total Number of Pages: 82)

Obituary (7 pages)

Folder Number One: Connie Lashowics [Library Director]; Providence Bulletin Obit; "The Forerunner-Rowland" by Ron Ray; The family chronology; Thomas Robinson Hazard [1791 to 1886]; Rowland Hazard Family Tree; Ron Ray letters from and to Dick B. and from Edith B.

Hazard n 1995; More notes on Hazard family tree; The National Cyclopedia-Rowland Gibson Hazard; Rhode Island Obit; Hazard in encyclopedia; Letter from Dick B.; Volume # 34 of American Biography; The National Cyclopedia on R. Hazard; Notes; Lt. Peter Hamilton Hazard obit and Helen Hazard Will; family tree and picture; T.P. Hazard Obit (38 pages)

Folder Number Two: Hazard Family tree; County scrapbook with Holly House picture; American Biography; Rowland's Shoes ad; Letter to Dick B. from Tom Bowles; "Sharing-Its Healing Power" by Ron Ray; More on Rowland Hazard; Rowland Hazard Obit in New York Times of December 22, 1945; Letter from Rowland Hazard to Ray Foote Purdy of February 5, 1938; Letter from Rowland Hazard to Chas Downing of March 1, 1937; Letter of thanks to Rowland Hazard from Publishers Association Dinner; Cincinnati newspaper clippings [1934]; The Forerunner articles; New York Times obit; Providence newspaper obit; Ron Ray notes and letter to Dick B.; Providence newspaper obit; Mel Barger letter to Dick B. to Donald Jones Recovery Services from Dick B. (32 pages)

Letter to Willard Hunter from Mel Barger (1 page)

Carl Jung (4 pages)

Ebby Thacher Materials [Ebby was rescued from alcoholism by Rowland Hazard, F. Shepard Cornell, and Cebra Graves; carried the message to his old drinking friend Bill Wilson; incited Wilson to go to Shoemaker's Calvary Rescue Mission and make a decision for Christ; and was the first to teach Wilson the Oxford Group life-changing ideas that were incorporated in the Twelve Steps. Bill called Ebby his sponsor] (Total Number of Pages: 33)

Letter to Dick B. from Melvin D. Barger (12/13/94) including pictures (4 pages)

Ebby's family home in Albany, New York [1915] (1 page)

Grapevine (Archives Committee) (2 pages)

Ebby's grave in Albany Rural Cemetery, includes map (2 pages)

Albany Cemetery Association with pictures (18 pages)

Heritage News (2 pages)

Letter from Bill DuVall to Larry about Bill's Rescue Mission experience (2 pages)

Photo of Winchester Cathedral Tombstone discussed on page 1 of Big Book (2 page)

Materials from the Founders' Homes

The Wilson House Materials [Bill Wilson was born in the now-restored Wilson House in East Dorset, Vermont. He was raised next door at the now-restored Griffith House. And Bill and Lois are buried down the road with other family members. The Wilson House is owned and operated as a non-profit entity and is headed up by Ozzie and Bonnie Lepper] (Total number of Pages: 81)

Pictures: 1 pages

Upcoming in 1998 (2 pages)

The Wilson House Newsletter (4 pages)

Dick B. What's New (1 pages)

Correspondence from Bonnie Lepper (2 pages)

Wilson House Seminar on Turning Point [May 17-18, 1997] Blue folder on A.A.'s Early Effective Spiritual Program; letter from Dick B. to Dennis; Dick B. to George; Dick B. to Dennis; and assorted notes (19 pages)

Griffith House Library Spiritual Holdings List of April 15, 1996 (3 pages)

Michael Galer notes (3 pages)

Folder: Letter to Ozzie and Bonnie from Ken Burns; list; Recovery Network; Contemplated pamphlets and ta pes; Spiritual Roots of A.A. (13 pages)

The Wilson House Newsletter (4 pages)

Letter and check receipt from Bonnie Lepper (2 pages)

Letter to Ozzie and Bonnie of 1997 from Dick B. (1 page)

Correspondence re May/97 Seminar (2 pages)

An Historical Approach to Early A.A.'s Spiritual Roots and Successes by Dick B. (20 pages)

Letter of thanks for anonymous check in 1996 (1 page)

Letter from Bonnie & Ozzie to Dick B. in 1996 (1 page)

Letter from Bonnie & Ozzie to Dick B. on August 4, 1995 (2 pages)

Dr. Bob's Home Materials (Total Number of Pages: 18)

Detroit News article of May 28, 1932 on presence of Oxford Group & Buchman (1 page)

Notes and quotes in the winter of 1993 (2 pages)

24

Ray Grumney, archivist, list (1 page)

St. Anthony Messenger magazine for December, 1992 (6 pages)

Welcome to Dr. Bob's Home pamphlet (4 pages)

Letter from Ray Grumney archivist, dated March , 1993 (1 page)

Dr. Bob paraphernalia (2 pages)

Manila folder with enclosed picture of Dr. Bob's Home (1 page)

Materials about Special Early A.A. Personalities

The Clarence Snyder Materials

[These materials were obtained from, among other sources, Grace Snyder (wife of Clarence), Dick Snyder (son of Clarence by Dorothy S.M.), Dick's former wife, a number of men sponsored by Clarence (John S., Steve F., Dick S., Clancy U., Barry W., Mitchell K., Dale M., and others), records and memorabilia collected by Danny S. (a sponsee of Grace Snyder's and the leader of one of Clarence's spiritual retreats. Story is "Home Brewmeister"] (Total Number of Pages: 1,965)

1. Pamphlets owned, authorized, contributed to, or written by Clarence; including Going Through the Steps; My Higher Power The Lightbulb; The Central Bulletin, Volumes I-II, Oct. 1942-Sept.1944, Cleveland Central Committee; The God Concept in Alcoholics Anonymous by Rev. George A. Little, D.D.; What Others Think of Alcoholics Anonymous by Friday Forum Luncheon Club, Akron A.A. Groups; Alcoholism and The Keeley Treatment, Dwight, Illinois; The Keeley Institute, Dwight, Illinois; Alcoholics Anonymous: An Interpretation of Our Twelve Steps; Mr. X and Alcoholics Anonymous by Rev. Dilworth Lupton, a sermon preached in 1939; A.A. Sponsorship Pamphlet written by Clarence in early 1944; Aims, Purposes and Functions of [Cleveland] Central Committee; Clarence Snyder: An Early A.A., Cleveland, Ohio; A.A. by Alcoholics Anonymous,

Cleveland, Ohio, circa early 1940's; Central Bulletin, Cleveland, Ohio, every issue from October 1941 to December, 1945; A.A.: January 1944 by The Alcoholic Foundation, New York; A.A. Sponsorship: Its Opportunities and Its Responsibilities; The Devil and A.A.; The Elrick Davis Articles, Liberty Magazine article by Morris Markey.

2. Copies of personal notes of Clarence Snyder on various A.A. subjects and its ideas: 6 pages of the beginning of an intended book on the history of A.A. in Clarence's own handwriting; 3 different pages in Clarence's hand on "personal inventory" items such as self-pity, lying, jealousy, fear, etc.; 3- page handwritten list of men and women whose personal stories were used or to be used for the original Big Book and whether they had "slipped" or not; many pages containing Clarence's thoughts and notes on talks he was planning or giving.

3. Copies of correspondence between Bill Wilson and early A.A. people and families: Letters to Clarence H. Snyder from Henrietta Seiberling; Letters from Bill Wilson to Clarence's former wife Dorothy; Letter to Clarence's former wife from Bill's lady friend Helen Wynn; Letters from Wilson to Clarence.

4. News articles and pictures about Clarence

5. Books and draft books about *Clarence: How it Worked* by Mitch K.; Draft of Mitch K. book submitted to Dick B. for editing;

6. Dick B.'s notes on interview of Clarence's son Dick, including three pages by Clarence's 1st wife: "Let me Tell About Anne Smith or I Knew Anne Smith or My First Meeting with Anne."

7. Dick B.'s notes on interview of Clarence's daughter-in-law "Mickey," including memorial article by Clarence's first wife Dorothy about Akron A.A. in 1938 and what AAs did.

8. Correspondence and memos on Clarence's battle with "New York" over royalties and power.

26

9.   Copies of materials from the Wilson Estate, the royalty agreement, and Lois Wilson's will showing the disposition of monies received from sale of books. Also, materials on Works Publishing Company, including stock certificate and financial report.

10.   Pamphlet by   Clarence's sponsee Clancy U. of Hawaii who got sober in 1940., including notes of The Twelve Steps and Scripture

11.   Materials of Ray M. of Hawaii who filmed many A.A. events.

12.   Memoranda and correspondence concerning acquisition of Clarence's personal papers by Mitch K., statement by Grace S. as to ownership, and proposed book on Clarence to be sponsored by Grace.

13.   Bibliography of Mitch K.

14.   Dozens of historical items about A.A. gathered by Clarence over the years from 1938 to his death and pertaining to A.A. history.

15.   Journals, memos, lists, and rosters kept by early Aas in Cleveland and in Akron, providing names, addresses, phones, sobriety dates, of the first 200 pioneers in A.A.; notes as to those in Akron who stayed sober and those who slipped and as to those few in New York who were sober in 1937 and 1938

16.   Programs and notes on spiritual retreats for Aas and their families which were established by Clarence in 1960, continued through his death, carried on by his wife Grace, and which continue to this day.

17.   Data on Clarence Snyder Hall owned by Hazelden

18.   Data on A.A. Pioneer Ed Andy, a friend of Clarence's who spoke at Clarence's spiritual retreats and who, after Clarence's death, was, at age 84, "the world's oldest living member of Alcoholics Anonymous."

19.   Obits and tributes on the death of Clarence's widow, Grace Moore
        Snyder

[In all, the Clarence Snyder materials consume about 7 inches of shelf
space width.]

Ed Andy Materials, Lorain, Ohio [Before his death, the pioneer AA
        with most sobriety] (Total Number of Pages: 9)

Bob Evans Materials [Bob E. was an A.A. pioneer who lived with Dr.
        Bob and Anne Smith] (Total Number of Pages: 24)

        Pamphlet and remarks on the Four Absolutes re readings and
                early Christian Fellowship (11 pages)

        Transcript of 1954 tape of Bob E. on early program (13 pages)

Earl Treat Materials [Earl founded of A.A. in Chicago. Story is "He
        Sold Himself Short" in the 3rd ed] (Total Number of Pages: 4)

Clancy Uterhardt Materials [Clancy was sponsored by Dr. Bob and
        then Clarence Snyder and lived many of his later sober years on
        the Island of Oahu in Hawaii] (Total Number of Pages: 138)

        A Sad Farewell (1 page)

        Complete Serenity Prayer (1 Page)

        Folder One :Assorted clippings, letters, pictures relevant to A.A.
                history (101 pages)

        Booklet about Clancy (24 pages)

        The Four Absolutes [frequently mentioned by Clancy at Hawii
                A.A. meetings] (9 pages)

        Folder Two: (2 pages)

Geraldine O. Delaney Materials [Friend of Bill and Lois Wilson; sober 50 years; died at 90; Founder and President of Little-Hill Alina Lodge Rehabilitation Center in New Jersey. Dick B.'s book *Hope!* tells the Gerry D. story and details her treatment program at Alina] (Total Number of Pages: 648)

Folder Number One: Little Hill Alina Lodge Treatment program (30 pages)

Folder Number Two: Little Hill Alina Lodge History (17 pages)

Folder Number Three: Dick B.'s Notes on the history (36 pages)

Folder Number Four: Interview of Alina CEO James Mell (4 pages)

Folder Number Five: Dick B.'s notes on the actual Alina program (11 pages)

Folder Number Six: Alina Lodge Family Program (51 pages)

Folder Number Seven: Philosophy of Geraldine D., with brochures and Dick B. interview and notes (30 pages)

Folder Number Eight: *Hope* book and news articles, pictures, and notes of Dick B. (45 pages)

Folder Number Nine: Notes on interview of male patient (6 pages)

Folder Number Ten: Further brochures on Alina Lodge program in action (59 pages)

Folder Number Eleven: Suggested book contents from mother of male patient (6 pages)

Folder Number Twelve: Obits and news articles on Hope Book

(15 pages)

Folder Number Thirteen: Materials used in preparation of Hope book, including interview notes, suggestions of patients and staff, pictures, brochures, copy of book (307 pages)

Folder Number Fourteen: Miscellaneous on Lodge and Gerry D. (16 pages)

Folder Number Fifteen: High Watch Farm Brochures, etc. (15 pages)

John Henry Fitzhugh Mayo Materials [Early AA; friend of Bill and Lois; argued unsuccessfully for retaining in the Big Book the Christian materials on which A.A. based its program. Story is "Our Southern Friend"] (Total Number of Pages: 82)

James Burwell Materials [Self-proclaimed early A.A. atheist in New York who successfully objected to the frequency with which God was mentioned in the Big Book; claimed to be the author of the idea "God as we understood Him" though this seems to have been an erroneous claim, Sam Shoemaker having authored the phrase and idea a decade before. Story is "The Vicious Cycle" in the 3rd ed.] (Total Number of Pages: 60)

Yellow folder (51 Pages)

Miscellaneous (9 Pages)

The Rev. Irving and Julia Harris Materials [Irving was Sam Shoemaker's Assistant Minister at Calvary in New York and edited *The Calvary Evangel* for a time. Irving and Julia lived in Calvary House. Julia staffed the Oxford Group book stall there. Both were credited by Bill Wilson as being inspirational in A.A.'s spiritual development and ideas. Irving Harris wrote *The Breeze of the Spirit*, which covers many details about Sam Shoemaker and Bill Wilson.] (Total Number of Pages: 332)

Folder of materials, including manuscript typewritten by Irving and detailing the discussions of Bill Wilson with Sam Shoemaker in Shoemaker's office before the 12 Steps were written. Julia supplied this and many other materials to Dick B. on the nature of the early program as it was conducted at Calvary House in New York. (30 pages)

Copies of The Evangel which Irving often edited and which was described as the virtual house organ of the Oxford Group. Contained articles by Shoemaker and other prominent in the church and Oxford Group in the early years in New York. (300 pages)

Manila envelope with picture (2 pages)

Judge John Toohey Materials [Toohey was prominent in early Chicago A.A. and wrote such articles as "God's Instrument" which was widely distributed as "Why We Were Chosen"] (Total Number of Pages: 5).

Harry M. Tiebout, M.D., Materials [Psychiatrist friend of Bill Wilson's who wrote extensively on the alcoholic, ego, and other subjects pertaining to alcoholism. He wrote "Observations on the 'Fundamental Phenomena' of A.A."] (Total Number of Pages: 40)

Lois Wilson Materials [Lois was the wife of Bill Wilson and co-founder of Al-Anon. Most of the materials concerning Lois can be found in connection with Stepping Stones materials and also in such writings of hers as "Lois Remembers"] (Total number of pages: 9)

Rosters of the Early A.A. Pioneers [Who wrote which stories in the Big Book, plus the names and addresses of the first 220 members of A.A.] (Total number of pages: 7)

Fragments of, on, and about A.A. History

The Original Draft Manuscripts of Dick B.'s First Books (Total Number of Pages 1,093)

Dick B., *A.A.'s Good Book Connection: The Oxford Group, Sam Shoemaker, Dr. Bob*. Fourth Draft, 9/3/91, 541 pp. (Unpublished draft.)

Dick B., *A.A.'s Good Book Connection: The Oxford Group, Sam Shoemaker, Dr. Bob*. Fifth Draft, 552 pp., plus 5 Appendices.

Miscellaneous Items pertaining to Early A.A. (Total Number of Pages: 336)

Folder Number One: Assorted Pamphlets and papers pertaining to A.A. History: The four AA of Akron pamphlets written at Dr. Bob's request; a Landmarks sheet; Origin of the Serenity Prayer; clippings from Edith Uterhardt and Father Paul Blaes; History of Cincinnati Area; Al Latch suggestions for "Improving Our Thinking," 1954; Reviews of Big Book in 1939; Elrick B. Davis Series in 1939 in The Plain Dealer; speeches of Dr. Bob and Bill together in Los Angeles in 1943; data tracking Cebra Graves; Care of Alcoholics by Sister Ignatia; Neibuhr's article for A.A. on Serenity Prayer; Seiberling fragment; Times article on A.A.; news article on demise of "God" in A.A.; Dick B.'s history fragments articles (269 pages)

Archival Materials of Ray G. at Dr. Bob's Home (33 pages)

Pamphlet: Spiritual Milestones by AA of Akron (16 pages)

Series of seven (7 pages)

October 23, 1939 (10 pages)

Date list (1 page)

Henry Parkhurst Materials [Parkhurst was Bill's partner in the Works Publishing Company Venture which published the First Edition

of Alcoholics Anonymous. Parkhurst's Story is "The Unbeliever"]
(Total Number of Pages: 4)

Dr. Walter Tunks Materials [Tunks was pastor to Harvey Firestone and Dr. Bob at the end of Bob's life. Tunks figured throughout A.A.'s formative years as the Episcopal Rector of St. Paul's Church in Akron who helped introduce Akron to the Oxford Group in 1933] (Total Number of Pages: 7)

Miscellaneous Items relating to A.A. History (Total Number of Pages: 215)

> Folder Number One: Miscellaneous items on Bill, Fitzhugh Mayo, Clarence Snyder (14 pages)
>
> Folder Number Two: Medical Inquiries and Observations by Benjamin Rush, M.D. [extract, 1818] (176 pages)
>
> Data from George Trotter (2 pages)
>
> Dear Willard Letter (6 pages)
>
> Notes on interviews of Dennis Cassidy (7 pages)
>
> Other miscellaneous historical items (10 pages)

Concluding Materials Pertaining to Dick B.'s Research

> Dick B.'s Newsletters on the Spiritual Roots of A.A. (Total Number of Pages: 184)
>
> Dick B. 's Correspondence with Ernest Kurtz, Ph.D. (Total Number of Pages: 13)
>
> Assorted Papers (Total number: 28)
>
> A.A. [A Religion–The Position of the Courts] (Total Number of

Pages: 26)

Dick B.'s Miscellaneous Historical Pamphlets and Materials [Particularly, *The Hidden Gospel of the Twelve Steps; Evolution of Alcoholics Anonymous* by Jim Burwell; *The Little Red Book*; *AA Dry Drunk*; *Stools and Bottles*; *Twelve Tremendous Steps That will work for anyone*; *The Evangel*; *My Higher Power: The Lightbulb* by Clarence Snyder; *The IWS Index to Alcoholics Anonymous*; *A Way of Life: AA*; *What Others Think of A.A.: A.A. on the Job*; *Anonymously They Help*; *AA Home Run*; *All Things Considered*; *A Dramatic Success*; *Progress through A.A.*; *an Open Meeting*; *Sportswriter's View*; *And the Ladies*; *Psychology Helps*; and other Early A.A. Pamphlets] (Total Number of Pages: 184)

The George Vondermuhll, Jr. Materials on The Oxford Group and Moral Re-Armament

Papers and Reports (Provided by George Vondermuhll, Jr.)

Anonymous, ASSEMBLY OF THE AMERICAS for the Moral Re-Armament of the Hemisphere. Petropolis, Brazil, 1961, paper, pp. 24. (5 copies)

Anon., DEMOCRACY'S INSPIRED IDEOLOGY. Undated, but obviously published in USA 1946 or 1947. Spiral bound, pp. 40. Largely photos and newspaper reports and editorials of MRA in the USA before and through WW II. (6 copies)

Anon., THE FIGHT TO SERVE. Moral Re-Armament, Inc., 1943, paper, pp.96. MRA and WW II, with special reference to MRA's fulltime volunteer workers. (2 copies)

Anon., FRANK BUCHMAN EIGHTY. London, 1958, cloth, pp. 214. Messages, photos, events celebrating the birthday. (5 copies)

Anon., AN IDEA TAKES WINGS. Miami, Florida, 1951,paper, pp.72, illustrated. The Miami-based airlines experience MRA and take it to the world. Exhilarating. (Also made into a movie.) (15 copies)

Anon., MIAMI ASSEMBLY REPORT. 1950, paper, ___ pp.? . Focus on Latin America, in _____ ? framework of labor and management in the Miami-based airlines and other industries.

Anon., SONGS FOR MORAL RE-ARMAMENT. Words only. OG and MRA songs plus favorite hymns . 1944, paper, pp.40. (2 copies)

Ibid., Mackinac Edition, including US and Canadian patriotic songs. 1946. paper, pp. 64. (One copy)

Anon., SONGS OF THE RISING TIDE. London, The Oxford Group, 1938. paper, pp.50. Full-size , words and music. (12 copies)

Anon., A SUMMIT CONFERENCE FOR THE MORAL RE-ARMAMENT OF THE WORLD. Caux, 1958, paper, pp. 50. A summary report. (2 copies)

Anon., YOU CAN DEFEND AMERICA, foreword by Gen. John J. Pershing. Washington, Judd & Detwiler, 1941,paper, pp. 16. Handbook for the home front. (15 copies)

Periodicals (Provided by George Vondermuhll)

PERIODICALS

A. Moral Re-Armament--in chronological order

NEW WORLD NEWS, Los Angeles
1947: 1 each for Jan., Apr., Dec.; 2 for Oct.; 3 each for May, June
1948: 5 for each month
1949: 5 each Jan, Feb, Mar, May, June, July; 4 Apr; 3 Aug; 1 Oct
1950: 3 June, July, Aug.

MRA INFORMATION SERVICE, Los Angeles
Published twice a month. Bound and indexed.

Vol. I	June 1952-May 1953	(2 copies)
Vol. II	June 1953-May 1954	(2 copies)
Vol. III	June 1954-May 1955	(2 copies)
Vol. IV	June 1955-May 1956	(2 copies)
Vol. VI	June 1957-May 1958	(3 copies)
Vol. VII	June 1958-May 1959	(2 copies)
Vol. VIII	June 1959-May 1960	(2 copies)
Vol. XII	June 1963-Aug.1964	(2 copies)

MRA INFORMATION SERVICE, London
Weekly
(1) Scattered issues, 1965,1967-69, 1972
(2) Complete, Jan 1968-Dec 1970 (in spring binder)
(3) Complete, Jan 1971-Dec 1973   "   "   "
(4) Complete, Jan 1974-Dec 1976   "   "   "

TOMORROW'S AMERICAN, Los Angeles
Weekly
Vol. 1, various issues, 1964-5, also complete in spring binder
Vol. 2,   "   "   1965-6,   "   "   "
     "   "
Vol. 3, 1966-7, complete in spring binder
== name changed to TOMORROW'S AMERICAN NEWS, Los Angeles
Vol.4, 1967
Vol.5, 1968
Vol.6, 1969

PERSPECTIVE, Up With People, Los Angeles
Newsletter, every two weeks, 1967-71

UP WITH PEOPLE NEWS, Los Angeles
April 1971 - May 1974
September 1974-Fall 1976

Pamphlets, Programs, Articles, Single Speeches (Provided by George Vondermuhll)

PAMPHLETS, PROGRAMS, ARTICLES, SINGLE SPEECHES (from 2 to 20 copies each) by the following:

Buchman, Frank
Campbell, Paul
Howard, Peter
Jaeger, Bill
Martin, Morris
Oberlander, Theodor
Pinsent, Roy
Thornton-Duesbery, J.P.
Wilson, Mary
Wood, Lawson
Up With People
Anonymous

BOOKS and/or PAMPHLETS in LANGUAGES other than English

Larger selections: French, German

Others: Arabic, Danish, Dutch, Finnish, Greek, Iranian, Norwegian, Portuguese, Russian, Spanish, Swedish, Turkish

The Danny Whitmore Historical Materials

[Inventory interrupted by possession of a portion in Mass. which were to go to Griffith Library]

The Historical Binders (Each binder is about 4 inches in width)

[There are 40 binders. Each binder contains approximately 220 items (including letters, pamphlets, bulletins, booklets, etc.). The total estimated number of items in all the binders combined is 8,800.]

1. Pre A.A. History

2. A.A. History, 1939

3 A.A. History, 1940

4. A.A. History Materials, 1941 to 1942

5. A. A. History Materials, 1943 to 1949

6. A.A. History Materials, 1950 to 1959

7. A.A. History Materials, 1950 to 1969

8. A.A. History Materials, 1970 to 1979

9. A.A. History Materials, 1980 to 1989

10. Cleveland Central Bulletins, October, 1942 to September, 1952

11. Cleveland Central Bulletins, October, 1952 to September, 1962

12. Cleveland Central Bulletins, January, 1978

13. Cleveland Central Bulletins, January 1978 to December, 1986

14. Silent Rostrum, 1957 to 1965

15. Silent Rostrum, 1966 to 1969

16. Silent Rostrum, 1970 to 1990

17. General Service Conference of A.A. Summary, 1951-1986; Final Report 1951 to 1955

18. General Service Conference of A.A., 1956 to 1963

19. General Service Conference of A.A. Final Report, 1964 to 1969

20. General Service Conference of A.A., Final Report, 1970 to 1975

21. General Service Conference of A.A., Final Report, 1976 to 1980

22. General Service Conference of A.A., Final Report, 1981 to 1985

23. General Service Conference of A.A., Final Report, 1986 to 1989

24. General Service Conference of A.A., Final Report, 1990 to 1994

25. Bill Wilson's Stories, Lois Wilson's Diaries

26. Early Books by Charles Clapp, Amelia Reynolds, Sharing, Du Maurier

27. Book Reviews of A.A. The Basic Text, 1939 to 1989 Early Box 459, 1967 to 1971. Medical Inquiries by Benjamin Rush, M.D.

28. Three Basic Text Study Groups

29. Discovering and Sharing Permanent Contented Sobriety

30. John Barley Corn Public Enemy # 1

32. A.A.

33. Oxford Group

34. MRA Today

35. Oxford Group (MRA, Faith at Work, OG Connection, Shoemaker, Calvary Church, Shoemaker's personal journals, A First Century Christian Fellowship, Four Absolutes, Shoemaker Sermons

36. Oxford Group: Friends of the O.G., Dr. Bob and Anne Smith, Ebby Thacher, Rowland Hazard, Fitz Mayo, Henrietta Sieberling, T. Henry and Clarace Williams, Frank Buchman, Oxford Group people, miscellaneous.

37 – 40 (not presently available though delivery requested of custodian in Mass.).

The Pamphlet Collection

(includes magazines and articles on alcoholism, addiction, religion, spirituality, recovery)

Reader's Digest 14 issues
Coronet 3 issue
The American Mercury 2 issue
Prevention 1 issue
U.S. News and World Report, 1 issue
New Yorker, 1 issue
Time Magazine, 15 issues
The Atlantic, 1 issue
Business Week, 1 issue
Good Housekeeping, 3 issues
Catholic Digest, 1 issue
Theosophy, 1 issue
Modern Maturity, 1 issue
National Geographic, 1 issue
Liberty, 8 issues
Argosy, 7 issues
McCall's, 1 issue
Family Circle, 1 issue
Science Illustrated, 1 issue
Fortune, 1 issue
Life, 7 issues
Sober Times, 1 issue
Seventeen Magazine, 1 issue
Look, 3 issues
Ladies Home Journal, 1 issue
Saturday Evening Post, 9 issues
Rising Tide, 1 issue
San Diego International Convention, 1 issue
Steps for Recovery, 1 issue
Newsweek, 1 issue
Women's Day, 1 issue
Alcohol Education Digest, 5 issues
Some Have Stopped Drinking, 1 issue
The Rape of the Law, 1 issue
Slump and Resurgence in Liquor Culture, 1 issue
Does Alcohol Aid Creative Ability, 1 issue
Scientific Temperance Journal, 1 issue
The Scientific Temperance Federation, 1 issue

Will You Help Keep the Law, 1 issue
Alcoholic Psychoses Before and After Prohibition, 1 issue
Report on behalf of the American Committee on International Relations,
    1 issue
The Wounds of a Friend, 1 issue
The Battle Cry, 1 issue
Prohibition with the People Behind It, 1 issue
Program, 15th National Convention of the Anti-Saloon League of
    America, 1 issue
Social Consequences of the Alcohol Problem, 1 issue
Self-control and Alcohol, 1 issue
Social Consequences of the Alcoholic's Desire, 1 issue
Alcohol and the Next Generation, 1 issue
The History of the Temperance Movement, 1 issue
The Evolution of Freedom, 1 issue
A New Deal in Liquor, 1 issue
The Eighteenth Amendment is Valid, 1 issue
Hold Fast America, 1 issue
Weekly Bulletin of the Department of Health, City of New York, 1 issue
An Enemy Hath Done This, 1 issue
The City of Me, 1 issue
Has Radical Temperance Opinion Prevented or Promoted Real
    Temperance Reform, 1 issue
Rejected Because of Family Connections, 1 issue
The Memorial to Educators, 1 issue
Effects of Alcoholic Drinks, 1 issue
The Job that Jack Lost, 1 issue
The Effect of Alcohol on the work of Typewriting, 1 issue
New Marksmanship Experiment, 1 issue
The Intemperance Factor in Poverty, 1 issue
$100,000,000 Saved Connecticut in Three Dry Years, 2 issues
Proceedings of the Board of Directors of the Anti-Saloon League of
    America, 1919 and 1927, 2 issues
Proceedings Sixth National Anti-Saloon Convention, 1901, 1 issue
Wet and Dry, 2 issues
Listen: Alcohol Education for Moderation or Abstinence? 1 issue
Listen: The Moral Basis of Education for Abstinence, 1 issue
Pamphlets of the Scientific Temperance Federation [on Prohibition], 14
issues

The International Student: Journal of Alcohol Studies. The Intercollegiate
       Association for Study of Alcohol, 170 issues
The Prohibition Situation, 1 issue
Mimeographed Typescript of *Alcoholics Anonymous* (1939)
AA Grapevine

Six Large Boxes of Audio and Video Cassette Tapes

Box 1: 16" x 10 ½" x 12 ½" inches

Box 2: 16" x 10 ½" x 12 ½" inches

Box 3: 16" x 10 ½" x 12 ½" inches

Box 4: 16" x 10 ½" x 12 ½" inches

Box 5: 16" x 10 ½" x 12 ½" inches

Box 6: 16" x 10 ½" x 12 ½" inches

Three Large Boxes of Pictures and Photographs

Box 1: 16" x 10 ½" x 12 ½" inches

Box 2: 16" x 10 ½" x 12 ½" inches

Box 3: 16" x 10 ½" x 12 ½" inches

The Earl Husband Bound Reprints

The Big Bender, Drunks Are Square Pegs, Drinking's Not The Problem
       (Charles Clapp, Jr.)
Early Friends of Alcoholics Anonymous (Silkworth, Tiebout, Shoemaker,
       Ignatia, Dowling)
Magazine Articles: From 1939 [On]
Daily Reprieve (2)
Non-Approved History of Alcoholics Anonymous: 1957-1985
Rock Bottom A.A. Prison Group
Pass It On: Book 1 (Mel Barger draft)

Pass It On: Book 2 (Mel Barger draft)

Religion and Alcoholics Anonymous: Volume I [primarily Roman Catholic Articles]

Medicine and Alcoholics Anonymous

The Emmanuel Movement and Richard Peabody

The Soul of Sponsorship [Fr. Robert Fitzgerald, S.J. on Father Dowling and Wilson]

A.A. History of General Services [Pages from the estate of Margaret Berger, A.A. secy. 1942-49]

Buchman And Buchmanism [Ph.D. Dissertation Thesis of Elston John Hill, 1970]

A.A. Story: 1976 [Kurtz Not-God manuscript]

Manuscript of A.A. Big Book: 1938

The Oxford Group [articles and pamphlets]

History of Alcoholics Anonymous: 1934-1939 [Pittman dissertation]

Theological Influence On Program of Recovery [copy of Charles Knippel Ph.D. dissertation]

The Dennis Cassidy Collection
of Recordings of All Bill Wilson's Public Talks

Over 150 Tapes of All Bill Wilson's Public Talks

[Inventory of tapes underway but interrupted by their possession by a custodian in Mass.

Explanatory Catalogs

[There are two catalogs which explain the sources and the recording process of the Wilson tapes. They also explain in detail the subject of each public talk and, in many cases, set forth a summary of the material Bill covered.]

Rare Items

Abraham Lincoln's Addresses on Temperance

Original Washingtonian Temperance Pledge Book (circa 1850)

Laminated Bill Wilson Obituary plus two other pages

Laminated Sister Ignatia Obituary

Laminated Draft of Alcoholics Anonymous First Edition Cover (Blue)

Laminated GSO Tribute to Lois Wilson

Facsimile of first issue of Grapevine (2 copies)

Article, "There Are No Proxies for Sobriety"

The Sober Press, Euclid, Ohio, December 1994 (Lots about the Creator, God, Jesus, Prayer)

Laminated Copy of Works Publishing, Inc. Stock Certificate dated June 20, 1940, certifying that Frank S. Shaw is the owner of 4 shares. Signed by Ruth Hock. Also, a photocopy of the first stock certificate.

Draft of Bill W. and Dr. Bob play by Shem

The Seven Points of Alcoholics Anonymous, published in 1955 by Inter-Group Office, Daytona Beach, Florida

Photograph of Rev. Sam Shoemaker inscribed to Sam by Bill Wilson in Christmas, 1957. The photo was given to Dick B. by Sam Shoemaker's daughters.

Part 2
Historical Books, Pamphlets, and Articles
on
Alcoholics Anonymous

Publications about Alcoholics Anonymous

AA The Best Way Just for Today, n.d. (D)

A History of Alcoholics Anonymous in Oregon: 1943-1983. OR: The Oregon Area Gen. Service History Committee of Alcoholics Anonymous, 1995 (D)

Alcoholics Anonymous. (Multilith volume). New Jersey: Works Publishing Co., 1939.

———. Multilith Manuscript. Published by Dr. Bob's Home.

———. Earlier multilith manuscript ("original"). owned by Clarence H. Snyder (spiral bound).

———. Earlier multilith manuscript ("original"). Reprinted by the Anonymous Press.

Alcoholics Anonymous: The Story of How More Than 100 Men Have Recovered from Alcoholism. New York City: Works Publishing Company, 1939 (reprint w/circus cover) (2).

Alcoholics Anonymous. NY: IWS, Inc., 1994. [Pamphlet reprint of portion of Third Edition, Original Manuscript of 1938, and directory] (17)

Alcoholics Anonymous. (A collection of 32 original stories from *Alcoholics Anonymous*–7 from the Second Edition and 25 from the First Edition–none of which is in the Third Edition. A spiral bound, paperback with replica of "circus cover" of First Edition. June, 1992) (2) D1.

Alcoholics Anonymous Study Edition. NY: IWS, Inc., 1994 (D)

45

Alcoholics Anonymous Workbook Edition. NY: IWS, Inc., 1995 (D)

An Unofficial Guide to the Twelve Steps. Written by AA Members in Texas. Edited by Paul O., 1993 (saddle-stitch paper).

Al-Anon Publications:

———. *Al-Anon: Faces Alcoholism* (D)

———. *Al-Anon's Favorite Forum Editorials* (D)

———. *Al-Anon Family Groups* (D)

———. *Al-Anon's Twelve Steps and Twelve Traditions* (D)

———. *Living with an Alcoholic with the Help of Al-Anon* (D)

———. *How Al-Anon Works for Families and Friends of Alcoholics* (D)

———. *One Day at a Time in Al-Anon* (D)

———. *Alateen: Hope for Children of Alcoholics* (D)

———. *First Steps: Al-Anon 35 Years of Beginnings* (D)

———. *Courage to Be Me: Living with Alcoholism* (D)

———. *From Survival to Recovery: Growing Up in an Alcoholic Home* (D)

———. *Living with Sobriety: Another Beginning* (D)

A Program for You: A Guide to the Big Book's Design for Living. MN: Hazelden, 1991 (D)

B., Dick. *Anne Smith's Journal, 1933-1939: A.A.'s Principles of Success.* 3rd ed. Kihei, HI: Paradise Research Publications, 1998 (5).

———. *By the Power of God: A Guide to Early A.A. Groups & Forming Similar Groups Today.* Kihei, HI: Paradise Research Publications, 2000 (5).

———. *Dr. Bob and His Library: A Major A.A. Spiritual Source.* 3rd ed. Kihei, HI: Paradise Research Publications, 1998 (5).

———. *Good Morning! Quiet Time,* Morning *Watch, Meditation, and Early A.A..* 2d ed. Kihei, HI: Paradise Research Publications, 1998 (5).

———. *Hope!: The Story of Geraldine D., Alina Lodge & Recovery.* Kihei, HI: Paradise Research Publications, 1997 (5).

———. *New Light on Alcoholism: God, Sam Shoemaker, and A.A.* New, rev. ed. Kihei, HI: Paradise Research Publications, 1999 (5).

———. *The Akron Genesis of Alcoholics Anonymous.* 3rd ed. Kihei, HI: Paradise Research Publications, 1998 (5).

———. *The Books Early AAs Read for Spiritual Growth.* 7th ed. Kihei, HI, CA: Paradise Research Publications, 1998 (5).

———. *The Golden Text of A.A.: God, the Pioneers, and Real Spirituality.* Kihei, HI: Paradise Research Publications, 1999 (5).

——. *The Good Book and The Big Book: A.A.'s Roots in the Bible.* 2d ed., Kihei, HI: Paradise Research Publications, 1997 (5).

——. *The Oxford Group & Alcoholics Anonymous: A Design for Living That Works.* New, rev. ed. Kihei, HI: Paradise Research Publications, 1998 (5).

——. *That Amazing Grace: The Role of Clarence and Grace S. in Alcoholics Anonymous.* San Rafael, CA: Paradise Research Publications, 1996 (5).

——. *Turning Point: A History of Early A.A.'s Spiritual Roots and Successes.* Kihei, HI: Paradise Research Publications, 1997 (5).

——. *Utilizing Early A.A.'s Spiritual Roots for Recovery Today.* Kihei, HI: Paradise Research Publications, 1999 (5).

——. A Collection of Statistics gathered by the author from lists prepared by AAs, by the families of A.A. founders, by biographers, by historians: Containing information on the original AAs by name and address and materials from Enoch Gordis, M.D., NIDA, SAMHSA, A.A. Membership Surveys.

——. and Bill Pittman. *Courage to Change: The Christian Roots of the 12-Step Movement.* Grand Rapids, MI: Fleming H. Revell, 1994.

——. and Bill Pittman. *Courage to Change: The Christian Roots of the Twelve-Step Movement.* Hazelden. 1998 (5).

B., Hamilton. *Getting Started in A.A.* MN: Hazelden, 1995 (D)

——. *Twelve Step Sponsorship: How it Works.* MN: Hazelden, 1996 (D)

B., Howard. *Leary: A Portrait of an Alcoholic.* CA: Fithian Press, 1996

B., Jim. *Evolution of Alcoholics Anonymous.* New York: A.A. Archives.

B., Mel. and Bill P. *The 7 Key Principles of Successful Recovery. Hazelden,* 1999.

B., Mel. Ebby: The Man Who Sponsored Bill W. MN: Hazelden, 1998 (2) D1.

——. Is there life after Sobriety? Toledo: Mel B., 1974. My Search for Bill W. Hazelden, 2000. erg, Steven L. Spirituality & Addiction. WV: The Bishop of Books, 1993 (D)

Bishop, Charles, Jr. The Washingtonians & Alcoholics Anonymous. WV: The Bishop of Books, 1992.

——. Alcoholism xxx. WV: The Bishop of Books, 1984 (D)

——. *Carrying the Message Comics, 1949.* WV: The Bishop of Books, 1993 (D)

——. and Bill Pittman. *The Annotated Bibliography of Alcoholics*

Anonymous, 1939-1989. WV: The Bishop of Books, 1989 (2) D1.

Blumberg, Leonard U. *Beware The First Drink: The Washingtonian Temperance Movement and Alcoholics Anonymous*. Seattle: Glen Abbey Books, 1991 (2) D1.

Book Reviews of Alcoholics Anonymous: A Collection of Twenty-Five Reviews of the Basic Text of Alcoholics Anonymous.

C., Stewart. *A Reference Guide to the Big Book of Alcoholics Anonymous*. Seattle: Recovery Press, 1986.

Clapp, Charles, Jr. *Drinking's Not the Problem*. New York: Thomas Y. Crowell, 1949.

Conrad, Barnaby. *Time Is All We Have*. New York: Dell Publishing, 1986 (2) D1.

Darrah, Mary C. *Sister Ignatia: Angel of Alcoholics Anonymous*. Chicago: Loyola University Press, 1992 (3) D1

E., Bob. *Handwritten note to Lois Wilson on pamphlet entitled "Four Absolutes."* (Copy made available to the author at Founders Day Archives Room in Akron, Ohio, in June, 1991).

———. Letter from Bob E. to Nell Wing. Stepping Stones Archives.

———. Record of Bob Evans of Akron, Ohio: Dictated to Bill Wilson on 6/18/1954 (partial transcript obtained from archivist at Dr. Bob's Home in Akron, Ohio).

Early Friends of Alcoholics Anonymous. Hardcover. Copies of articles by and about Dr. William Duncan Silkworth, Dr. Harry M. Tiebout, Rev. Sam Shoemaker, Sister Mary Ignatia, and Father Edward Dowling, S.J..

Fifty Years of Freedom in the Mountain State. WV: Alcoholics Anonymous Area 73, 1992

First Steps: Al-Anon . . . 35 Years of Beginnings. New York: Al-Anon Family Group Headquarters, 1986.

Ford, Betty, with Chris Chase. *The Times of My Life*. New York: Harper and Row, 1978 (2) D1.

Ford, John C. *Depth Psychology, Morality and Alcoholism*. Massachusetts: Weston College, 1951 (2) D1.

Gray, Jerry. *The Third Strike*. Minnesota: Hazelden, 1949 (3) D1.

H., Paul. *Things My Sponsors Taught Me*. MN: Hazelden, 1987 (D)

Halvorson, Ron and Valerie Deilgat. *Living Free: A Guide to Forming and Conducting a Recovery Ministry*. CA: Recovery Publications, 1992.

Hartigan, Francis. *Bill W.: A Biography of Alcoholics Anonymous*

Cofounder Bill Wilson. NY: St. Martin's Press, 2000.

Hunter, Willard, with assistance from M. D. B. *A.A.'s Roots in the Oxford Group.* New York: A.A. Archives, 1988.

———. Draft page on Conversation with Garrett Stearly re Buchman, Shoemaker, himself, and Bill Wilson at Calvary Church.

Index to The Big Book Alcoholics Anonymous (saddle-stitch paper back), n.d.

J., *A Simple Program: A Contemporary Translation of the Book Alcoholics Anonymous.* NY: Hyperion, 1996 (D)

Johnson, Vernon E. *God, Help Me to Be Me: Spiritual Growth During Recovery.* MN: Johnson Institute, 1991.

K., Mitchell. *How It Worked: The Story of Clarence H. Snyder.* NY: AA Big Book Study Group, 1999. (2)

Knippel, Charles T. *Samuel M. Shoemaker's Theological Influence on William G. Wilson's Twelve Step Spiritual Program of Recovery.* Ph. D. dissertation. St. Louis University, 1987.

Kurtz, Ernest. *Not-God: A History of Alcoholics Anonymous.* Exp. ed. Minnesota: Hazelden, 1991 (2) D1.

———. *AA: The Story.* A revised edition of *Not-God.* San Francisco: Harper & Row, 1988 (2) D1.

———. *The Collected Ernie Kurtz.* WV: The Bishop of Books, 1999 (D)

Last Major Talk of Doctor Bob Smith, Cleveland, Ohio, 1950. FL: Life Enrichment Retreat, n.d. (Among Clarence Snyder's treasures, reprint, with Clarence's signature and margin notes) (2).

Learning to Live (saddle-stitch paper back index of Big Book, 12 x 12, AACA, *As Bill Sees It*).

Lifestyles of the Clean & Sober Souvenir Convention Guide. [Seattle Convention], 1995 (D)

M., Dr. Earle. *Physician, Heal Thyself!* MN: CompCare, 1989 (D)

M., Stanley. *The Glumlot Letters: A Devil's Discourse on Sobriety, Recovery and the Twelve Steps of Alcoholics Anonymous.* CA: Capizon Publishing, 1997.

Mann, Marty. *Marty Mann's New Primer on Alcoholism: How People Drink, How to Recognize Alcoholics, and What to Do about Them.* New York: Holt, Rinehart and Winston, 1958 (2) D1

———. *Marty Mann Answers Your Questions About Drinking and Alcoholism.* NY: Holt, Rinehart and Winston, 1969 (D).

Markey, Morris. *Alcoholics and God.* Liberty Magazine, 1939 (reprint copy).

Martin, Conrad. *Cornerstones of Sobriety and Sanity*. Creative Flow, Inc.

Martin, Francis. *Prayers for Recovery: Talks with God for Your Twelve Step Program*. TN: New Directions, 1990.

Maxwell, Milton A. *The Washingtonian Movement*. Milton A. Maxwell, 1979 (saddle-stitched pamphlet, reprint of article in *Quarterly Journal of Alcohol Studies*, September, 1950).

——. *The Alcoholics Anonymous Experience*. NY: McGraw-Hill, 1984 (D)

Mooney, A. J. and Eisenberg, Arlene and Eisenberg, Howard. *The Recovery Book*. NY: Workman Publishing Company, 1992

Morreim, Dennis C. *Changed Lives: The Story of Alcoholics Anonymous*. Minneapolis: Augsburg Fortress, 1991 (2) D1.

Morse, Robert M, M.D., and Daniel K. Flavin, M.D. "The Definition of Alcoholism." *The Journal of the American Medical Association*. August 26, 1992, pp. 1012-14.

My Spiritual Journey: Finding Hope and Encouragement along the Way and Life Recovery New Testament. IL: Tyndale House Publishers, 1995.

Non Approved History of A.A., Book1 and Book 2. Hardcover. Draft prepared by Bob Pearson. CT: Robert Pearson Associates Writing Services, 1985.

O., Paul Dr. *There's More to Quitting Drinking Than Quitting Drinking*. CA: Sabrina, 1995 (D)

Our Devilish Personalities. MN: Hazelden, 1975 (D)

P., Wally. *But, for the Grace of God . . .: How Intergroups & Central Offices Carried the Message of Alcoholics Anonymous in the 1940s*. West Virginia: The Bishop of Books, 1995 (2).

Pittman, Bill. *AA The Way It Began*. Seattle: Glen Abbey Books, 1988 (2) D1.

——. *Practice These Principles and What is the Oxford Group?*. MN: Hazelden, 1997 (2) D1.

——. *Stepping Stones to Recovery*. WA: Glen Abbey Books, 1988 (D)

——. and Todd Weber. *Drop the Rock: Removing Character Defects*. Seattle: Glen Abbey Books, 1993 (2) D1.

Poe, Stephen E., and Frances E. *A Concordance to Alcoholics Anonymous*. Nevada: Purple Salamander Press, 1990 (2) D1.

Raphael, Matthew J. *Bill W. and Mrs. Wilson*. MA: University of Mass., 2000.

Recovery Devotional Bible: New International Version. MI: Zondervan

Publishing House, 1993.

Robertson, Nan. *Getting Better Inside Alcoholics Anonymous*. New York: William Morrow & Co., 1988 (2) D.

Rudy, David R. *Becoming Alcoholic: Alcoholics Anonymous and the Reality of Alcoholism*. IL: Southern Illinois University Press, 1986 (3) D1.

S., Clarence. *Going through the Steps*. 2d ed. Altamonte Springs, FL: Stephen Foreman, 1985. (Also copies published earlier by Roger Bunn). (3).

——. *My Higher Power–The Lightbulb*. 2d ed. Altamonte Springs, FL: Stephen Foreman, 1985.

Seiberling, John F. *Origins of Alcoholics Anonymous*. (A transcript of remarks by Henrietta B. Seiberling: transcript prepared by Congressman John F. Seiberling of a telephone conversation with his mother, Henrietta in the spring of 1971): Employee Assistance Quarterly. 1985; (1); pp. 8-12.

Shem, Samuel and Janet Surrey. *Bill W. and Dr. Bob*. New York: Samuel French, Inc., 1990.

Sikorsky, Igor I., Jr. *AA's Godparents*. Minnesota: CompCare Publishers, 1990 (2) D1.

——. Manuscript of *AA's Godparents*, n.d. (D)

Smith, Bob and Sue Smith Windows. *Children of the Healer*. Illinois: Parkside Publishing, 1992. (1 inscribed by Bob and Betty to Dick B.) (2)

Sobriety Calendars for Various Years (11) D11

Stein, Benjamin J. *"Hollywood: God Is Nigh."* Newsweek, December 12, 1986.

Stoop, David and Stephen Arterburn. *The Twelve Step Life Recovery Devotional*. Wheaton, IL: Tyndale House Publishers, 1991.

Stools and Bottles. MN: Hazelden, 1995 (D).

Stools and Battles: Daily Thoughts and Meditations For A.A. Members. MN: Coll-Webb Co., 1955.

"Strong Tea." Alcoholics Anonymous and The Four Absolutes. CA: Lucky Bill Tapes (reprint of July 1976 issue of *24 Magazine*, author unknown).

The Cost of Substance Abuse to America's Health Care System. NY: A CASA Report, 1994.

The Dove Locator to the Big Book of Alcoholics Anonymous. MO: Locator Publications, 1987 (D)

The Life Recovery Bible: The Living Bible. IL: Tyndale House Publishers, 1992. (2).

The Little Big Book. NY: AA-BBSG, *n.d.* (D)

The Little Red Book. Rev. MN: Hazelden, 1996.

The Little Red Book: An Interpretation of the Twelve Steps of the Alcoholics Anonymous Program. MN: Coll-Webb Company, 1957 (D1).

The 4ᵗʰ Edition. NY: Big Book Study Group, n.d. ISBN 0-9663282-2-1. (Reprint of First Edition of the Alcoholics Anonymous.)

The San Diego AA Coordinator. San Diego Central Office, 1995 (D)

The Twelve Steps of Alcoholics Anonymous. Hazelden

Thomsen, Robert. *Bill W.* New York: Harper & Row, 1975 (3) D1.

Twelve Steps and the Older Member. Older Member Press, 1964 (2) D1.

Van V., Ellie, ed. *Dairy of Two Motorcycle Hobos.* Canada: Gratitude Press Canada, 1998 (D)

Walker, Richmond. *For Drunks Only.* Minnesota: Hazelden, n.d. (2).

———. *The 7 Points of Alcoholics Anonymous.* Seattle: Glen Abbey Books, 1989 (2) D1.

Washington Temperance Society: 1842. (Hardcover reprint of original articles.)

We in Recovery. Premier Issue, 1995, Pittsburgh, Pennsylvania (D)

Webb, Terry. *Tree of Renewed Life: Spiritual Renewal of the Church through the Twelve-Step Program.* New York: Crossroad, 1992 (2) D1.

Wholey, Dennis. The Courage to Change: Personal Conversations about Alcoholism with Dennis Wholey. Boston: Houghton Mifflin Company, 1948 (2) D1.

———. When the Worst That Can Happen Already Has. NY: Berkeley Books, 1992.

Wilson, Bill. How The Big Book Was Put Together. New York: A.A. General Services Archives, Transcript of Bill Wilson Speech delivered in Fort Worth, Texas, 1954.

———. *Bill Wilson's Original Story.* Bedford Hills, New York: Stepping Stones Archives, n.d., a manuscript whose individual lines are numbered 1 to 1180.

———. "Main Events: Alcoholics Anonymous Fact Sheet by Bill." November 1, 1954. Stepping Stones Archives. Bedford Hills, New York.

———. "Our Destiny Can Surely Be Made Secure." Talk to Dutch Groups, 10th Anniversary, The Hague, n.d.

———. "The Fellowship of Alcoholics Anonymous." *Quarterly Journal of Studies on Alcohol.* Yale University, 1945, pp. 461-73.

———. *W. G. Wilson Recollections.* Bedford Hills, New York: Stepping Stones Archives, September 1, 1954 transcript of Bill's dictations to Ed B.

———. *Why Alcoholics Anonymous is Anonymous.*

Wilson, Jan R., and Judith A. Wilson. *Addictionary: A Primer of Recovery Terms and Concepts from Abstinence to Withdrawal.* New York: Simon and Schuster, 1992 (3) D1

Wilson, Lois. *Lois Remembers.* New York: Al-Anon Family Group Headquarters, 1987 (2) D1.

Windows, Sue Smith. (daughter of A.A.'s Co-Founder, Dr. Bob). Typewritten Memorandum entitled, *Henrietta and early Oxford Group Friends, by Sue Smith Windows.* Delivered to the author of this book by Sue Smith Windows at Akron, June, 1991.

———. Article on Lois Wilson's hosting A.A.'s oldtimers at Stepping Stones, mentioning Sue and her husband, Bob Smith and his wife, Johnny and Elsie R., Al L., Ed A., and Clarence S.

Wing, Nell. *Grateful to Have Been There: My 42 Years with Bill and Lois, and the Evolution of Alcoholics Anonymous.* Illinois: Parkside Publishing Corporation, 1992.

Women Pioneers in Recovery. MN: Hazelden Pittman Archives Press, 1999 (D)

Publications Approved by Alcoholics Anonymous

AA Everywhere-Anywhere. NY: Alcoholics Anonymous World Services, Inc., 1995 [San Diego] (D)

A.A. Service Manual, The, 1987 Edition. New York: Alcoholics Anonymous World Services, Inc., 1969.

AA in Prison: Inmate to Inmate. NY: Alcoholics Anonymous World Services, Inc., 1991.

AA Fact File. NY: General Service Office of A.A., 1956 (D)

AA Grapevine: Spirituality in AA., April, 1994. NY: The AA Grapevine, Inc., 1944.

A.A. Grapevine, The: "RHS"—issue dedicated to the memory of the Co-

Founder of Alcoholics Anonymous, DR. BOB. New York: A.A. Grapevine, Inc., 1951 (two copies).

AA Grapevine Various Issues (73) D73

AA Grapevine Workbook. NY: The AA Grapevine, Inc., 1993 (D)

AA Group, The: Where it all begins. Rev. ed. NY: Alcoholics Anonymous World Services, Inc., 1990 (2).

A Brief Guide to Alcoholics Anonymous. New York: Alcoholics Anonymous World Services, Inc., 1972.

Alcoholics Anonymous. 3rd ed. New York: Alcoholics Anonymous World Services, Inc., 1976 (27) D1.

Alcoholics Anonymous. 2d ed. (Beautifully covered copies of each reprint) 13 (D)

Alcoholics Anonymous. 3rd ed. (Beautifully covered copies of each reprint) 54 (D)

Alcoholics Anonymous 3rd ed.(Spanish Language Edition) 1 (D)

Alcoholics Anonymous. 1st ed. New Jersey: Works Publishing, 1939 (reprint with "circus" cover).

Alcoholics Anonymous. 2d ed. New York City: Alcoholics Anonymous World Services, Inc., 1955 (2) D1

Alcoholics Anonymous Comes of Age. New York: Alcoholics Anonymous World Services, Inc., 1957.

A Newcomer Asks . . . York, England: A.A. Sterling Area Services, n.d.

As Bill Sees It: The A.A. Way of Life . . . *selected writings of A.A.'s Co-Founder.* New York: Alcoholics Anonymous World Services, Inc., 1967 (2) D1.

Best Cartoons from the Grapevine. NY: Cornwall Press, 1990 (D)

Best of Bill from the Grapevine, The: Faith, Fear, Honesty, Humility, Love. NY: The AA Grapevine, Inc., 1986.

Best of the Grapevine. New York: The A.A. Grapevine, Inc., 1985 (2) D1.

Best of the Grapevine, Volume II. New York: The A.A. Grapevine, Inc., 1986 (2) D1.

"Bill W.: 1895 - 1971." *AA Grapevine*, March, 1971

Bill W. *A.A. Tradition: How It Developed.* NY: Alcoholics Anonymous World Services, Inc., 1983.

Came to Believe. New York: Alcoholics Anonymous World Services, Inc., 1973 (2) D1.

Co-Founders of Alcoholics Anonymous, The: Biographical sketches. Their Last Talks. New York: Alcoholics Anonymous World

Services, Inc., 1972, 1975 (7).

Daily Reflections. New York: Alcoholics Anonymous World Services, Inc., 1991 (2) D1.

DR. BOB and the Good Oldtimers. New York: Alcoholics Anonymous World Services, Inc., 1980. (4) D1

DR. BOB and the Good Oldtimers: (Spanish Language Edition) (1) D

"Fifty Years with Gratitude" NY: Alcoholics Anonymous World Services, Inc., 1985 [Quebec Convention](D)

Grapevine Binder, 13 issues (13) D

44 Questions. New York: Works Publishing, Inc., 1952.

Inside AA: Understanding the Fellowship and Its Service Agencies. NY: Alcoholics Anonymous World Services, Inc., 1974 (2) D2.

"Jack Alexander Article about AA, The." (A reprint from *The Saturday Evening Post,* 1941.)

Language of the Heart, The. Bill W.'s Grapevine Writings. New York: The A.A. Grapevine, Inc., 1988.

Living Sober: Some Methods A.A. Members have used for not drinking. NY: Alcoholics Anonymous World Services, Inc., 1975 (2) D1.

Members of the Clergy Ask about Alcoholics Anonymous. New York: Alcoholics Anonymous World Services, 1961, 1979-revised 1992, according to 1989 Conference Advisory Action.

Pass It On. New York: Alcoholics Anonymous World Services, Inc., 1984. (3) D1

Questions & Answers on Sponsorship. New York: Alcoholics Anonymous World Services, Inc., 1976 (3).

The A.A. Service Manual Combined with Twelve Concepts for World Service. NY: Alcoholics Anonymous World Services, Inc. [covering several periods of time] (11) D10

The Danny W. Collection of A.A. Conference Approved Pamphlets on a wide variety of topics over a period of many years (325 pamphlets)

The Forty-Fourth Annual Meeting of The General Service Conference, 1994 (D)

The Forty-Fifth Annual Meeting of The General Service Conference, 1995 (D)

The Forty-Sixth Annual Meeting of the General Service Conference, 1996

The Home Group: Heartbeat of A.A. A Collection of Articles

Reprinted from the A.A. Grapevine. NY: The AA Grapevine, Inc., 1993 (D)

The Third Legacy Manual of A.A. World Service. NY: Alcoholics Anonymous Publishing, 1955 (D)

The Thirtieth Annual Meeting of the General Service Conference of Alcoholics Anonymous, 1980 (D)

This is A.A. . . . An Introduction to the A.A. Recovery Program. New York: Alcoholics Anonymous World Services, Inc., 1984 (2).

Three Talks to Medical Societies by Bill W., Co-Founder of Alcoholics Anonymous. NY: Alcoholics Anonymous World Services, Inc., 1988.

Twelve Concepts For World Service by Bill W., 1962 and 1978 (2) D2

Twelve Steps and Twelve Traditions. New York: Alcoholics Anonymous World Services, Inc., 1953 (5) D1.

Twelve Traditions Illustrated, The. NY: Alcoholics Anonymous World Services, Inc., 1971.

Pamphlets Circulated in Early A.A.

A.A. God's Instrument. Chicago: Chicago Area Alcoholics Anonymous Service Office, 1954.

A. A. Sponsorship: Its Opportunities and Its Responsibilities. Cleveland: Cleveland Ohio District Office, 1944 (located in Clarence Snyder archives box of Dick B.).

Alcoholics Anonymous: An Interpretation of our Twelve Steps. Washington, D.C.: Paragon Creative Printers, 1944 (2)

Alcoholics Anonymous Approach Program. Jackson, Michigan, n.d.

A Manual for Alcoholics Anonymous. Akron: AA of Akron, Alcoholics Anonymous Group No. 1 (plus two sixth revised edition copies).

Andy, Ed R. *Gossip*: Lorain, Ohio, n.d.

———. *Resent Somebody. . . .* Lorain, Ohio, n.d.

Central Bulletin, Volumes I - III. Cleveland Central Committee, October, 1942 - December, 1945 (located in Clarence Snyder archives box of Dick B.).

Clarence Snyder Binder with Guidance of God and Four Absolutes used in early A.A. plus personal stories of pioneers.

Delahanty, Edward J., M.D. *The Therapeutic Value of the Twelve Steps of A.A.* Salt Lake City, UT: Alcoholism Foundations, n.d.

Devil and A.A., The. Chicago: Chicago Area Alcoholics Anonymous Service Office, 1948.

Four Absolutes, The. Cleveland: Cleveland Central Committee of A.A., n.d. (3).

G., Clyde. *My Quiet Time.* Cleveland: Alcoholics Anonymous, n.d.

Guide to Serenity, A. Cleveland: The Cleveland District Office of Alcoholics Anonymous, n.d.

Guide to the Twelve Steps of Alcoholics Anonymous, A. Akron: AA of Akron, n.d. (2)

Handles and Hodge Podge, comp. a member of Alcoholics Anonymous. Cleveland: The Cleveland District Office of Alcoholics Anonymous, n.d.

Handles for Sobriety, comp. A Member of Alcoholics Anonymous. Cleveland: The Cleveland District Office of Alcoholics Anonymous, n.d.

"It's All in the Mind" Chicago: Chicago Area Alcoholics Anonymous Service Office, n.d.

Making a Start in Alcoholics Anonymous: A Guide for the Beginners. Knoxville: East Tennessee Intergroup A.A., n.d.

New Way of Life, The: A.A. Cleveland: The Cleveland District Office of Alcoholics Anonymous, n.d.

Second Reader for Alcoholics Anonymous. Akron: AA of Akron, n.d.

Smith, Roy. *Emergency Rations*: cast thy burden upon the Lord, and he shall sustain thee. Psalm 55:22. Cleveland: The Cleveland District Office of Alcoholics Anonymous, n.d.

Spiritual Milestones in Alcoholics Anonymous. Akron: A.A. of Akron (three copies, 1974, 1986, 1989).

T., John. *A.A.: God's Instrument.* Chicago: Chicago Area Alcoholics Anonymous Service Office, n.d.

Twelve Steps of AA and The Bible. From the collection of Clancy U., n.d.

What Others Think of A.A. Akron: Friday Forum Luncheon Club, circa 1941.

Wood, Charles L. *Prayers for Alcoholics.* Cincinnati: Foreword Movement Publications, n.d. From a Midwest Intergroup Office.

Alcoholics Anonymous: Pro, Con, and Evaluated

B., Mel. *New Wine: The Spiritual Roots of the Twelve Step Miracle.*

Hazelden Foundation, 1991 (2) D1.

Baker, John. *Celebrate Recovery*. (Four pamphlets on the Twelve Steps).

Bartosch, Bob and Pauline. *A Bridge to Recovery*. La Habra, CA: Overcomers Outreach, Inc., 1994.

Bishop, Charlie, Jr. and Pittman, Bill. *To Be Continued...The Alcoholics Anonymous World Biography 1935-1994*. Wheeling, WV: The Bishop of Books, 1994 (2).

Bobgan, Martin and Deidre. *12 Steps to Destruction: Codependency Recovery Heresies*. Santa Barbara, CA: EastGate Publishers, 1991 (2) D1.

Bufe, Charles. *Alcoholics Anonymous: Cult or Cure?* 1st ed. San Francisco: Sharp Press, 1991 (2) D1

——. *Alcoholics Anonymous: Cult or Cure?* 2d. ed. (D)

Burns, Dr. Cathy. *Alcoholics Anonymous Unmasked: Deception and Deliverance*. Mt. Carmel, PA: Sharing, 1991 (2) D1.

Burns, Robert E., C.S.P. *The Catholic Church and Alcoholics Anonymous*. Columbia, 31: 15-16, May, 1952.

Burwell, Jim. *Bill Wilson Letters to Jim Burwell*

C., Chuck. *A New Pair of Glasses*. Irvine, CA: New-Look Publishing Company, 1984 (2) D1.

Chambers, Cal. *Two Tracks-One Goal: How Alcoholics Anonymous Relates to Christianity*. Langley, B.C., Canada: Credo Publishing Corporation, 1992.

Cline, Earl W. *AA: The New Mystery Cult*. Long Beach: C & R Communications, 1985 (D)

Clinebell, Howard. *Basic Types of Pastoral Care & Counseling: Resources for the Ministry of Healing & Growth*. Rev. and enlarged. Nashville: Abingdon Press, 1990 (inscribed to Dick B. by author)

——. *Basic Types of Pastoral Counseling*. Nashville: Abingdon Press, 1966 (D)

——. *Understanding and Counseling Persons with Alcohol, Drug, and Behavioral Addictions*. Rev. and enl. ed. Nashville: Abingdon Press, 1998.

——. *Well Being: A Personal Plan for Exploring and Enriching the Seven Dimensions of Life: Mind, Body, Spirit, Love, Work, Play, Earth*. San Francisco: Harper, 1992. (Inscribed to Dick B. by author.)

Ciccolini, Samuel R. *God, A.A., and Akron: A Golden Anniversary*

Tribute. Akron: Interval Brotherhood Home, 1985.

Costantino, Frank. *Holes in Time: The Autobiography of a Gangster.* 2d ed. Dallas, TX: Acclaimed Books, 1986. (3) D1

Cunningham, Loren. *Is That Really You, God?: Hearing the Voice of God.* Seattle, WA: YWAM Publishing, 1984 (2) D1.

Davis, Martin M. *The Gospel and the Twelve Steps: Developing a Closer Relationship with Jesus.* San Diego, CA: Recovery Publications, Inc., 1993.

Doe, Father John. *Sobriety and Beyond.* Indianapolis: The S.M.T. Guild, 1980 (2) D1

Dorsman, Jerry. *How to Quit Drinking Without A.A.: A Complete SelfHelp Guide.* DE: New Dawn Publishing Company, 1991 (D)

Dowling, The Reverend Edward, S.J. *Catholic Asceticism and the Twelve Steps.* St. Louis, MO, The Queen's Work, Brooklyn, 1953.

Doyle, Paul Barton. *In Step with God: A Scriptural Guide for Practicing 12 Step Programs.* Brentwood, TN: New Directions, 1989. (2nd ed. with Ishee–two copies in all.)

Dunn, Jerry G. *God is for the Alcoholic.* Chicago: Moody Press, 1965 (2) D1.

Ellis, Albert and Emmett Belten. *When A.A. Doesn't Work for You.* NJ: Barricade Books, 1992 (D)

Fingarette, Herbert. *Heavy Drinking: The Myth of Alcoholism as a Disease.* Berkeley, CA: University of California Press, 1988 (2) D1.

Fitzgerald, Robert. *The Soul of Sponsorship: The Friendship of Fr. Ed Dowling, S.J. and Bill Wilson in Letters.* Hazelden, 1995 (2).

Gilliam, Marianne. *How Alcoholics Anonymous Failed Me: My Personal Journey to Sobriety Through Self-Empowerment.* New York: Eagle Brook, 1998 (D)

Gorski, Terrence T. *Understanding the Twelve Steps: A Guide for Counselors, Therapists, and Recovering People.* Independence, MO: Herald House/Independence Press, 1989 (D)

Grateful Members. *The Twelve Steps for Everyone . . . Who Really Wants Them.* MN: CompCare, 1977 (2) D1

Guidebook for Overcomers Outreach: 12 Step Support Groups (D)

Hemfelt, Robert and Fowler, Richard. *Serenity: A Companion for Twelve Step Recovery.* Nashville, TN: Thomas Nelson Publishers, 1990.

Jellinek, E. M. *The Disease Concept of Alcoholism.* New Haven, CN: College and University Press, 1960 (2)D1.

K., Mitchell. *How It Worked: The Story of Clarence H. Snyder and the Early Days of Alcoholics Anonymous in Cleveland, Ohio.* NY: AA Big Book Study Group, 1997. (Inscribed to Dick B. by the author.)

Kavanaugh, Philip. *Magnificent Addiction: Discovering Addiction as Gateway to Healing.* CA: Asland Publishing, 1992.

Kessel, Joseph. *The Road Back: A Report on Alcoholics Anonymous.* New York: Alfred A. Knopf, 1962 (3) D1.

Ketcham, Katherine, and William Asbury. *Beyond The Influence: Understanding and Defeating Alcoholism.* (Draft edition.)

Kurtz, Ernest and Katherine Ketcham. *The Spirituality of Imperfection: Modern Wisdom from Classic Stories.* New York: Bantam Books, 1992 (2) D1.

Landry, Mim J. *Overview of Addiction Treatment Effectiveness.* Rev. ed., 1997. U.S. Department of Health and Human Services.

Larson, Joan Mathews. *Seven Weeks to Sobriety: The Proven Program to Fight Alcoholism Through Nutrition.* New York: Fawcett Columbine, 1992 (2) D1

————. *Alcoholism-The Biochemical Connection: A Breakthrough Seven-Week Self-Treatment Program.* NY: Villard Books, 1992 (D)

Lomas, Tom. *40 Days to Freedom: Live the Miracle!* FL: Freedom Ministries, 1994.

Martin, Father Joseph C. *No Laughing Matter: Chalk Talks on Alcohol.* San Francisco: Harper & Row, 1982 (D)

May, Gerald G. *Addiction & Grace: Love and Spirituality in the Healing of Addictions.* Harper San Francisco, 1988 (D)

McCrady, Barbara and William R. Miller. *Research on Alcoholics Anonymous: Opportunities and Alternatives.* NJ: Rutgers Center of Alcohol Studies, 1993 (D)

McGee, Robert S., Pat Springle, and Susan Joiner. *Rapha's Twelve Step Program for Overcoming Chemical Dependency.* 2d ed. TX: Rapha Publishing/Word, Inc., 1995.

McNeil, Robert Dean. *Valiant for Truth Clarence True Wilson and Prohibition: A story of Prohibition and one of its leading advocates.* OR: Oregonians Concerned about Addiction Problems, 1992. (Inscribed to Dick B. by the author.)

McQ., Joe. *The Steps We Took.* Little Rock, AR: August House Publishers, Inc., 1990 (2) D1.

Mellon, John C. *Finding Jesus in Sobriety: A Millennial Translation of* the Gospel of Mark. IL: Markos Books, 1999.

Miller, J. Keith. *A Hunger for Healing: The Twelve Steps as a Classic Model for Christian Spiritual Growth*. San Francisco: HarperSanFrancisco, 1991 (2) D1.

Morreim, Dennis C. *The Road to Recovery: Bridges between the Bible and the Twelve Steps*. MN: Augsburg Fortress, 1990 (D)

Nelson, James Douglas. *Awakening: Restoring Health through the Spiritual Principles of Shalom, Jesus and the Twelve Step Recovery Program*. PA: Tab Books, Inc., 1989.

O., Dr. Paul. *There's More to Quitting Drinking than Quitting Drinking*. Laguna Niguel, CA: Sabrina Publishing, 1995.

O., Peter. *Serenity's Prayer: Asking for Recovery. Surviving Our Daily Struggles*. NY: East River/Saratoga Inc., 1997.

Ozment, Robert V. *But God Can*. NJ: Fleming H. Revell Company, 1962 (D)

P., Bob. *Unforgettable Bill W.* Excerpt from *Reader's Digest*, April, 1986.

P., Homer. *Turning It Over: A Third Step Guide for Recovering People*. MN: Hazelden, 1999

P., Wally. *Back to Basics: The Alcoholics Anonymous Beginners' Classes. Take All 12 Steps in Four One-Hour Sessions*. Tucson, AZ: Faith With Works Publishing Company, 1997.

Parham, A. Philip. *Letting God: Christian Meditations for Recovering Persons*. San Francisco: Harper & Row, 1987.

Pawlak, Vic. *Drug Abuse: A Realistic Primer for Parents*. AZ: Do It Now Foundation, n.d.

Peale, Norman Vincent. *The Positive Power of Jesus Christ: Life-Changing Adventures in Faith*. Pauling, NY: Foundation for Christian Living, 1980 (2) D.

———. *The Power of Positive Thinking*. Pauling, NY: Peale Center for Christian Living, 1978 (2) D1.

———. "Twelve Tremendous Steps that Will Work for Anyone." *Guideposts Magazine*, 1989

Peck, M. Scott. *The Road Less Traveled: A New Psychology of Love, Traditional Values and Spiritual Growth*. NY: A Touchstone Book, 1978.

Peele, Stanton. *Diseasing of America: How We Allowed Recovery Zealots and the Treatment Industry to Convince Us We Are Out of Control*. San Francisco: Jossey-Bass Publishers, 1995.

————. and Charles Bufe. *Resisting 12-Step Coercion*. Tucson, AZ: Sharp Press, 2000.

Pittman, Bill. *The 12 Step Prayer Book*. WA: Glen Abbey Books, 1990 (D)

Playfair, William L. *The Useful Lie*. Wheaton, IL: Crossway Books, 1991 (2) D1.

Powter, Susan. *Sober . . . And Staying That Way: This Missing Link in the Cure for Alcoholism*. NY: Simon & Schuster, 1997.

Prayers for the Twelve Steps: A Spiritual Journey. CA: Recovery Publications Inc., 1993.

Preston, John, Nicolette Varzos, and Douglas Liebert. *Every Session Counts: Making the Most of Your Brief Therapy*. CA: Impact Publishers, 1995.

Program for You, A: A Guide to the Big Book's Design for Living. Hazelden Foundation, 1991.

Ragge, Ken. *More Revealed: A Critical Analysis of Alcoholics Anonymous and the Twelve Steps*. Henderson, NV: Alert! Publishing, 1991 (2) D1.

Ryan, Dale and Juanita. *The Twelve Steps A Spiritual Kindergarten: Christian Perspectives on the Twelve Steps*. CA: Christian Recovery International, 1999.

Life Recovery Bible, The: The Living Bible. Wheaton, IL: Tyndale House Publishers, Inc., 1992.

Seiden, Jerry. *Divine or Distorted?: God As We Understand God*. San Diego, CA: Recovery Publications, Inc., 1993.

Self-Help Sourcebook, The: Your Guide to Community and Online Support Groups. 6th.ed. compiled and edited by Barbara J. White and Edward J. Madara. Denville, NJ: American Self-Help Clearinghouse, 1994.

Spiritual Journeys and Mental Exercises in Alcoholics Anonymous, n.d.

Stafford, Tim. *The Hidden Gospel of the 12 Steps. Christianity Today*, July 22, 1991.

The Fourth Edition (D)

Taintor, Eliot. *September Remember*. NY: Prentice-Hall, 1945 (D)

Taylor, G. Aiken. *A Sober Faith: Religion and Alcoholics Anonymous*. NY: Macmillan, 1954 (D)

The Twelve Steps: A Spiritual Journey. Rev. ed. CA: RPI, 1988 (D)

The 12 Steps: A Way Out. CA: Recovery Publications, 1987 (D)

The Light That Heals: A Modern Testimony of Spiritual Therapy. CT:

Older Member Press, 1970 (D)

Trimpey, Jack. *Rational Recovery: The New Cure for Substance Addiction.* New York: Pocket Books, 1996 (2) D1.

———. *Revolutionary Alternative for Overcoming Alcohol and Drug Dependence, A: The Small Book.* Rev. ed. NY: Delacorte Press, 1992 (2) D1.

U.S. Department of Health and Human Services. Substance Abuse and Mental Health Services Administration. *National Household Survey on Drug Abuse: Main Findings 1996.* Rockville, MD: SAMHSA, Office of Applied Studies, 1998.

Vaillant, George E. *The Natural History of Alcoholism: Causes, Patterns, And Paths to Recovery.* Cambridge, MA: Harvard University Press, 1983 (D)

———. *The Natural History of Alcoholism Revisited.* Cambridge, MA: Harvard University Press, 1995.

Way Home, The: A Spiritual Approach to Recovery. Orlando, FL: Bridge Builders, Inc., 1996.

White, William L. *Slaying The Dragon: The History of Addiction Treatment and Recovery in America.* Bloomington, IL: Chestnut Health Systems/Lighthouse Institute, 1998 (2) D1

Williams, Jerry. *Keep Coming Back: It Works*. Scott Valley, CA: Star Lodge Publications, n.d. (D)

Part 3
Spiritual History and Roots of Alcoholics Anonymous

The Bible—Versions of and Books About

Abingdon Bible Commentary, The. New York: Abingdon Press, 1929 (2).

Authorized (King James) Version. New York: Thomas Nelson, 1984.

Begbie, Harold. *The Bible in Story and Pictures.* 2 vols. New and Old Testament. NY: H. S. Stuttman, 1956 (2) D2

Bochmuehl, Klaus. *Listening to the God Who Speaks: Reflections on God's Guidance from Scripture and the Lives of God's People.* CO: Helmers & Howard, 1990.

Bryan, William Jennings. *The Bible and Its Enemies.* Chicago: The Bible Institute Colportage Assn., 1921 (D)

Catholic Encyclopedia, The. New York: Robert Appleton Company, 1912. (Extract from Volume XV on *Yahweh*, *Jehovah*.)

Divine Name That Will Endure Forever, The. NY: Watch Tower Bible and Tract Society of Pennsylvania. (A study of God's name, "Jehovah," and its importance.)

Every Catholic's Guide to the Sacred Scriptures. Nashville: Thomas Nelson, 1990.

Fenelon. *Let Go.* PA: Whitaker House, 1973. (Inscribed to Dick B. by Dr. Bob's daughter-in-law, Betty Smith.)

Gibran, Kahlil. *Jesus The Son of Man.* NY: Knopf, 1958 (D)

Goodspeed, Edgar J. *The New Testament: An American Translation.* Chicago: The University of Chicago Press, 1923 (D)

Harnack, Adolph. *The Expansion of Christianity in the First Three Centuries.* New York: G. P. Putnam's Sons, Volume I, 1904; Volume II, 1905. (In the Johnston collection).

Harrell, Irene Burk and Alie Harrell Benson. *The Manufacturer's Handbook: The 4-in-1 Gospel for King's Kids*. NC: Star Books, 1987 (D)

Hill, Harold. *Bible Answers for King's Kids*. NJ: Fleming H. Revell, 1984 (D)

——. *God's In Charge Here*. NJ: Fleming H. Revell, 1982 (D)

"Jehovah." (Extract of pages on "Jehovah," collected by a Canadian A.A. and sent to Dick B.)

Jukes, Andrew. *The Names of GOD in Holy Scripture*. Michigan: Kregel Publications, 1967 (2) D.

Kierkegaard, Soren. *Edifying Discourses: A Selection*. NY: Harper & Brothers, 1958 (D)

Law, William. *The Power of the Spirit*. PA: Christian literature Crusade, 1971.

Lytle, Clyde Francis, ed. *Leaves of Gold*. PA: Coslett Publishing, 1948 (D)

Lewis, C. S. *Christian Reflections*. Michigan: William B. Eerdmans, 1967 (D)

——. *Reflections on the Psalms*. NY: Harcourt, Brace, 1958 (D)

——. *Surprised By Joy*: The Shape of My Early Life. NY: Harcourt, Brace, 1955 (D)

——. *Till We Have Faces*. NY: Time Reading Program, 1956 (D)

Life Recovery Bible, The. Wheaton, IL: Tyndale House Publishers, 1992.

Mears, Henrietta C. *What the Bible is All About*. Rev. ed. Dallas, TX: Chaplain Ray International Prison Ministry, 1983 (D)

McKnight, Edgar V. *Opening The Bible: A Guide To Understanding The Scriptures*. Broadman Press, 1967 (D)

Megivern, James J. *Official Catholic Teachings: Bible Interpretation*. North Carolina: McGrath Publishing Company, 1978.

Moffatt, James. *A New Translation of the Bible*. New York: Harper & Brothers, 1954 (2) D1

——. *A New Translation of the New Testament*. NY: Hodder & Stoughton, 1913 (D)

New Catholic Encyclopedia. Washington D.C.: The Catholic University of America, 1967. (Extract on *Jehovah, Yahweh, Jehovah's Witnesses*.)

Phillips, J. B. *The New Testament in Modern English*. New York: The Macmillan Company, 1958.

Puskas, Charles B. *An Introduction to the New Testament*. Mass.:

Hendrickson Publishers, 1989.

Schaeffer, Francis A. *He is There And He is not Silent*. IL: Tyndale House Publishers, 1972 (D)

Schaff, Philip. *History of the Christian Church*. MI: Wm B. Eerdmans, 1956. Two Volumes

Spurgeon, C. H. *Twelve Sermons For The Troubled and Tried*. Fleming H. Revell, 1862-92 (D)

Strong, James. *The Exhaustive Concordance of the Bible*. Iowa: Riverside Book and Bible House, n.d.

The Guideposts Parallel Bible. NY: Zondervan, 1981 (D)

The NIV Exhaustive Concordance. Grand Rapids, MI: The Zondervan Corporation, 1990 (D)

Vine's Expository Dictionary of Old and New Testament Words. NJ: Fleming H. Revell, 1981 D

Young's Analytical Concordance. Grand Rapids, Michigan, Robert Young., n.d. (D)

Quiet Time and Inspirational Books, Pamphlets and Bible Devotionals Popular with Dr. Bob and Early AAs, As Well As More Recent "Meditation" Books

The Early Quiet Time Books, Devotionals, and Pamphlets the Pioneers Used

À Kempis, Thomas. *The Imitation of Christ*. England: Penguin Group, 1952 (3) D2.

Allen, James. *As a Man Thinketh*. New York: Peter Pauper Press, Inc., n.d. (5) D2

Carruthers, Donald W. *How to Find Reality in Your Morning Devotions*, State College, PA., n.d.

Chambers, Oswald, *My Utmost for His Highest*. Oswald Chambers Publication Assn. 1963 (3)D1.

——. *Studies in the Sermon on the Mount*. MI: Discovery House, 1960. (2)

Clark, Glenn. *I Will Lift Up Mine Eyes*. New York: Harper & Row, 1937.

Drummond, Henry. *The Greatest Thing in the World*. Fleming H. Revell, 1968. (3) D2

Dunnington, Lewis L. *Handles of Power*. New York: Abingdon-

67

Cokesbury Press, 1942 (2) D1.

Fosdick, Harry Emerson. *The Meaning of Prayer*. New York: Association Press, 1915. (6) D4

Gordon, S. D. *Quiet Talks on Prayer* NJ: The Christian Library, 1984 (2) D1.

Holm, Nora Smith. *The Runner's Bible: Compiled and Annotated for the Reading of Him Who Runs*. New York: Houghton Mifflin Company, 1913. (4) D1

Jones, E. Stanley. *Abundant Living*. New York: Abingdon-Cokesbury Press, 1942 (3) D1

———. *Victorious Living*. New York: Abingdon Press, 1936 (2) D1.

———. *The Christ of the Mount: A Working Philosophy of Life*. New York: The Abingdon Press, 1931.

Sheldon, Charles M. *In His Steps: "What Would Jesus Do?"* New York: Books, Inc., n.d. (4) D1

The Upper Room: Daily Devotions for Family and Individual Use. Edited by Grover Carlton Emmons. Nashville: Department of Home Missions, Evangelism, Hospitals Board of Missions, Methodist Episcopal Church, South. (Reprint of the first issue of this quarterly: April, May, June, 1935).

———. January-March, 1941, issue.

———. July-August, 1993, issue.

———. November-December, 1997, issue.

———. (Almost complete set of photocopies of all quarterlies from April, 1935 to June, 1939.)

———. Index by Dick B. prepared and used to locate verses popular and studied in early A.A.

Tileston, Mary W. *Daily Strength for Daily Needs*. New York: Grosset and Dunlap, 1934 (2) D1.

Other, Recent "Meditation" Books

B., Mel. *Walk in Dry Places*. MN: Hazelden, 1996.

Chambers, Oswald. *The Place of Help: A Book of Devotional Readings*. NY: Grosset & Dunlap, 1936 (D)

Cordes, Liane. *The Reflecting Pond*. MN: Hazelden, 1981 (D)

Daily Affirmations: For Adult Children of Alcoholics. FL: Health Communications, Inc.,1985(D)

Daily Reflections: A Book of Reflections by A.A. Members for A.A.

68

Members. New York: Alcoholics Anonymous World Services, Inc., 1990.

Dayton, Tian. *The Soul's Companion: Connecting with the Soul through Daily Meditations*. FL: Health Communications, Inc., 1995.

Each Day a New Beginning: Daily Meditations for Women. MN: Hazelden, 1982 (D)

Hager, Wesley H. *Whom God Hath Joined Together: A Devotional Guide for Husband and Wife*. Nashville: The Upper Room, 1962 (D)

Keep It Simple. NY: Harper-Hazelden, 1985 (D)

Marshall, Catherine. *Adventures in Prayer*. Carmel, NY: Guideposts, n.d.

Meditations on the Twelve Steps. Nashville: Thomas Nelson, n.d. (D)

Myers, Warren and Ruth. *How to Have a Quiet Time*. CO: Navpress, 1989.

Parham, A. Philip. *Letting God: Christian Meditations for Recovering Persons*. San Francisco: Harper & Row, 1987 (2) D1.

Prescott, D. M. *A New Day: Daily Readings for Our Time*. New ed. London: Grosvenor Books, 1979 (2) (D1).

The Two Listeners. *God Calling*. Edited by A. J. Russell. Ohio: A Barbour Book, 1985 (4) D1.

Twenty-Four Hours a Day, Rev ed. MN: Hazelden, 1975 (3) D1.

Publications by or about the Rev. Samuel Moor Shoemaker, Jr.

Shoemaker, Samuel Moor, Jr., "A 'Christian Program.'" In *Groups That Work: The Key to Renewal . . . for Churches, Communities, and Individuals*. Compiled by Walden Howard and the Editors of *Faith At Work*. Michigan: Zondervan, 1967.

———. "Act As If." *Christian Herald*. October, 1954 (2).

———. "A First Century Christian Fellowship: A Defense of So-called Buchmanism by One of Its Leaders." Reprinted from the *Churchman*, circa 1928.

———. "And So from My Heart I Say . . ." *The A.A. Grapevine*. New York: The A.A. Grapevine, Inc., September, 1948.

———. *. . . And Thy Neighbor*. Waco, Texas: Word Books, 1967 (2) D1.

———. *A Young Man's View of the Ministry*. New York: Association Press, 1923.

———. *Beginning Your Ministry*. New York: Harper & Row Publishers,

1963 (2) D1.

———. *By the Power of God.* New York: Harper & Brothers, 1954 (2) D1.

———. *Calvary Church Yesterday and Today.* New York: Fleming H. Revell, 1936 (2) D1.

———. *Children of the Second Birth.* New York: Fleming H. Revell, 1927 (2) D1.

———. *Christ and This Crisis.* New York: Fleming H. Revell, 1943.

———. *Christ's Words from the Cross.* New York: Fleming H. Revell, 1933 (2) D1.

———. *Confident Faith.* New York: Fleming H. Revell, 1932.

———. *Creative Relationships* [in the title, *Together.* ed. By Glenn Clark]. NY: Abingdon-Cokesbury, 1956 (D)

———. *Extraordinary Living for Ordinary Men.* Michigan: Zondervan, 1965 (2) D1.

———. *Faith at Work.* A symposium edited by Samuel Moor Shoemaker. Hawthorne Books, 1958 (2) D1.

———. *Freedom and Faith.* New York: Fleming H. Revell, 1949 (2) D1.

———. *Get Going Through Small Groups.* NY: Guideposts (D)

———. *God and America.* New York: Book Stall, 61 Gramercy Park North, New York, n.d.

———. *God's Control.* New York: Fleming H. Revell, 1939 (2) (D1).

———. *How to Become a Christian.* New York: Harper & Brothers, 1953 (4) D1.

———. "How to Find God." *The Calvary Evangel.* July, 1957, pp. 1-24.

———. *How to Help People.* Cincinnati: Forward Movement Publications, 1976.

———. *How You Can Find Happiness.* New York: E. P. Dutton & Co., 1947 (2) D1.

———. *How You Can Help Other People.* New York: E. P. Dutton & Co., 1946 (3) D1.

———. *If I Be Lifted Up.* New York: Fleming H. Revell, 1931 (3) D1.

———. *In Memoriam: The Service of Remembrance.* Princeton: The Graduate Council, Princeton University, June 10, 1956.

———. *Living Your Life Today.* New York: Fleming H. Revell, 1947 (2) (D1).

———. "Lord, Teach Us to Pray." *Creative Help for Daily Living* (Foundation for Christian Living, Pawling, New York) 28, no. 2 (1977), Part ii.

———. *Morning Radio Talk No. 1, by Reverend Samuel M. Shoemaker,*

American Broadcasting Co., 1 page transcript of program for October 4, 1945.

———. *My Life-Work and My Will.* Pamphlet, Christian ministry conference, Concord, N.H., circa 1930 (2).

———. *National Awakening.* New York: Harper & Brothers, 1936 (2) (D).

———. *One Boy's Influence.* New York: Association Press, 1925.

———. *Realizing Religion.* New York: Association Press, 1923 (4) D1.

———. *Religion That Works.* New York: Fleming H. Revell, 1928 (2) D1.

———. *Revive Thy Church.* New York: Harper & Brothers, 1948 (2) D1.

———. *Sam Shoemaker at His Best.* New York: Faith At Work, 1964.

———. *So I Stand by the Door and Other Verses.* Pittsburgh: Calvary Rectory, 1958.

———. *Steps of a Modern Disciple.* Atlanta, GA: Lay Renewal Publications, 1972.

———. *The Breadth and Narrowness of the Gospel.* New York: Fleming H. Revell, 1929.

———. *The Calvary Evangel, monthly articles in.* New York. Calvary Episcopal Church.

———. *The Church Alive.* New York: E. P. Dutton & Co., Inc., 1951 (2) D1.

———. *The Church Can Save the World.* New York: Harper & Brothers, 1938 (4) D1.

———. *The Conversion of the Church.* New York: Fleming H. Revell, 1932 (3) D1.

———. "The Crisis of Self-Surrender." *Guideposts.* November, 1955.

———. *The Experiment of Faith.* New York: Harper & Brothers. 1957 (4) D2.

———. *The Gospel According to You.* New York: Fleming H. Revell, 1934 (3).

———. *The Guideposts Trilogy* [faith, prayer, healing] NY: Guideposts Associates, 1962 (D)

———. *The James Houston Eccleston Day-Book: Containing a Short Account of His Life and Readings for Every Day in the Year Chosen from His Sermons.* Compiled by Samuel M. Shoemaker, Jr. New York: Longmans, Green & Co., 1915.

———. "The Spiritual Angle." *The A.A. Grapevine.* New York: The A.A. Grapevine, Inc., October, 1955.

———. "The Way to Find God." *The Calvary Evangel*, August, 1935 (2).

———. *They're on the Way.* New York: E. P. Dutton, 1951 (2) D1.

————. "Creative Relationships." In *Together*. New York: Abingdon Cokesbury Press, 1946.

————. "The Twelve Steps of A.A.: What They Can Mean to the Rest of Us." *The Calvary Evangel*. New York: The Evangel, 1953.

————. "Those Twelve Steps As I Understand Them." *Best of the Grapevine: Volume II*. New York: The A.A. Grapevine, Inc., 1986.

————. "12 Steps to Power." *Faith At Work News*. Reprint. 1983 (4)

Transcript of Reverend Samuel M. Shoemaker's Talk to Third International A.A. Convention, 25th A.A. Anniversary, Sunday, July 3, 1960, ll:00 A.M., Memorial Stadium, Long Beach.

Transcript prepared by Rev. Samuel Shoemaker as to Bill Wilson's remarks at the annual AA dinner, celebrating Bill Wilson's 20th anniversary, on Tuesday, November 9, 1954, at the Grand Ballroom of the Commodore Hotel. Title: "The Story of the Foundings of AA."

————. *Twice-Born Ministers*. New York: Fleming H. Revell, 1929 (2) D1.

————. *Under New Management*. Grand Rapids: Zondervan Publishing House., 1966 (2) D1.

————. *What the Church Has to Learn from Alcoholics Anonymous*. Reprint of 1956 sermon. (2.)

————. *With the Holy Spirit and with Fire*. New York: Harper & Brothers, 1960 (4) D2.

A Guide to Calvary Episcopal Church: 125th Anniversary 1855-1980. Pittsburgh: Calvary Episcopal Church, 1980.

"Buchman Religion Explained to 1,000." *New York Times*. May 27, 1931.

Callahan, Griffin C. *Kairos Moments Remembered: Taking Hurdles for Our Coach*. WV: Griffin C. Callahan, 1999. (Inscribed to Dick B. by author and references to Shoemaker, the Oxford Group, and Pittsburgh days.)

"Calvary Mission." Pamphlet. New York: Calvary Episcopal Church, n.d.

"Calvary Mission Celebrates Its First Anniversary" *Calvary Evangel*, February, 1917. (Excerpt.)

"Campus Calls by Dr. Shoemaker Foster Chain of Religious Cells." *New York Tribune*. February 25, 1951.

Centennial History: Calvary Episcopal Church, 1855-1955. Pittsburgh: Calvary Episcopal Church, 1955 (2) D1.

"Church Ejects Buchman Group." *New York Times*. November 8, 1941.

"Crusaders of Reform." *Princeton Alumni Weekly*. June 2, 1993.

Cuyler, John Potter, Jr. *Calvary Church in Action*. New York: Fleming H. Revell, 1934.

Day, Sherwood S. "Always Ready: S.M.S. As a Friend." *The Evangel* (New York: Calvary Church, July-August, 1950).

Gammon, Roland. *Faith Is A Star*. N. Y. E. P. Dutton, 1963 (D)

Get Changed; Get Together; Get Going: A History of the Pittsburgh Experiment. Pittsburgh: The Pittsburgh Experiment, n.d.

Harris, Irving. *The Breeze of the Spirit*. New York: The Seabury Press, 1978 (2) D1.

———. "S.M.S.—Man of God for Our Time." *Faith At Work* (January-February, 1964).

"Houseparties Across the Continent." *The Christian Century*. August 23, 1933.

*Howard, Walden. *Groups the Work: the key to Renewal for Churches, Communities, and Individuals*. Michigan: Zondervan, 1967 (D)

Knippel, Charles Taylor. *Samuel M. Shoemaker's Theological Influence on William G. Wilson's Twelve Step Spiritual Program of Recovery (Alcoholics Anonymous)*. Dissertation. St. Louis University, 1987.

Steps To a New Beginning: Leading Others to Christ Through the Twelve Step Process. Nashville: Thomas Nelson, 1993 (D)

"Listening to God Held Daily Need." *New York Times*. December 4, 1939.

Moyes, John S. *In Journeyings Often*. Melbourne: Oxford University Press, 1949 (D)

Norton-Taylor, Duncan. "Businessmen on Their Knees." *Fortune*. October, 1953.

Olsson, Karl A. "The History of Faith at Work" (five parts). *Faith at Work News*. 1982-1983.

Peale, Norman Vincent. "The Unforgettable Sam Shoemaker." *Faith At Work*. January, 1964.

———. "The Human Touch: The Estimate of a Fellow Clergyman and Personal Friend." *The Evangel* (New York: Calvary Church, July-August, 1950).

Pitt, Louis W. "New Life, New Reality: A Brief Picture of S.M.S.'s Influence in the Diocese of New York." *Faith at Work*, July-August, 1950.

"Pittsburgh Man of the Year." *Pittsburgh Post Gazette*. January 12, 1956.

Sack, David Edward. *Sam Shoemaker and the "Happy Ethical Pagans."* Princeton, New Jersey: paper prepared in the Department of Religion, Princeton University, June, 1993.

"Sam Shoemaker and Faith at Work." Pamphlet on file at Faith At Work, Inc., 150 S. Washington St., Suite 204, Falls Church, VA 22046.

Schwartz, Robert. "Laymen and Clergy to Join Salute to Dr. S. M. Shoemaker." *Pittsburgh Press*. December 10, 1961.

"Sees Great Revival Near." *New York Times*. September 8, 1930.

Shoemaker, Helen Smith. *I Stand by the Door*. New York: Harper & Row, 1967 (3) D1.

———. *Power Through Prayer Groups*. NJ: Fleming H. Revell, 1958 (D)

———. *Prayer & Evangelism*. Waco, TX: Word Books, 1974 (D)

———. *Prayer and You*. NY: Fleming H. Revell Company, 1958 (D)

———. *The Secret of Effective Prayer*. NJ: Fleming H. Revell Company, 1955 (D)

Sider, Michael J. *Taking the Gospel to the Point: Evangelicals in Pittsburgh and the Origins of the Pittsburgh Leadership Foundation*. Pittsburgh: Pittsburgh Leadership Foundation, n.d.

"Soul Clinic Depicted By Pastor in Book." *New York Times*. August 5, 1927.

"Ten of the Greatest American Preachers." *Newsweek*. March 28, 1955.

The Calvary Evangel. Eight different issues during the period from 1939 to 1941. (In the personal collection of Rev. Shoemaker's assistant minister, Rev. W. Irving Harris, and containing articles by Shoemaker and Harris: both credited by Bill Wilson as wellsprings of A.A.)

The Pittsburgh Experiment's Groups. Pittsburgh: The Pittsburgh Experiment, n.d.

Tools for Christian Living. Pittsburgh: The Pittsburgh Experiment, n.d.

"Urges Church Aid Oxford Group." *New York Times*. January 2, 1933, p. 26.

Whiston, Lionel A. and Walden Howard. *Marriage is for Living*. Michigan: Zondervan, 1968 (D)

Wilson, Bill. "I Stand by the Door." *The A.A. Grapevine*. New York: The A.A. Grapevine, Inc., February, 1967.

Woolverton, John F. "Evangelical Protestantism and Alcoholism 1933-1962: Episcopalian Samuel Shoemaker, The Oxford Group and Alcoholics Anonymous." *Historical Magazine of the Protestant*

Episcopal Church 52 (March, 1983).

Publications by or about The Oxford Group and Oxford Group People

Adam, Karl. *Extracts from Moral Re-Armament and Christianity in the West.* "Vaterland," organ of the Roman Catholic party, Lucerne Switzerland, 1952.

A Day in Pennsylvania Honoring Frank Nathan Daniel Buchman in Pennsburg and Allentown. Oregon: Grosvenor Books, 1992 (5) D1.

Addison, H. A. *Daw Nyein Tha: Joyful Revolutionary.* India: Friends of Moral Re-Armament, 1969.

Allen, Geoffrey Francis. *He That Cometh.* New York: The Macmillan Company, 1933 (2) D1

——. *Christ The Victorious.* NY: The Macmillan Company, 1935 (D).

Almond, Harry J. *Foundations for Faith.* 2d ed. London: Grosvenor Books, 1980 (5) D1.

——. *Iraqi Statesman: A Portrait of Mohammed Fadhel Jamali.* Salem, OR: Grosvenor Books, 1993 (3) D1.

An Approach To "Remaking The World." London: Moral Re-Armament, 1948.

Appel. Joseph H. *A World Cruise Log.* NY: Harper & Brothers Publishers, 1926 (D).

Arnold, Minister President Karl. *Road From Ruin.* Dusseldorf, 1949 (4)

Austin, H. W. "Bunny". *Frank Buchman As I Knew Him.* London: Grosvenor Books, 1975 (3) D1.

——. *Moral Re-Armament: The Battle for Peace.* London: William Heinemann, 1938 (4) D1.

—— and Phyllis Konstam. *A Mixed Double.* London: Chatto and Windus, 1969 (D)

Bach, Marcus. *They Have Found a Faith.* NY: The Bobbs-Merrill Company, 1946 (D)

——. *Strange Sects and Curious Cults.* NY: Dodd, Mead, 1961 (D)

Barnes, Stanley. *200 Million Hungry Children.* London: Grosvenor Books, 1980.

Barrett, Michael. *Footprints: some personal memories.* England: Linden Hall, 1991.

Batterson, John E. *How to Listen to God*. N.p., n.d.

Bayless, W. N. *The Oxford Group: A Way of Life*, n.d.

Becker, Mrs. George. "Quiet Time in the Home." N.p., n.d.

Begbie, Harold. *Broken Earthenware: A Footnote in Narrative To Professor William James's Study in Human Nature "The Varieties of Religious Experience."* London: Hodder and Stoughton, n.d.

——. *Life Changers*. New York: G. P. Putnam's Sons, 1927 (6) D.

——. *More Twice-Born Men*. NY: G. P. Putnam's Sons, 1923 (2) D1

——. *Religion And The Crisis*. London: Cassell & Company, 1913 (D)

——. *Souls in Action: The Crucible of the New Life: Expanding the Narrative of Twice-Born Men*. New York: Hodder & Stoughton, 1911 (2) D1

——. *The Ordinary Man and The Extraordinary Thing*. NY: Hodder & Stoughton, n.d. (D)

——. *Twice-Born Men*. New York: Fleming H. Revell, 1909 (4)D2.

Belden, David C. *The Origins and Development of the Oxford Group (Moral Re-Armament)*. D. Phil. Dissertation, Oxford University, 1976 (not in collection, owned by David Belden).

Belden, Kenneth D. *Beyond The Satellites: Is God is Speaking-Are We Listening?* London: Grosvenor Books, 1987 (4) D1.

——. *Meeting Moral Re-Armament*. London: Grosvenor Books, 1979 (3) D1.

——. *Reflections on Moral Re-Armament*. London: Grosvenor Books, 1983 (5) D1.

——. *The Hour of the Helicopter*. Somerset, England: Linden Hall, 1992 (3) D1.

——. *Theatre and the Task of the Century*. London: Moral Re-Armament, 1968.

——. *The Story of The Westminster Theatre*. London: Westminster Productions, 1965 (D)

——. *Where There's Change There's Hope*. London: The Friends of the Westminster Theatre, 1972.

——. and Stell Belden, *Husband & Wife are One . . . But Which One*. London: Grosvenor Books, 1982.

Belk, J. B. *A Faith to Move Nations*. Moral Re-Armament, Inc., 1969 (3)

Bennett, John C. *Social Salvation: A Religious Approach to the Problems of Social Change*. New York: Charles Scribner's Sons, 1935 (3) D1.

Benson, Clarence Irving. *The Eight Points of the Oxford Group*. London: Humphrey Milford, Oxford University Press, 1936. (3) D1

Birdwood, Field Marshal Lord. *In My Time: Recollections and Anecdotes*. London: Skeffington, n.d. (D)

Bishop of Leicester, The, Chancellor R. J. Campbell and the Editor of the "Church of England Newspaper." *Stories of our Oxford House Party.*, July 17, 1931.

Blair, David. *For Tomorrow-Yes!* Compiled and edited from David Blair's Notebook by Jane Mullen Blair & Friends. New York: Exposition Press, 1981.

Blair, Emily Newell. "The Oxford Group Challenges America." *Good Housekeeping*, October, 1936. (2)

Blake, Howard C. *Way to Go: Adventures in Search of God's Will*. Burbank, CA: Pooh Stix Press, 1992 (3).

Bockmuehl, Klaus. *Listening to the God who Speaks*. Colorado: Helmers & Howard, 1990 (2)

Boobbyer, Brian. *Fit For Life*. London: A Freeway Publication, 1990 (4) D1

Boobbyer, Juliet and Joanna Sciortino. *Columbia*. England: Fowler Wright Books, 1981.

Bowerman, David A. *Poems in a Time of War*. London: Linden Hall, 1992

Braden, Charles Samuel. *These Also Believe*. New York: The Macmillan Company, 1951 (2) D1.

Bradley, Francis. *The American Proposition: A New Type of Man*. NY: Moral Re-Armament, Inc., 1977 (9) D1.

Brodersen, Paul. *The Church and the Destiny of Nations*. New York: Moral Re-Armament, 1953.

Brown, J. C. *The Oxford Group Movement: Is it of God or of Satan?* London: Pickering & Inglis, 1932 (2) D1.

Brown, Philip Marshall. *The Venture of Belief*. New York: Fleming H. Revell, 1935 (2) D1.

Buchman, Frank N. D. *Remaking the World*. London: Blandford Press, 1961 (15).

———. *Remaking the World*. New, Rev ed., Blandford Press, 1953 (5) D1.

———. *Remaking the World*. Abridged Preliminary. London: Wm. Heinemann, 1941.

———. *Remaking the World*. Abridged Preliminary. Washington, D.C.:

Moral Re-Armament, 1945 (2) D2.

———. *The Making of A Miracle*. London: The College of the Good Road, 1952 (2)

———. *The Revolutionary Path: Moral Re-Armament in the thinking of Frank Buchman*. London: Grosvenor, 1975 (3) D1.

———. *Where Personal Work Begins*. Extracts and notes from talks given at the Lily Valley Conference near Kuling, China 1-13 August, 1918. London: Grosvenor Books, 1984.

———, and Sherwood Eddy. *Ten Suggestions for Personal Work*????

Buchman House, Lehigh County Historical Society Inventory Sheets of Frank Buchman Library.

Burns, Vincent Godfrey. *Flame Against the Night*. Washington, D.C.: New World Books, 1960 (D) [inscribed by author to Frank Buchman]

"Calvary's Eviction of Buchman." *Time Magazine*, November 24, 1941.

Cameron, M.A. *Kindling A Purpose: "Economics: Brake or Throttle?"* circa 1980

Campbell, Annejet. *Listen for a change*. London: Grosvenor Books, 1986

Campbell, Paul. *A Dose of My Own Medicine*. London: Grosvenor Books, 1992 (4) D1.

———. *The Art of Remaking Men*. Bombay: Himmat Publications, 1970 (3) D1.

———. *Modernising Man*. Middlesex: Grosvenor Books, 1968 (2) D1

——— and Peter Howard. *America Needs an Ideology*. London: Frederick Muller, Ltd., 1957 (8) D1.

——— and Peter Howard. *Remaking Men*. New York: Arrowhead Books, 1954 (7) D1.

——— and Peter Howard. *The Strategy of St. Paul*. London: Grosvenor Books, 1956 (3) D1

——— and Peter Howard. *A Story of Effective Statesmanship*. London: Blandford Press, 1956 (6) D1

Cantrill, Hadley. *The Psychology of Social Movements*. New York: John Wiley & Sons, Inc., 1941 (3) D1.

Carey, David E. *A Personal Story*, 1982.

Carey, Walter, Bishop of Bloemfontein. *The Group System and the Catholic Church*. Archives of the Episcopal Church, Austin, Texas, n.d.

Caulfied, Entwistle, Viney. *Live Wires: A Tribute to Frank N. D. Buchman from his friends on the occasion of his sixtieth birthday*.

NY: The Oxford Group, June 4, 1938.

Chesteron, G. K. *The Well and The Shallows*, circa 1935, pp. 435-39.

Christiansen, Ane, and Rasmussen. *How To Create a Sing-Out.* 6th ed. Los Angeles: Pace Publications, 1968 (4)

Church Information Board of the Church Assembly. *Moral Re-Armament: A study prepared by The Social and Industrial Council of the Church Assembly.* Church House, Westminster, 1955.

Clapp, Charles, Jr. *The Big Bender*. New York: Harper & Row, 1938 (2).

———. *Drinking's Not the Problem*. New York: Thomas Y. Crowell, 1949 (2)

———. *Drunks are Square Pegs*. NY: Island Press, 1942 (2) D1.

Clark, Walter Houston. *The Oxford Group: Its History and Significance*. New York: Bookman Associates, 1951 (4) D1.

———. *The Psychology of Religion*. NY: Macmillan, 1958 (D)

Coggan, Donald. *Cuthbert Bardsley: Bishop, Evangelist, Pastor*. London: Collins, 1989 (D)

Cook, Sydney and Garth Lean. *The Black and White Book: A Handbook of Revolution*. London: Blandford Press, 1972.(2)

Cooper, Neville. *How should Government and Industry manage People and Money?* London, 1981

———. *People Profit and Participation*. London, 1980.

Copeman, Fred. *Reason In Revolt*. London: Blandford Press, 1948 (2) D1.

Crossman, R. H. S. *Oxford and the Groups*. Oxford: Basil Blackwell, 1934 (2) D1.

Crothers, Rachel. *Susan and God*. New York: Harper & Brothers, 1939 (3) D1.

*Crowley, Patrice. *Pickle Bill of Pickle Hill*. PA: Town & Gown, 1978, pp. 38-50.

Cumbers, Frank, ed. Daily Readings from W. E. Sangster. NJ: Fleming H. Revell Company, 1966 (D)

Cust, Sylvia. *Mallee Roots to New Horizons*. Sydney, Australia, 1990.

Davies, Horton. Christian Deviations: Essays in Defence of the Christian Faith. London: SCM Press, 1956

Day, Sherwood Sunderland. *The Principles of the Group*. Oxford: University Press, n.d.

Dilly, Rex. *Discovering Moral Re-Armament*. London: A Freeway Publication, 1995.

Dinger, Clair M. *Moral Re-Armament: A Study of Its Technical and Religious Nature in the Light of Catholic Teaching.* Washington, D.C.: The Catholic University of America Press, 1961.

"Discord in Oxford Group: Buchmanites Ousted by Disciple from N.Y. Parish House." *Newsweek.* November 24, 1941.

Dodds, T. C. 'Dickie', *Hit Hard and Enjoy It.* England: The Cricketer Ltd., 1976 (2)

Dorsey, Theodore H. *From a Far Country: The Conversion Story of a Campaigner for Christ.* Huntington, Indiana: Our Sunday Visitor Press, n.d.

Drakeford, John W. *People to People Therapy.* New York: Harper & Row, 1978 (2).

Driberg, Tom. *The Mystery of Moral Re-Armament: A Study of Frank Buchman and His Movement.* New York: Alfred A. Knopf, 1965 (4) D1.

——. *MRA: A Critical Examination by Tom Driberg.* London: The Shenval Press, 1962 (D)

Eckman, Gosta. *Experiment with God: Frank Buchman Reconsidered.* London: Hodder & Stoughton, 1972 (3).

Eister, Allan W. *Drawing Room Conversion.* Duke University Press, 1950 (4) D1

Elliott, Hugh P. *Dawn in Zimbabwe: Concept for a Nation.* London: Grosvenor Books, 1980.

——. *Darkness and Dawn in Zimbabwe.* London: Grosvenor Books, 1978 (2)

Elwin, Verrier. *The Tribal World.* Calcutta: Oxford University Press, 1965 (D)

Entwistle, Basil. *Japan's Decisive Decade.* London: Grosvenor Books, 1985 (3).

——. *Making Cities Work.* Pasadena, CA: Hope Publishing House, 1990 (2).

—— and John McCook Roots. *Moral Re-Armament: What Is It?* Pace Publications, 1967 (12) D2.

Evans, Claire. *Freewoman.* Oxford: Becket Publications, 1979 (2).

Ferguson, Charles W. *The Confusion of Tongues.* Garden City: Doubleday, Doran Company, Inc., 1940.

—— *The New Books of Revelations: The Inside Story of America's Astounding Religious Cults.* NY: Doubleday, Doran & Company, Inc., 1931 (2) D1.

————. *Naked to Mine Enemies: The Life of Cardinal Wolsey*. Boston: Little, Brown, 1958 (D)

Foot, Stephen. *African Tale*. London: Blandford Press, 1955 (D)

————. *Life Began Yesterday*. New York: Harper & Brothers, 1935 (4) D1.

————. *Life Begins Today*. South Africa: Juta & Co., Limited, n.d. (2).

————. *Three Lives- And Now*. New and Rev. ed. London: Heinemann, 1937 (D).

Ford, John C., S.J. *Moral Re-Armament and Alcoholics Anonymous*. NCCA "Blue Book," Vol 10, 1968.

Forde, Eleanor Napier. *Guidance: What It Is and How to Get It*. Paper presented by Eleanor Napier Forde at Minnewaska, NY, September, 1927.

————. *The Guidance of God*. London: The Oxford Group, 1927 (5) D1.

Foss, Denis. *Lionheart: The story of Leo Exton: 1887 to 1960*. England: Linden Hall, 1985.

————. *Shoot a Line: A Merchant Mariner's War*. England: Linden Hall, 1992 (2)

Foss, Hannen. *The Riches of Christmas*. London: Blandford Press, 1951.

Foss, Hannen and William Cameron Johnson. *Where Do We Go From Here?* NY: Duell, Sloan and Pearce, 1955 (2).

Foss, Patrick. *Climbing Turns: A Pilot's Story in War and Peace*. England: Linden Hall, 1990.

Frank Buchman-80. Compiled by His Friends. London: Blandford Press, 1958 (5) D1.

Gandhi, Rajmohan. *A Writer's Duty*. London: Grosvenor Books, 1977.

————. *America's Role-An Asian Perspective*. Richmond, VA: MRA Books (2)

————. *Cracks and Bridges: The Encounter of Cultures*. MN: House of Hope Presbyterian Church, 1994 (D)

Gordon, Anne Wolrige. *Peter Howard Life and Letters*. London: The Oxford Group, 1969 (14)D1

Gray, Betty. *Watersheds: Journey to a Faith*. London: Grosvenor, 1986 (2) D1.

Grensted, L.W. *The Person of Christ*. New York: Harper & Brothers, 1933 (4, 1 autographed)D1

————. *This Business of Living*. London: Student Christian Movement Press, 1939 (D).

Grogan, William. *John Riffe of the Steelworkers*. New York:

Coward—McCann, 1959 (5) D1.

Groups in South Africa 1930, The. South Africa: The Groups, 1930.

Guldseth. Mark O. *Streams: The Flow of Inspiration from Dwight Moody to Frank Buchman.* Alaska: Fritz Creek Studios, 1982 (5) D1.

Gundersen, Paul. *Thankful at Every Turn.* Finland: Nakyma, 1991 (2)

Hadden, Richard M. "Christ's Program for World-Reconstruction: Studies in the Sermon on the Mount." *The Calvary Evangel*, 1934-35, pp. 11-14, 44-49, 73-77, 104-07, 133-36.

Hagedorn, Hermann. *The Bomb that fell on America.* New York: Association Press, 1948 (2).

Hamilton, A. S. Loudon. *MRA: How It All Began.* London: Moral Re-Armament, 1968.

———. *Some Basic Principles of Christian Work.* The Oxford Group, n.d.

———. "Description of the First Century Christian Fellowship." Vol. 2, *The Messenger*, June, 1923.

Hamlin, Bryan T. *Moral Re-Armament and Forgiveness in International Affairs.* London: Grosvenor, 1992 (3) D1.

Hanna, David. *"Come Up and See Me Some Time": An Uncensored Biography of Mae West.* NY: Tower Publications, Inc., 1976.

Hansford, Robert. *Who Says We're Buffaloed?* MI: Moral Re-Armament, 1964 (4)

Hannen and Cameron. *Where Do We Go from Here?: A Simple Guide to The World We Live in, What Makes it Tick, and What to do about it.* London: Blandford Press, n.d. (3)

Hannon, Peter. *Who's Side is God On?*

———. *Southern Africa: What Kind of Change?* 3rd ed. Johannesburg 2000, 1977 (D).

Hardy, Web. *Informational Talk at 32 AA Groups.* Dallas, Texas, March, 1990.

Hardiman, James W. *The Crowning Experience.* NY: Random House, 1960 (6) D2

Harriman, Jarvis. *Matched Pair: The Elys of Embassy Row.* AZ: Pooh Stix Press, 1999. (2)

Harris, W. Irving. *Out in Front: Forerunners of Christ. A Study of the Lives of Eight Great Men.* New York: The Calvary Evangel, 1942.

———. *The Breeze of the Spirit.* New York: The Seabury Press, 1978.

Harrison, Marjorie. *Saints Run Mad.* London: John Lane, Ltd., 1934.

Henderson, Michael. *A Different Accent.* Richmond, VA: Grosvenor

Books USA, 1985 (3) D1.

——. *All Her Paths Are Peace: Women Pioneers in Peacemaking*. CT: Kumerian Press, 1994 (3) D1.

——.. *Forgiveness Factor, The: Stories of Hope in a World of Conflict.*. London: Grosvenor Books, 1996 (2) D1.

——. *From India with Hope*. London: Grosvenor, 1971 (D)

——. *Hope for a Change: Commentaries by an Optimistic Realist*. Salem, OR: Grosvenor Books, 1991 (2) D1.

——. *On History's Coattails: Commentaries by an English Journalist in America*. Richmond, VA: Grosvenor USA, 1988 (3) D1.

Henson, Herbert Hensley. *The Oxford Groups*. London: Oxford University Press, 1933 (3) D1

——. *The Group Movement*. 2d ed. London: Oxford University Press, 1934 (D)

Herman, E. *Creative Prayer*. London: James Clarke & Co., Ltd., 1921 (2) D1.

Hicks, Roger. *How Augustine Found Faith: Told in his own words from F. J. Sheed's translation of The Confessions of St. Augustine*. N.p., 1956.

——. *How to Read the Bible*. London: Moral Re-Armament, 1940.

——. *Letters to Parsi*. London: Blandford Press, 1950 (7) D1.

——. *The Endless Adventure*. London: Blandford Press, 1964 (5) D1.

——. *The Lord's Prayer and Modern Man*. London: Blandford Press, 1967 (3) D1.

Hofmeyr, Agnes Leakey. *Beyond Violence: A True story of hurt, hate, and hope*. Johannesburg, 1990 (3) D1

Hofmeyr, Bremer. *How to Change*. New York: Moral Re-Armament, n.d.

——. *How to Listen*. London: The Oxford Group, 1941 (2).

Hogue, Meta. *Paul Hogue: Oxford Group-Moral Re-Armament Lifetime Soldier*. MS: 1998.

Holme, Reginald. *A Journalist for God: The memoirs of Reginald Holme*. London: A Bridge Builders Publication, 1995.

Holmes-Walker, Wilfrid. *The New Enlistment*. London: The Oxford Group, circa 1937.

Howard, Peter. *A Renaissance That Unites East and West*. London: MRA, n.d. (2)

——. *An Idea To Win the World*. London: Blandford Press, 1955 (4) D1.

——. *Beaverbrook: A Study of Max the Unknown*. London: Hutchinson of London 1964 (5)D1

83

———. *Beyond Communism to Revolution*. London: The Oxford Group, 1963 (3).

———. *Britain and the Beast*. London: Heinemann, 1963 (7) D1.

———. *Diplomats*, The. London: Blandford Press, 1964 (D)

———. *Design for Dedication*. Chicago: Henry Regenry Company, 1964 (10) D2.

———. *Fighters Ever*. London: William Heinemann Ltd., 1941 (7) D1.

———. *Frank Buchman's Secret*. Garden City: New York: Doubleday & Company, Inc., 1961. (103) D 1

———. *Happy Deathday*. London: Westminister Productions Ltd., 1967 (2).

———. *Ideas Have Legs*. London: Frederick Muller, Ltd., 1945 (6) D2.

———. *Innocent Men*. London: William Heinemann, 1941 (9) D1.

———. *Men on Trial*. London: Blandford Press, 1945 (5) D1

———. *Pickle Hill*. London: Blandford Press, 1960 (2).

———. *The Ladder*. London: Blandford Press, 1960 (2).

———. *The World Rebuilt: The true story of Frank Buchman and the achievements of Moral Re-Armament*. New York. Duell, Sloan & Pearce, 1951. (11) D1

———. *That Man Frank Buchman*. London: Blandford Press, 1946 (12) D1.

———. *Tomorrow Will Be Too Late*. New York: Moral Re-Armament, 1964 (11)

———. *We Are Tomorrow*. London: Blandford Press, 1954 (D).

——— and Cecil Broadhurst. *The Vanishing Island*., Philips, n.d. (5)

———. and Anthony.. *Space is So Startling*. London, 1962.

——— and Alan Thornhill. *Music at Midnight*. London: Blandford Press, 1962.

——— and Alan Thornhill. *The Hurricane*. London: Blandford Press, 1960.

*Hovelsen, Leif. .*The Flying Horseman*. MI: National Ski Hall of Fame Press, 1983.

———. *Out of the Evil Night*. London: Blandford Press, 1959.

Howell, Edward. *Escape To Live*. London: Longmans, Green, 1947 (6) D1.

Hunter, T. Willard, with assistance from M.D.B. *A.A.'s Roots in the Oxford Group*. New York: A.A. Archives, 1988.

———. *Press Release*. Buchman Events/Pennsylvania, October 19, 1991.

———. *"It Started Right There" Behind the Twelve Steps and the Self-help*

Movement. Oregon: Grosvenor Books, 1994 (3) D2.

——. *The Spirit of Charles Lindbergh: Another Dimension*. Lanham, MD: Madison Books, 1993 (2) D1.

——. *Uncommon Friends' Uncommon Friend*. A tribute to James Draper Newton, on the occasion of his eighty-fifth birthday. (Pamphlet, March 30, 1990).

——. *World Changing Through Life Changing*. Thesis, Newton Center, Mass: Andover-Newton Theological School, 1977.

Hutchinson, Michael. *A Christian Approach to Other Faiths*. London: Grosvenor Books, 1991 (2) D.

——. *The Confessions*. (privately published study of St. Augustine's *Confessions*).

Jaeger, Clara. *Philadelphia Rebel: The Education of a Bourgeoise*. VA: Grosvenor, 1988 (4) (D1)

——. *Annie: Annie Jaeger tells her own story*. London: Grosvenor Books, 1968.

——. *Never To Lose My Vision*: The Story of Bill Jaeger. London: Grosvenor Books, 1995

*Jaeger, William. *The World Struggle of Ideologies*. Los Angeles: The College of the Good Road, 1950.

Jones, Olive M. *Inspired Children*. New York: Harper & Brothers, 1933 (2) D1.

——. *Inspired Youth*. New York: Harper & Brothers, 1938.

Kitchen, V. C. *I Was a Pagan*. New York: Harper & Brothers, 1934 (2) D1.

Koenig, His Eminence Franz Cardinal. *True Dialogue*. Oregon: Grosvenor USA, 1986 (2) D1.

Langcroft, Peggy. *Theirs By Right*. London: Blandford Press, n.d. (2).

Landau, Rom. *Arm The Apostles*. London: Nicholson & Watson, 1938 (D)

——. *God is My Adventure*. London: Unwin Books, 1935 (2) D1.

Laun, Ferdinand. *Unter Gottes Fuhring*. The Oxford Group, n.d. (Plus German version, 1934) D

Layman with a Notebook, The. *What Is the Oxford Group?* London: Oxford University Press, 1933. (3) D1

Lean, Garth. *Brave Men Choose*. London: Blandford Press, *1961 (13)*.

——. *Cast Out Your Nets: Sharing Your Faith with Others*. London: Grosvenor, 1990 (4) D1

——. *Frank Buchman: A Life*. London: Constable, 1985 (4) D1.

——. *Frank Buchman: A Life: Notes for Study*. London: Grosvenor, 1986 (D).

——. *God's Politician: William Wilberforce's Struggle*. London: Darton, Logman & Todd, 1980.

——. *Good God, It Works*. London: Blandford Press, 1974 (3) D1.

——. *John Wesley*, Anglican. London: Blandford Press, 196 4 (6) D1

——. *Joyful Remembrance*. London: Executors of Garth D. Lean, 1994.

——. *On the Tail of a Comet: The Life of Frank Buchman*. Colorado Springs: Helmers & Howard, 1988 (3) D1.

——. *Strangely Warmed: The Amazing Life of John Wesley*.

——, and Morris Martin. *New Leadership*. London: William Heinemann, 1936.

Leon, Philip. *A Philosopher's Quiet Time*. N.p., n.d.

——. *The Philosophy of Courage or the Oxford Group Way*. New York: Oxford University Press, 1939. (6) D1

"Less Buchmanism." *Time*, November 24, 1941.

Lester, John and Pierre Spoerri. *Rediscovering Freedom*. London: Grosvenor, 1992.

Letter 7, The: The South African Adventure. A Miracle Working God Abroad. Oxford: The Groups, A First Century Christian Fellowship, 1930.

Libby, Lucile Tretheway. *My Search for Faith*, 1981.

Limburg, Kay. *All Things Are Possible*. CA: Kimberly Press, Inc., 1992 (2)

Lunn, Arnold and Garth Lean. *Christian Counter-Attack*. London: Blandford Press, 1969 (2) (D1).

Lunn, Sir Henry S. *Chapters From My Life*. London: Cassell & Co., 1918 (D).

——. *Unkilled For So Long*. London: George Allen & Unwin, 1968 (D)

Lowery, Bob. *The Unbeatable Breed: People and events in Northern Manitoba*. Canada: The Prarie Publishing Company, 1981

—— and Garth Lean. *The Cult of Softness*. London: Blandford Press, 1965.

——. *The New Morality*. London: Blandford Press, 1964 (10)

Macaulay, Rose. *Going Abroad*. NY: Harper & Brothers, 1934 (D)

Maccassey, Sir Lyndon. *The Oxford Group And Its Work of Moral Re-Armament*. London, 1954 (3)

Macintosh, Douglas C. *Personal Religion*. New York: Charles Scribner's Sons, 1942 (3) D

Mackay, Malcom George. *More than Coincidence*. Edinburgh: Saint Andrew Press, 1979 (2) (D).

Macmillan, Ebenezer. *Seeking and Finding*. New York: Harper & Brothers, 1933 (2) D1.

Magor, Cliff and Edna Magor. *The Song of a Merryman: Ivan Menzies*. London: Grosvenor Books, 1976.

Mann, Ronald. *Moving the Mountain*. London: Aldersgate Productions, 1995.

Marcel, Gabriel. *Fresh Hope for the World: Moral Re-Armament in Action*. London: Longman's, 1958 (D)

Margetson, The Very Reverend Provost. *The South African Adventure*. The Oxford Group, n.d.

Marsh, Peter and Hugh Elliott. *Hope For Today: A Selection of Daily Readings*. London: Grosvenor Books, 1995 (3).

Marhsall, Peter. *Mr. Jones, Meet The Master: Sermons and Prayers of Peter Marshall*. NY: Fleming H. Revell, 1950 (D)

Martin, Morris H. *Always a Little Further: Four Lives of a Luckie Felowe: A Memoir*. Tucson, AZ: Elm Street Press, 2001.]

———. *Born to Live in the Future*. Up With People, 1991 (2).

———. *The Thunder and the Sunshine*. Washington, D.C.: MRA, n.d. (2) D1

*Mathison, Richard R. *Faiths, Cults and Sects of America: From Atheism to Zen*. Indianapolis: Bobbs-Merrill, 1960 (D)

McAll, Frances. *So What's the Alternative?* London: Moral Re-Armament, 1974.

———. *Hurdles are for Jumping*. Oxford: New Cherwell Press, 1998 (2) D1

Milne, J. W. H. *What the Oxford Group Movement Did for Ottawa*. Winnipeg, Canada: Manitoba Free Press, May 2, 1933.

Molony, John N. *Moral Re-Armament*. Melbourne: The Australian Catholic Truth Society Record, June 10, 1956 (2) D1.

Moral Re-Armament. *An Idea Takes Wings*. NY: Moral Re-Armament, April-May, 1951.

Moral Re-Armament. *The Golden Age of MRA*. NY: Moral Re-Armament, n.d. (2)

Moral Re-Armament. *You Can Defend America*. Washington, D.C.: Moral Re-Armament, 1941.

Moral Re-Armament. *The Fight To Serve: Moral Re-Armament and The War*. Washington, D.C.: Moral Re-Armament, circa 1943.

Moral Re-Armament. *Ideology and Co-Existence*. NY: Moral Re-Armament, 1959 (2).

Moral Re-Armament. *What is MRA?* Washington, D.C., 1992 (6).

Moral Re-Armament: Vital for the Future. London: Grosvenor Books, 1983 (2)

Morrison, G. Cecil. *The Life and Times of G. Cecil Morrison*. Ontario: Gai-Garet Design & Publication, Ltd., 1990.

Morrison, J. M. *Honesty and God*. Edinburgh: The Saint Andrew Press, 1966 (2)

———. *The Statesman's Dream and Other Poems*. Edinburgh: Collins, 1957 (2).

Mottu, Philippe. *The Story of Caux*. London: Grosvenor, 1970 (4) D1.

Mowat, R. C. *Climax of History*. London: Blandford Press, 1955 (7) D1.

———. *Modern Prophetic Voices: From Kierkegaard to Buchman*. Oxford: New Cherwel Press, 1994 (3) D1.

———. *The Message of Frank Buchman*. London: Blandford Press, n.d. (4)

———. *Report on Moral Re-Armament*. London: Blandford Press, 1955 (7).

———. *Creating the European Community*. London, 1973.

———. *Decline and Renewal: Europe Ancient and Modern*. Oxford: New Cherwel Press, 1991.

———. *Ruin and Resurgence: The History of Europe 1939-1965*. London: Blandford Press, 1966 (D)

———. *Spiritual Forces in International Politics*. Oxford: New Cherwel Press, 1998 (3) D1.

Moyes, John S. *American Journey*. Sydney: Clarendon Publishing Co., n. d.

Murray, Robert H. *Group Movements Throughout the Ages*. New York: Harper & Brothers. 1935. (3) D1

Niebuhr, Reinhold. *Christianity and Power Politics*. NY: Charles Scribner's Sons, 1948

Niel's Legacy : The Story of an American Boy Who Lived at the Heart of a World Family. [Nathaniel Jennings Ely, May 6, 1939 to January 3, 1952] By his family and friends.

Newton, Eleanor Forde. *I Always Wanted Adventure*. London: Grosvenor, 1992 (3) D1.

———. *Echoes From The Heart*. Fort Myers Beach, Florida, 1986 (2) D1.

Newton, James Draper. *Uncommon Friends: Life with Thomas Edison,*

Henry Ford, Harvey Firestone, Alexis Carrel, & Charles Lindbergh. New York: Harcourt Brace, 1987 (3) D1.

Nichols, Beverley. *The Fool Hath Said*. Garden City: Doubleday, Doran & Company, 1936 (3)D

——. *Powers That Be*. London: Jonathan Cape, 1966 (D)

Orglmeister, Peter. *An Ideology for Today*. Pamphlet, 1965 (8)

Peaston, Monroe. *Personal Living: An Introduction to Paul Tournier*. NY: Harper & Row, 1972 (D)

Perkiomen School. *Perkiomen: Here's to You: A Centennial History of Perkiomen School* [the school attended by Frank N. D. Buchman]..

Perry, Edward T. *God Can Be Real*. Moral Re-Armament, Inc., 1969 (14).

Petrocokino, Paul. *A Man of Many Loves*. London: Grosvenor Books, 1986.

——. *The New Man for the New World: A Study of the Sermon on the Mount*. Cheshire: Paul Petrocokino, n.d. (2)

——. *The Right Direction*. Great Britain: The City Press of Chester, Ltd., n.d.

——. *An Experiment: Try This For a Fortnight*. Privately published pamphlet, n.d.

Philips, Frederik. *45 Years With Philips: An Industrialists's Life*. Dorset: Blandford Press, 1978 (2).

Phillimore, Miles. *Just for Today*. Privately published pamphlet, 1940 (6).

Piguet, Charles and Michel Sentis. *The World at the Turning: Experiments in Moral Re-Armament*. London: Grosvenor, 1982 (3)

Powell, Lyman P. *The Better Part*. Indianapolis: Bobbs-Merrill, 1933 (D)

Prestwich, Irene. *Irene Prestwich of Tirley Garth: A Personal Memoir*.

Pribram, John G. *Horizons of Hope: An Autobiography*. Oklahoma, 1991 (3)

Proctor, Marjorie. *The World My Country: The Story of Daw Nyein Tha of Burma*. London: Grosvenor Books, 1976 (3).

Rawl, Ray. *The Oxford Group Connection*, Pamphlet, n.d.

Raynor, Frank D. *The Finger of God: A Book About the Group Movements*. London: Group Publications, Ltd., 1934.

Reaching the Millions. New World News No. 7, n.d.

Readers' Digest, May, 1967. *Sing Out America*.

Readers' Digest, January, 1968. *They're Out to Remake The World.*

Redwood, Hugh. *God in the Shadows.* London: Hodder & Stoughton, 1932 (2) D2

———. *God in the Slums.* n.d. (D)

———. *Kingdom Come.* London: Hodder & Stoughton, 1934 (2) D1.

———. *God in the Everyday.* London: Rich & Cowan, 1936 (D)

Reynolds, Amelia S. *New Lives for Old.* New York. Fleming H. Revell, 1929.

Reynolds, Bert. *Industry at its Best.* England: Industrial Pioneer Publications, 1991.

Rodzinski, Halina. *Our Two Lives: The story of an extraordinary marriage and a brilliant career in music.* NY: Charles Scribner's Sons, 1976.

Roots, The Right Reverend Herbert, Bishop of Hankow, China. *The Two Options.* The Oxford Group, 1934.

Roots, John McCook. *An Apostle to Youth.* Oxford, The Oxford Group, 1928 (2).

———. *Chou: An Informal Biography of China's Legendary Chou En-Lai.* NY: Doubleday & Company, 1978.

———. *Modernizing America.* Los Angeles: Pace Publications, 1965 (28) D1.

Rose, Cecil. *Betting and Gambling.* Rev. ed. London: Student Christian Movement Press, 1935 (D)

———. *When Man Listens.* New York: Oxford University Press, 1937. (3)

Rose, Howard J. *The Quiet Time.* New York: Oxford Group at 61 Gramercy Park, North, 1937.

———. *The Quiet Time.* (Pamphlet.)

Ruffin, R.W.B. *Are We Free Enough to Care?* Richmond, VA: MRA Books, circa 1982

———. Breakthroughs in Peacemaking: The Moral and Spiritual Dimension of Statecraft, 1993 (D)

Russell, Arthur J. *For Sinners Only.* London: Hodder & Stoughton, 1932 (4) D1.

———. *One Thing I Know.* New York: Harper & Brothers, 1933 (3) D1.

———. *God at Eventide: Companion Volume to God Calling.* NY: Dodd Mead & Co., 1950 (D)

Sangster, W. E. *God Does Guide Us.* New York: The Abingdon Press, 1934 (2) D1.

———. *Let Me Commend.* NY: Abingdon-Cokesbury Press, 1958 (2) D2

————. *The Craft of Sermon Construction*. London: The Epworth Press, 1949 (D)

————. *The Path To Perfection: An Examination And Restatement of John Wesley's Doctrine of Christian Perfection*. NY: Abingdon-Cokesbury, 1943 (D)

Schollgen, Werner. *The Basic Problem of Education in Morals*. Germany: Reprint of chapter from Aktuelle Moral-probleme, 1955 (2).

Selbie, W. B. *Aspects of Christ*. NY: Hodder & Stoughton, n.d. (D)

————.*The Fatherhood of God*. NY: Charles Scribner's Sons, 1936 (D)

Sherry, Frank H. and Mahlon H. Hellerich. *The Formative Years of Frank N. D. Buchman*. (Reprint of article at Frank Buchman home in Allentown, Pennsylvania).

Simpson, Don. *Katie Woo: Pioneer Educator from Hong Kong*. Australia: Katie Woo Memorial Trust Fund., 1997 (D)

Skard, Oyvind. *Ideological Strategy*. London: Blandford Press, 1954 (2)

Slattery, Sarah Lawrence. *I Choose*. MA: The University Press, 1969 (10) D1.

Smith, Alec. *Now I Call Him Brother*. United Kingdom: Marshalls, 1984 (2).

Spencer, F. A. M. *The Meaning of the Groups*. London: Methuen & Co., Ltd., 1934 (2) D1.

Spoerri, Theophil. *Basic Forces in European History*. Los Angeles: The College of the Good Road, 1950.

————. *Dynamic out of Silence: Frank Buchman's Relevance Today*. Translated by John Morrison. London: Grosvenor Books, 1976 (5) D1.

Spoerri, Pierre. *Who are the True Europeans?* London: Moral Re-Armament, 1967.

Strachey, Ray. *Group Movements of the Past and Experiments in Guidance*. London: Faber & Faber Limited, 1934 (2) D1

Streeter, Burnett Hillman. *Reality: A New Correlation of Science and Religion*. London: Macmillan, 1943 [originally published in 1927] (2) D1.

————. *The God Who Speaks*. London: Macmillan & Co., Ltd., 1936 (4) D1.

Tappert, Theodore G. *History of the Lutheran Theological Seminary at Philadelphia: 1864-1964* [the seminary attended by Frank N.D. Buchman].

The College of the Good Road. Los Angeles, 1950.

The Crowning Experience: Book of the Film. NY: Moral Re-Armament, n.d.

The Missing Dimension of Statecraft. London: Grosvenor Books, 1993 (2)

The Rise of a New Spirit: 1940 MRA Year.

Thornhill, Alan. *One Fight More.* London: Frederick Muller, 1943 (3) D1.

———. *The Significance of the Life of Frank Buchman.* London: Moral Re-Armament, 1952 (3).

———. *Best of Friends: A Life of Enriching Friendships.* United Kingdom, Marshall Pickering, 1986 (4) D1

———. *Bishop's Move.*

———. *Give A Dog A Bone.* London: Westminster Productions, 1964 (D)

———. *Hide Out*

———. *Mr. Wilberforce, MP.*

Thornton-Duesbury, Julian P. *Sharing.* The Oxford Group. n.d.

———. *The Oxford Group: A Brief Account of its Principles and Growth.* London: The Oxford Group, 1947 (2).

———. *The Open Secret of MRA: An examination of Mr. Driberg's "critical examination" of Moral Re-Armament.* London: Blandford, 1964 (2).

———. *A Visit to Caux: First-hand experience of Moral Re-Armament in action.* London: The Oxford Group, 1960.

Tournier, Paul. *A Listening Ear: Reflections on Christian Caring.* MN: Augsburg, 1987.

———. *Guilt & Grace: A Psychological Study.* NY: Harper & Row, 1962 (D)

———. *Learn To Grow Old.* NY: Harper & Row, 1971 (D)

———. *Secrets.* Virginia: John Knox Press, 1963 (D)

———. *The Healing of Persons.* NY: Harper & Row, 1965 (D)

———. *The Meaning of Persons.* NY: Harper & Row, 1957 (D)

———. *Medicine of the Whole Person.* Waco, TX: Word Books, 1973 (D)

———. *The Person Reborn.* NY: Harper & Row, 1966 (2) D2

———. *The Whole Person in a Broken World.* NY: Harper & Row, 1947 (D)

———. *To Resist or Surrender?* VA: John Knox Press, 1968 (D)

———. *To Understand Each Other.* VA: John Knox Press, 1972 (D)

Truman, Harry S. Press Release on Moral Re-Armament. U.S.S.

Missouri, April 12, 1943.

Twitchell, H. Kenaston. *Frank Buchman: Twentieth Century Catalyst.* NY: Moral Re-Armament, 1947 (5).

——. *How Do You Make Up Your Mind?.* New York: Moral Re-Armament, n.d. (3)

——. *More Sanity in Sex And Now. . . Aids.* Richmond, VA: Grosvenor, 1978 (2)

——. *Regeneration in the Ruhr.* Princeton: Princeton University Press, 1981 (9) D1.

——. *Supposing Your Were Absolutely Honest.* New York: Moral Re-Armament, n.d. (4) D1

——. *The Strength of a Nation: Absolute Purity.* New York: Moral Re-Armament, n.d. (2)

Twitchell, Hanford. *Poems,* n.d. (Spiral bound, mimeographed notebook)

Tyndale-Biscoe, John. *For God Alone: The Life of George West, Bishop of Rangoon.* Oxford: The Amate Press, 1984.

Unknown Christian. *How to Live The Victorious Life.* London: Marshall Brothers., n.d.

Usher-Wilson, Rodney N. *As If For You Alone-God's Love*, 1981.

——. *No Human Affair.* Princeton, NJ: 1981 (8)

——. *Suicide or Adoration.* NY: Vantage Press, 1971 (9)

——. *The Mystery of Human Existence.* NY: Moral Re-Armament, 1976.

——. *Worship is a Modern Necessity.* NY: Moral Re-Armament, 1975 (8)

Valentine, Denys. *Jesus & Zaccheus.* London, Blandford Press., n.d. (7)

Van Baalen, J. K. *The Chaos of Cults: A Study in Present-Day Isms.* 2d rev. enl. ed. Michigan: Wm B. Eerdmans, 1956 (5) D5

Van Dusen, Henry P. "Apostle to the Twentieth Century: Frank N. D. Buchman." *The Atlantic Monthly,* Vol. 154, pp. 1-16, July 1934. (2)

——. "The Oxford Group Movement: An Appraisal." *The Atlantic Monthly.* Vol. 154, pp. 230-252 (August 1934).

Vickers, Virginia. *Spin a Good Yarn: The Story of W. Farrar Vickers.* Leeds: M.T. Co., 1978.

Viney, Hallen. *How Do I Begin?* The Oxford Group, 61 Gramercy Park, New York., 1937. (4)

——. *Which Way Is Right?* London: Moral Re-Armament, 1968 (2).

Von Teuber, Eugene. *Step Ahead of Disaster.* London: Grosvenor, 1993

(2)

Vrooman, Lee. *The Faith That Built America*. New York: Arrowhead Books, Inc., 1955 (3) D1.

Waddy, Charis. *The Skills of Discernment*. London: Grosvenor Books, 1977 (2)

——. *The Muslim Mind*. 3rd ed. London: Grosvenor, 1990.

Walter, Howard A. *Soul Surgery: Some Thoughts On Incisive Personal Work*. Oxford: The Oxford Group, 1928 (2).

Watt, Frederick B. *Great Bear: A Journey Remembered*. Yellowknife, Northwest Territories, Canada: The Northern Publishers, 1980 (2) D1.

——. *Who Dare to Live*. Toronto: The Macmillan Company, 1943.

Weatherhead, Leslie D. *A Plain Man Looks at the Cross*. NY: Abingdon Press, 1955 (2) D2

——. *A Shepherd Remembers*. NY: Abingdon-Cokesbury Press, 1938 (D)

——. *Discipleship*. London: Student Christian Movement Press, 1934 (2) D1.

——. *Discipleship*. Rev. ed. London: SCM Press, 1958.

——. *How Can I Find God?* London: Fleming H. Revell, 1934 (2).

——. *In Quest of a Kingdom* .NY: Abingdon-Cokesbury Press, 1944 (D)

——. *Key Next Door*. NY: Abingdon Press, 1960 (D)

——. *Over His Own Signature*. NY: Abingdon Press, 1940 (2) D2

——. *Personalities of the Passion*. NY: Abingdon Press, 1953 (D)

——. *Psychology and Life*. New York: Abingdon Press, 1935 (3) D1

——. *Psychology Religion and Healing*. NY: Abingdon-Cokesbury, 1951 (D).

——. *The Christian Agnostic*. NY: Abingdon Press, 1965 (D)

——. *The Immortal Sea*. London: The Epworth Press, 1953 (D)

——. *The Mystery of Pain*. Nashville: The Upper Room, 1946.

——. *The Resurrection and the Life*. NY: Abingdon-Cokesbury Press, 1958 (D)

——. *The Transforming Friendship: A Book about Jesus and Ourselves*. NY: Abingdon-Cokesbury Press, 1931 (2) D2

——. *The Will of God*. NY: Abingdon-Cokesbury Press, 1954 (D)

—— *Thinking Aloud in War-Time*. NY: Abingdon-Cokesbury Press, 1940 (D).

——. *This is the Victory*. NY: Abingdon-Cokesbury Press, 1951 (D)

——. *When the Lamp Flickers*. NY: Abingdon-Cokesbury Press, 1958

(D)

——. *Wounded Spirits.* NY: Abingdon Press, 1962 (D)

West, The Right Rev. George. *The World That Works.* London: Blandford, 1945 (6) D1.

Which Way Cambodia? Friends of Moral Re-Armament, n.d.

Which Way Sri Lanka? Friends of Moral Re-Armament, n.d.

Whyte, Alexander. *The Nature of Angels.* London: Hodder & Stoughton, 1930.

Wilhelmsen, Jens J. *Man and Structures.* London: Grosvenor Books, 1977.

Williams, Hugh Steadman. *Skeletons.* London: Westminster Productions, 1987.

Wilson, Mary. *God's Plan in History* (1 set of 5 volumes) London: Grosvenor Books, 1960-83.

Williamson, Geoffrey. *Inside Buchmanism.* New York: Philosophical Library, Inc., 1955 (3) (D).

Winslow, Jack C. *Church in Action.* ???

——. *Modern Miracles.* London: Hodder & Stoughton, 1968.

——. *Vital Touch with God: How to Carry on Adequate Devotional Life.* The Evangel, 8 East 40th St., New York, n.d.

——. *When I Awake.* London: Hodder & Stoughton, 1938.

——. *Why I Believe in the Oxford Group.* London: Hodder & Stoughton, 1934.

—— and Verrier Elsin. *The Dawn of Indian Freedom.* London: George Allen & Unwin, 1931 (D).

Wishard, Charles Scoville. *Thoughts Along The Way.* Spring Valley, California, 1988 (3).

Without and Within [Poems], n.d..

Wood, Denise H. *Experiencing Pasadena.* CA: All Saints Episcopal Church, 1984.

---

* Index by Dick B. of Oxford Group Reading Lists of the Early A.A. period. *

Books by or about Oxford Group & A.A. Christian Mentors

A Gentleman with a Duster. *Painted Windows: Studies in Religious*

Personality. NY: G. P. Putnam's Sons, 1922 (D)

Atkins, Gaius Glenn and Charles Samuel Braden. *Procession of the Gods.* NY: Harper & Brothers, 1936 (D)

Braden., Charles S. *The World's Religions*, Rev. NY: Abingdon Press, 1939 (D)

Bushnell, Horace. *The New Life.* London: Strahan & Co., 1868 (2) D1.

———. *Christ and His Salvation.* NY: Charles Scribner's Sons, 1908 (2) D2

Chapman, J. Wilbur. *Life and Work of Dwight L. Moody.* Philadelphia: Universal Publishing, 1900 (3). D1

Cheney, Mary B. *Life and Letters of Horace Bushnell.* New York: Harper & Brothers, 1890.

De Remer, Bernard D. *Moody Bible Institute: A Pictorial History.* Chicago: Moody Press, 1960.

D Drummond, Henry. *Addresses.* Philadelphia: Henry Altemus, 1892. (Includes *The Greatest Thing in the World*, *Pax Vobiscum*, *The Changed Life*, *"First," How to Learn How*, *What is a Christian?*, *The Study of the Bible*, *A Talk on Books*.) (3) D1

———. *A Life for a Life.* NY: Fleming H. Revell Company, 1897 (D).

———. *Natural Law in the Spiritual World.* Potts Edition. NY: John B. Alden Publisher, 1887 (6) D-5.

———. *The Ascent of Man.* NY: James Pott & Co. Publishers, 1894 (2) D,

———. *The Changed Life.* NJ: Fleming H. Revell Company (reprint), n.d. (2) D1

———. *The Greatest Thing in the World and Other Addresses.* London: Collins, 1953 (5) D2.

———. *The Ideal Life.* NY: Dodd, Mead and Company, 1898 (2) D (1 plus partial copy)

———. *The New Evangelism and Other Addresses.* New York: Dodd, Mead And Company, 1899 (3) D1.

Eddy, Sherwood. *A Pilgrimage of Ideas or The Re-Education of Sherwood Eddy.* New York: Farrar & Rinehart, 1934.

———. *Eighty Adventurous Years: The Autobiography of Sherwood Eddy.* NY: Harper & Brothers, 1955 (D)

———. *You Will Survive after Death.* NY: Rinehart & Co., 1950 (D)

Edwards, Robert L. *Of Singular Genius, of Singular Grace: A Biography of Horace Bushnell.* Cleveland: The Pilgrim Press, 1992 (2) D.

Findlay, James F., Jr. *Dwight L. Moody: American Evangelist 1837-1899.* Chicago: The University of Chicago Press, 1969 (2) D.

Fitt, Emma Moody, *Day by Day with D. L. Moody*. Chicago: Moody Press, n.d.

———. *The D. L. Moody Year Book: A Living Daily Message from the Words of D.L. Moody*. East Northfield, Mass: The Bookstore, 1900.

Guldseth, Mark O. *Streams*. Alaska: Fritz Creek Studios, 1982 .

Goodspeed, Edgar Johnson. *Strange New Gospels*. Chicago: The University of Chicago Press, 1931.

Hopkins, C. Howard. *John R. Mott, a Biography*. Grand Rapids: William B. Erdmans Publishing Company, 1979 (3) D1.

James, William. *Habit.* NY: Henry Holt & Co., 1890 (D)

———. *On Some of Life's Ideals*. NY: Henry Holt & Company, 1900 (D)

———. *On Vital Reserves*. Westminster, MD: Christian Classics, Inc., 1988 [originally published in 1907] (D)

———. *Psychology*. NY: Henry Holt & Co., 1892 (D)

———. *The Energies of Men*. NY: Moffat, Yard and Company, 1911 (D)

———. *The Principles of Psychology: Volume I.* NY: Henry Holt & Co., 1893 (D)

———. *The Principles of Psychology: Volume II.* NY: Henry Holt & Co., 1893 (D)

———. *The Will to Believe: And Other Essays in Popular Philosophy*. London: Longmans Green and Company, 1903 (D)

———. *Talks to Teachers on Psychology*. New ed. Henry Holt and Company, 1899.

———. *Varieties of Religious Experience, The*. New York: First Vintage Books/The Library of America, 1990. (3) D1

Jung, C. G. *The Psychogenesis of Mental Disease.* NY: Pantheon Books, 1960 (D)

———. *Psychology & Religion*. New Haven: Yale University Press, 1938 (D)

Mann, A. Chester. *F. B. Meyer: Preacher, Teacher, Man of God.* NY: Fleming H. Revell Company, 1929.

Meyer, F. B. *Five Musts*. Chicago: Moody Press, 1927 (3) D1.

———. *The Secret of Guidance*. New York: Fleming H. Revell, 1896 (3) D1

Moody, Dwight L. *Heaven: Where It Is; Its Inhabitants; And How to Get There.* Toronto: Rose-Belford Publishing Company, 1880.

———. *How to Study the Bible*. Philadelphia: Henry Altemus Company,

1897 (D)

———. *Secret Power: Or, The Secret of Success in Christian Life and Christian Work*. Chicago: F. H. Revell, 1881 (2) D.

———. *The Way to God*. Chicago: F. H. Revell, 1884 (D)

Moody, Paul D. *My Father: An Intimate Portrait of Dwight Moody*. Boston: Little Brown, 1938 (2) D1.

Moody, William R. *The Life of D. L. Moody*. New York: Fleming H. Revell, 1900 (4) D2

Mott, John R. *Addresses and Papers: Volume IV The Young Men's Christian Association*. New York: Association Press, 1947 (D)

———. *Decisive Hour of Christian Missions. The*. NY: Student Volunteer Movement, 1910 (D)

———. *Evangelism for the World Today*. NJ: Harper Brothers, 1938.

———. *Evangelization of the World in This Generation, The*. London, 1901 (3) D1.

———. *Five Decades and a Forward View*. 4th ed. New York: Harper & Brothers, 1939 (2) D1.

———. *Larger Evangelism, The*. New York: Abingdon-Cokesbury Press, 1944.

———. *Pastor and Modern Missions, The: A Plea For Leadership in World Evangelization*. New York: Student Volunteer Movement For Foreign Missions, 1904.

———. *The Present World Situation*. NY: Student Volunteer Movement For Foreign Missions, 1914.

Pollock, J. C. *Moody: A Biographical Portrait of the Pacesetter in Modern Mass Evangelism*. New York: Macmillan, 1963 (2) D1.

Plowright, B. C. *Rebel Religion: Christ, Community, and Church*. NY: Round Table Press, 1937 (D)

Rollins, Wayne G. *Jung and the Bible*. Atlanta: John Knox Press, 1983 (D)

Rosell, Garth M., and Richard A. G. Dupuis. *The Memoirs of Charles G. Finney: The Completely Restored Text*. MI: Zondervan Publishing House, 1989.

* Schaer, Hans. *Religion and the Cure of Souls in Jung's Psychology*. NY: Pantheon Books, 1950 (D)

Smith, George Adam. *The Life of Henry Drummond*. New York: McClure, Phillips & Co., 1901 (4) D1.

Speer, Robert E. *A Christian's Habits*. Philadelphia: The Westminster Press, 1911 (D)

————. *Christian Realities*. NY: Fleming H. Revell, 1935 (D)

————. *Marks of a Man, The*. New York: Hodder & Stoughton, 1907 (2) D1.

————. *Principles of Jesus, The*. New York: Fleming H. Revell Company, 1902 (2) D1.

————. *Servants of the King*. NY: Missionary Education Movement, 1914 (D)

————. *Studies of the Man Christ Jesus*. New York: Fleming H. Revell, 1896.

————. *Five Minutes a Day*. Philadelphia: The Westminster Press, 1953. (D)

————. *The Finality of Jesus Christ*. NY: Fleming H. Revell, 1933 (D)

Stewart, George, Jr. *Life of Henry B. Wright*. New York: Association Press, 1925 (4) D2

————. *The Crucifixion in our Street*. NY: George H. Doran, 1927 (D) [inscribed by author to Frank Buchman]

Trumbull, H. Clay. *Individual Work For Individuals*. NY: The International Committee of Young Men's Christian Associations, 1901.

————. *The Evangelization of the World*. The Connecticut Magazine. Volume VIII, No. 3, n.d.

Wheeler, W. Reginald. *A Man Sent From God: The Biography of Robert E. Speer*. NJ: Fleming H. Revell Company, 1956 (D)

Wright, Henry B. *The Will of God and a Man's Lifework*. New York: The Young Men's Christian Association Press, 1909. (4) D1.

Christian and Other Religious Literature Pertaining to Early A.A.

The Books of "Dr. Bob's Library"

[Books owned, studied, recommended, and loaned to others by Dr. Bob, co-founder of A.A., and his wife Anne Ripley Smith, whom Bill W. called the "Mother of A.A."]

[In their respective comments and writings, Dr. Bob and his wife Anne indicated that Dr. Bob and probably his wife read and recommended (1) "all" the Oxford Group and (2) "all" the Sam Shoemaker books published by late 1939 when AAs began meeting in the Smith Home and then King School. (3) Also, "all" the Quiet Time books listed above and published by 1949. **This list will include those which were named as read, owned by the family, or mentioned by others in connection with the Smiths. The remainder are covered in the Oxford Group Mentors, Oxford Group, Shoemaker, Bible, and Quiet Time lists. For the complete list of items in Dr. Bob's Library or that were read and recommended by him, see Dick B.,** ***Dr. Bob and His Library***, **3rd ed.]**

Bible

Authorized (King James) Version. National Publishing Company, 1978.

About the Bible

Williams, R. Llewelyn. *God's Great Plan: A Guide to the Bible*. 6th ed. London: The Covenant Publishing Company, 1973 [first published in 1939] (2) D1.
The Fathers of the Church: The Apostolic Fathers. CIMA Publishing, 1947.

Christian Classics

Brother Lawrence. *The Practice of the Presence of God*. PA: Whitaker House, 1982 (2) D1.
The Confessions of St. Augustine. Trans. by E. B. Pusey. New York: Cardinal ed., Pocket Books, 1952 (2) D1.

The Life and Teachings of Jesus Christ

Barton, George A. *Jesus of Nazareth: A Biography*. New York: The Macmillan Company, 1922.
Fosdick, Harry Emerson. *The Man from Nazareth: As His Contemporaries Saw Him*. New York: Harper & Brothers, 1949 (2) D1.
Gilkey, Charles Whitney. *Jesus and Our Generation*. Chicago: The University of Chicago Press, 1925.

Glover, T. R. *The Jesus of History*. New York: Association Press, 1919 (2) D1.

Harris, Irving. *An Outline of the Life of Christ*. New York: The Oxford Group, 1935.

Ligon, Ernest M. *The Psychology of Christian Personality*. New York: The Macmillan Company, 1942 (3) (D2).

Oursler, Fulton. *The Greatest Story Ever Told: A Tale of the Greatest Life Ever Lived*. New York: Doubleday & Company, 1949. (3) D1

Stalker, James. *The Life of Jesus Christ*. New York: Fleming H. Revell Company, 1891 (5) D2.

Devotionals (See the section on Quiet Time above)

Healing

Barbanell, Maurice. *Parish The Healer*. Spec. London: Psychic Book Club, 1938 (D)

Brownell, Louise. *Life Abundant For You.* CA: The Aquarian Ministry, 1928 (D)

Clark, Glenn. *How to Find Health through Prayer*. 3rd ed. New York: Harper & Brothers, 1940.

Fillmore, Charles. Christian Healing. MO: Unity School of Christianity, 1919 (3) D1.

Fox, Emmet. *Power through Constructive Thinking*. 12th ed. New York: Harper & Brothers, 1940 (2) D1

Hickson, James Moore. *Heal the Sick*. London: Methuen & Co., 1924

Willitts, Ethel R. *Healing in Jesus' Name*. Detroit: Ethel R. Willitts, Evangelist, 1931 (2) D1.

Prayer

Clark, Glenn. *Clear Horizons Volume IV*. MN: Macalester Park Publishing Company, 1943 (D)

———. *Fishers of Men*. 1948 ed. MN: Macalester Park Publishing Co., 1928 (2) D1.

———. *God's Reach*. MN: Macalester Park Publishing Company, 1951 (2) D1.

———. *How to Find Health through Prayer* New York: Harper & Row,

1940 (2) D1.

———. *I Will Lift Up Mine Eyes*. NY: Harper & Brothers, 1937 (D).

———. *The Lord's Prayer and Other Talks on Prayer from the Camp Farthest Out*. MN: Macalester Park Publishing Company, 1932.

———. *The Man Who Talks with the Flowers: The Life Story of Dr. George Washington Carver*. MN: Macalester Park Publishing Co., 1939 (2) D1

———. *The Man Who Tapped The Secrets of the Universe*. VA: The University of Science and Philosophy, 1946 (D)

———. *The Song of the Souls of Men*. MN: Macalester Park Publishing Company, n.d. (D).

———. *The Soul's Sincere Desire*. Boston. Little, Brown, and Company, 1925. (3) D1

———. *Touchdowns for the Lord: The Story of "Dad" A. J. Elliott*. MN: Macalester Park Publishing Company, 1947.

———. *Two or Three Gathered Together*. New York: Harper & Brothers, 1942. (2)

———. *Water of Life*. MN: The Macalester Park Company, 1931 (D)

———, and Louise Miles Clark. *Stepping Heavenward: The Spiritual Journal of Louise Miles Clark*. MN: Macalester Park Publishing Co., 1950 (2) D1.

Daily, Starr. *Recovery*. MN: Macalester Park Publishing Company, 1948 (2) D1.

Eddy, Mary Baker. *Christian Science Textbook with Key to the Scriptures*. Published by the Trustees under the Will of Mary Baker Eddy, 1916 (3) D2.

Fillmore, Charles and Cora. *Teach Us to Pray*. MO: Unity School of Christianity, 1945 (2) D1.

Fosdick, Harry Emerson. *A Great Time to Be Alive*. New York: Harper & Brothers, 1944 (3) D1

———. *On Being a Real Person*. New York: Harper & Brothers, 1943 (2) D1

———. *The Manhood of the Master*. NY: Association Press, 1913 (2) D1.

———. *The Meaning of Faith*. NY: The Abingdon Press, 1917 (3) D2.

———. *The Meaning of Service*. NY: The Abingdon Press, 1920 (4) D3.

Fox, Emmet. *Alter Your Life*. New York: Harper & Brothers Publishers, 1921 (2) D1.

———. *Find and Use Your Inner Power*. San Francisco: Harper, 1937 (2) D1.

————. *Getting Results by Prayer* (1933); *You Must Be Born Again* (1936); *The Great Adventure* (1937). Reprints. CA: DeVorss & Co., 1961.

————. *The Lord's Prayer: An Interpretation.* CA: DeVorss & Company, 1932.

————. *The Sermon on the Mount.* NY: Harper & Brothers, 1934 (2) D1

————. *Your Heart's Desire* (= pp. 168-77 of *Power through Constructive Thinking*, listed above). Owned in pamphlet form by Dr. Bob.

Heard, Gerald. *A Preface to Prayer.* New York: Harper & Brothers, 1944 (3) D2.

Jones, E. Stanley. *Along the Indian Road.* London: Hodder and Stoughton Ltd, 1939 (2) D1.

————. *Christ and Human Suffering.* New York: The Abingdon Press, 1933 (2) D1.

————. *Christ at the Round Table.* NY: Grosset & Dunlap Publishers, 1928 (3) D1

————. *Christ's Alternative to Communism.* NY: Abingdon-Cokesbury Press, 1935 (D)

————. *The Choice Before Us.* New York: The Abingdon Press, 1937 (2) D1.

————. *The Christ of the American Road.* New York: Abingdon-Cokesbury Press, 1944 (3) D1.

————. *The Christ of the Indian Road.* New York: The Abingdon Press, 1925. (3) D2

————. *The Christ of Every Road.* NY: The Abingdon Press, 1930 (D)

————. *Is The Kingdom of God Realism?* NY: Abingdon-Cokesbury, 1950 (D)

————. *The Way to Power and Poise.* NY: Abingdon-Cokesbury Press, 1949 (D)

Laubach, Frank C.. *Prayer* (*Mightiest Force in the World*). NY: Fleming H. Revell, 1956 (2)

Laymon, Charles. *A Primer of Prayer.* Nashville, TN: Tidings, 1949 (2).

Mosely, Rufus. *Perfect Everything.* MN: Macalester Park Publishing, 1949. ???

Parker, William R., and Elaine St. Johns. *Prayer Can Change Your Life: Experiments and Techniques in Prayer Therapy.* New ed. New York: Prentice Hall Press, 1957 (3) D2.

Rawson, F. L. The Nature of True Prayer. England: The Society for

Spreading The Knowledge of True Prayer, 1918 (2) D1.

The Sermon on the Mount

Chambers, Oswald. *Studies in the Sermon on the Mount.* London: Simpkin Marshall, Ltd. n.d. (2) D1

Jones, E. Stanley. *The Christ of the Mount: A Working Philosophy of Life.* New York: The Abingdon Press, 1931 (3) D1.

Love

Kagawa, Toyohiko. *Love: The Law of Life.* Philadelphia: The John C. Winston Company, 1929. (4) D1

The Oxford Group (See the section on The Oxford Group above, books prior to 1940.)

Samuel M. Shoemaker, Jr. (See also the section above on the Rev. Samuel Moor Shoemaker, Jr., books prior to 1940.)

Shoemaker, Samuel M. Jr. *Three Levels of Life.* (Pamphlet from *Confident Faith*, located at Stepping Stones.)

———. *What If I Had But One Sermon to Preach.* (Pamphlet from *Religion That Works*, located at Stepping Stones.)

Religion and the Mind

Allen, James. *Heavenly Life.* New York: Grosset and Dunlap, n.d. (2) D1

James, William. *The Varieties of Religious Experience.* New York: New American Library, 1958.

Jung, Carl. *Modern Man in Search of a Soul.* New York: Harcourt Brace Jovanovich Publishers, 1933 (2) D1.

Liebman, Joshua Loth. *Peace of Mind.* New York: Simon & Schuster, 1946. (A copy is also located at Stepping Stones and inscribed by Bill W. to Dr. Bob.) (2) D1

Link, Henry C. *The Rediscovery of Man.* New York: The Macmillan Company, 1938 (2) D.

Lupton, Dilworth. *Religion Says You Can.* Boston: The Beacon Press, 1938 (3) D1.

Trine, Ralph Waldo. *In Tune with the Infinite: Or Fullness of Peace, Power, and Plenty*. Indianapolis: The Bobbs-Merrill Company, 1897 (2) D1.

———. *The Man Who Knew*. London: G. Bell and Sons, 1940 (D).

Troward, Thomas. *The Edinburgh Lectures on Mental Science*. New York: Dodd, Mead And Company, 1909 (3) D2.

Miscellaneous Books That Were Part of Dr. Bob's Library

Carnegie, Dale. *How To Win Friends and Influence People*. NY: Simon & Schuster, 1937 (D)

Douglas, Lloyd C. *Forgive Us Our Trespasses*. NY: Grosset & Dunlap, 1932 (D)

———. *The Robe*. Boston: Houghton Mifflin, 1942 (D)

Fosdick, Harry Emerson. *As I See Religion*. NY: Grosset & Dunlap, 1932 (D)

Gheon, Henri. *Secrets of the Saints*. NY: Sheed & Ward, 1944 (D)

Lieb, Frederick G. *Sight Unseen: A Journalist Visits the Occult*. NY: Harper & Brothers, 1930 (D).

Maugham, W. Somerset. *The Razor's Edge*. Philadelphia: The Blakiston Company, 1953 D

Moseley, J. R. *Perfect Everything*. MN: Macalester, n.d. (Extract.)

Noyes, Alfred. *The Unknown God*. New York: Sheed & Ward, 1934 (D)

Oursler, Fulton. *The Happy Grotto: A Journalist's Account of Lourdes*. Surrey: The World's Work, 1957 (2) (D2)

Ouspensky, Peter D. *Tertium Organum*, 2d American ed., auth. and rev. NY: Alfred A. Knopf, 1944 (2).

Peabody, Richard R. *The Common Sense of Drinking*. 1933 (D)

Peale, Norman Vincent. *The Art of Living*. New York: Abingdon-Cokesbury Press, 1937 (2) D.

Seabury, David. *The Art of Selfishness*. NY: Garden City Publishing, 1937 (2) D1

Sheean, Vincent. *Lead Kindly Light: Ghandi & The Way to Peace*. NY: Random House, 1949 (2) D1.

Sheen, Fulton J. *Peace of Soul*. NY: McGraw Hill, 1949 (2) D1.

Teachings of the Temple. Halcyon, California: The Temple of the People, 1925 (D)

Werber, Eva Bell. *Quiet Talks with the Master*. CA: DeVorss Publications, 1964. [originally published 1936.] (2) D1

Werfel, Franz. *The Song of Bernadette.* NY: The Viking Press, 1943 (D)
White, Stewart Edward. *The Rose Dawn.* NY: Doubleday, Page & Co., 1920 (D)

Background Books A.A. Pioneers Read on Christianity, Healing, and Religion; and Books Helpful in Understanding the Pioneers' Beliefs

Allen, Charles L. *All Things are Possible Through Prayer.* NJ: Fleming H. Revell, 1958 (D)
——. *God's Seven Wonders for You.* NJ: Fleming H. Revell, 1987 (D)
——. *God's Psychiatry.* NJ: Fleming H. Revell, 1953 (2) D2
——. *Healing Words.* NJ: Fleming H. Revell, 1951 (D)
——. *Perfect Peace.* NY: Guideposts, 1979 (D)
——. *Roads to Radiant Living.* NY: Fleming H. Revell, 1952 (D)
——. *The Life of Christ.* NJ: Fleming H. Revell, 1962 (D)
——. *The Lord's Prayer: An Interpretation.* NJ: Fleming H. Revell, 1953 (D)
——. *The Secret of Abundant Living.* NJ: Fleming H. Revell, 1980 (D)
——. *The Touch of the Master's Hand.* NJ: Fleming H. Revell, 1956 (D)
——. *The Twenty-third Psalm: An Interpretation.* NJ: Fleming H. Revell, 1961 (D)
——. *Victory in the Valleys of Life.* NJ: Fleming H. Revell, 1981 (D)
——. *What I Have Lived By.* NJ: Fleming H. Revell, 1976 (D)
——. *When the Heart is Hungry.* NJ: Fleming H. Revell, 1955 (D)
——. *You are Never Alone.* NJ: Fleming H. Revell, 1978 (D)
Allen, James. *The Mastery of Destiny.* NY: The Knickerbocker Press, 1909 (D)
——. *As You Think.* San Rafael, CA: The Classic Wisdom Collection, 1991 (D)
——. *Morning and Evening Thoughts.* NY: The Peter Pauper Press, 1966 (D)
Allen, James Lane. *The Choir Invisible.* NY: The Macmillan Company, 1897 (2) D2
——. *A Kentucky Cardinal.* NY: The Macmillan Company, 1905
An Unknown Christian. *How to Live the Victorious Life.* New Popular ed. London: Marshall, Morgan & Scott, Limited, n.d.
Armstrong, April Oursler. *The Tales Christ Told.* NY: Doubleday & Co., 1959 (D)
Babson, Roger W. *New Tasks for Old Churches.* NY: Fleming H. Revell,

1922 (D)

Barton, Bruce. *The Man Nobody Knows: A Discovery of the Real Jesus.* IN: Bobbs-Merrill, 1925. (3) D1

——. *The Book Nobody Knows.* Gross & Dunlap, 1926 (2) D.

——. *He Upset World.* Indianapolis: Bobbs-Merrill, 1922 (D)

——. *What Can A Man Believe?* Grosset & Dunlap, 1927 (D)

Beard, Rebecca. *Everyman's Goal: The Expanded Consciousness,* VT: Merrybrook Press, 1951 (2) D1

——. *Everyman's Mission. The Development of the Christ-Self.* NY: Harper & Brothers, 1952 (D)

——. *Everyman's Search.* VT: Merrybrook Press, 1950 (D)

Bennett, Arnold. *How To Live On Twenty-Four Hours a Day.* NY: The Bookman, 1925 (3) D3

——. *Mental Efficiency.* NY: George H. Doran, 1911 (D)

——. *The Human Machine.* NY: George H. Doran, n.d. (D)

——. *The Feast of St. Friend.* NY: George H. Doran, 1911 (D)

Bennett, John C. *Christianity and Our World.* NY: Hazen Books on Religion, 1936 (D)

——. *Christianity and Communism.* NY: Association Press, 1948 (D)

——. *Christians and the State.* NY: Charles Scribner's Sons, 1958 (D)

Bunyan, John. *Pilgrim's Progress.* NY: American Tract Society, n.d. (D)

Braden, Charles. *The World's Religions, revised.* NY: Abingdon Press, 1954 (D)

——. *Varieties of American Religion.* Chicago: Willett Clark & Co., 1936 (D)

Browne, Lewis. *This Believing World: A Simple Account of the Great Religions of Mankind.* Rev ed. NY: The Macmillan Company, 1935 (3) D1

——. *The World's Great Scriptures: An Anthology of the Sacred Books of the Ten Principal Religions.* NY: The Macmillan Company, 1946 (D)

——. *How Odd of God: An Introduction to the Jews.* NY: The Macmillan Company, 1934 (D)

Carrel, Alexis. *Man The Unknown.* NY: Halcyon House, 1933 (D)

Chambers, Oswald. *Biblical Psychology.* Ohio: God's Revivalist Office, 1914 (D).

——. *Conformed to His Image.* London: Marshall, Morgan & Scott, 1950 (D)

——. *Daily Thoughts for Disciples.* Michigan, Zondervan, 1976 (D)

——. *God's Workmanship*. IL: Van Kampen Press, 1953 (D)

——. *If You Will Ask*. MI: Discovery House Publishers, 1958 (D)

——. *The Psychology of Redemption*. London: Simpkin Marshall, 1941 (D)

——. *Workmen of God*. PA: Oswald Chambers Publications Assn., 1965 (D) [Other books by Oswald Chambers—from the personal library of Rev. W. Irving Harris—declared by Bill Wilson to be one of those who, along with Harris's wife Julia and Shoemaker himself, inspired the A.A. program]:

——. *As He Walked: Talks on Christian Experience*. Oswald Chambers Publications Assn, n.d.

——. *Bringing Sons Unto Glory*. (*Studies in the Life of Our Lord*.) Reprint. Oswald Chambers Publications Assn., 1958.

——. *Disciples Indeed*. Reprint. Oswald Chambers Publications Assn., 1955.

——. *If Thou Wilt Be Perfect. . . . Talks on Spiritual Philosophy*. London: Simpkin Marshall, 1941.

——. *If Ye Shall Ask . . .* Reprint. Oswald Chambers Publications Assn., 1958.

——. *Our Portrait in Genesis*, Reprint. Oswald Chambers Publications Assn., 1957.

——. *Shade of His Hand: Talks on the Book of Ecclesiastes*. London: Simpkins Marshall, 1941.

——. *The Philosophy of Sin and other Studies in the Problems of Man's Moral Life*. London: Simpkin Marshall, 1941. (2)

——. *The Psychology of Redemption*. Reprint. Oswald Chambers Publications Assn., 1955.

Clark, Francis *E. Christian Endeavor in All Lands: A Record of Twenty-Five Years of Progress*. Official ed. The United Society of Christian Endeavor, 1908 (2) D1

——. *Memoirs of Many Men in Many Lands: An Autobiography*. Boston: United Society of Christian Endeavor, 1922 (2) D1.

Clark, Glenn. *A Manual of the Short Story Art*. NY: The Macmillan Company, 1926 (D)

——. *A Man's Reach: The Autobiography of Glenn Clark*. MN: Macalester Park Publishing Company, 1977 (D)

——. *Come Follow Me: Living with Jesus of Galilee 2000 Years Ago*. MN: Macalester Park Publishing Company, 1952 (D)

Daily, Starr. *Release*. NY: Harper & Brothers, 1942 (D)

————. *Well-Springs of Immortality*. MN: Macalester Park Publishing Company, 1941 (D)

————. *You Can.* Los Angeles: G & J Publishing, 1956 (D)

Dunnington, Lewis L. *More Handles of Power.* NY: Abingdon-Cokesbury, 1954 (D)

Du Plessis, J. *The Life of Andrew Murray of South Africa.* London: Marshall Brothers, 1919 (D).

Emerson, Ralph Waldo. *The Portable Emerson,* New ed. NY: Penguin Books, 1981 (D)

Farrar, Frederic William. *Farrar's Life of Christ.* OH: The World Publishing Company, 1913 (D)

Fosdick, Harry Emerson. *Adventurous Religion.* NY: Harper & Brothers, 1926 (D)

————. *A Faith For Tough Times.* NY: Harper & Brothers, 1952 (2) D2

————. *A Guide to Understanding The Bible.* NY: Harper & Brothers, 1938 (D)

————. *Assurance of Immortality, The.* NY: The Macmillan Company, 1924 (D)

————. *Dear Mr. Brown: Letters to a Person Perplexed about Religion.* NY: Harper, 1961 (D)

————. *On Being Fit to Live With.* NY: Harper & Brothers, 1946 (D)

————. *Jesus of Nazareth.* NY: Random House, 1959. (D)

————. *A Pilgrimage To Palestine.* NY: The Chatauqua Press, 1928 (D)

————. *Power to See It Through, The: Sermons on Christianity Today.* NY: Harper & Brothers, 1935 (D).

————. *Second Mile, The.* NY: Association Press, 1917 (D)

————. *Secret of Victorious Living, The.* NY: Harper & Brothers, 1934 (D)

————. *Successful Christian Living.* NY: Harper & Brothers, 1937 (D)

————. *Living Under Tension.* NY: *Harper & Brothers, 1941 (D)*

————. *The Challenge of the Present Crisis.* NY: Association Press, 1918 (D)

————. *The Hope of the World.* NY: Garden City Books, 1933 (2) D2

————. *The Life of Saint Paul.* NY: Random House, 1961 (D)

————. *The Modern Use of the Bible. NY*: The Macmillan Company, 1924 (D)

————. *What is Vital in Religion.* NY: Harper & Brothers, 1955 (D)

————. *Twelve Tests of Character.* NY: George H. Doran Company, 1923 (D)

——. ed., *Great Voices of the Reformation: An Anthology*. NY: Random House, 1952 (D)

Fox, Emmet. *Around the Year with Emmet Fox: A Book of Daily Readings*. NY: Harper & Row, 1952 (D)

——.*Be Still: A Treatment Against Fear: Spiritual Key to Psalm XLVI*. Harper & Row, Publishers, 1934.

——. *Diagrams For Living: The Bible Unveiled*. NY: Harper & Row, 1968 (D)

——. *Make Your Life Worth While*. New York, Harper & Row, 1946 (2) D1.

——. The Golden Key. Enlarged and Revised. CA: De Vorss & Co., nd. (Originally published 1931) (2) (D1)

——. Sparks of Truth. NY: Grosset & Dunlap, 1937 (D)

——. Stake Your Claim. NY: Harper & Brothers, 1952 (D)

——. The Seven Main Aspects of God. CA: De Vorss & Co., n.d. (Originally published: 1942)

Getting The Most Out of Life: An Anthology from The Reader's Digest. NY: 1946 (D)

Glover, T. R. *Jesus in the Experience of Men*. NY: Grosset & Dunlap, 1921 (D)

——. *The Nature and Purpose of a Christian Society*. NY: George H. Doran, 1922 (D)

Goodspeed, Edgar. *A Life of Jesus*. NY: Harper & Brothers, 1950 (D)

——. *How Came the Bible?* NY: Abingdon-Cokesbury, 1940 (D)

——. *How to Read the Bible*. Philadelphia: John C. Winston, 1946 (D)

Gordon, S. D. *Quiet Talks on Power*. NY: Fleming H. Revell, 1903 (D)

Gunnarsson, Gunnar. *The Good Shepherd*. NY: Bobbs-Merrill, 1940 (D)

Heard, Gerald. *Is God Evident?: An Essay Towards a Natural Theology*. London: Faber & Faber, n.d. (D)

——. *Man The Master*. NY: Harper & Brothers, 1941 (D)

—— *The Third Morality*. NY William Morrow, 1937 (D)

Holmes, Ernest. *Alcoholism: Its Cause and Cure From the viewpoint of Science of Mind*. Los Angeles, CA: Science of Mind Publications, 1941 (D).

Holmes, Marjorie. *How Can I Find You, God?* NY: Doubleday & Co., 1975 (D).

——. *Two From Galilee: A Love Story*. Old Tappan, NJ: Fleming H. Revell, 1972 (D).

110

────. *Who Am I, God?* NY: Doubleday & Company, 1971 (D).

Howe, Reuel L. *Man's Need and God's Action.* Greenwich, CT: Seabury Press, 1957 (D)

Huxley, Aldous. *Brave New World.* NY: The Modern Library, 1932 (D)

Jones, E. Stanley. *A Song of Accents: A Spiritual Autobiography.* NY: Abingdon Press,1968 (D)

────. *Christian Maturity.* NY: Abingdon Press, 1957 (D)

────. *Conversion.* NY: Abingdon Press, 1959 (D)

────. *Growing Spiritually.* NY: Abingdon Press, 1953 (D)

────. *In Christ.* NY: Abingdon, 1961 (D)

────. *Mastery: The Art of Mastering Life.* NY: Abingdon Press, 1955 (D).

────. *The Word Became Flesh.* NY: Abingdon Press, 1963.(D)

Kagawa, Toyohiko. *Meditations on the Cross.* NY: Willett, Clark & Company, 1935 (D)

────. *The Challenge of Redemptive Love.* NY: The Abingdon Press, 1940 (D)

Kelly, Thomas. *The Sanctuary of the Soul: Selected Writings of Thomas Kelly.* Nashville: Upper Room Books, 1997. (Society of Friends–the Quakers-explanations of the inner light.)

Kennedy, G. A. Studdert. *The New Man in Christ.* London: Hodder and Stoughton, 1932 (D)

Laymon, Charles M. *The Lord's Prayer in its Biblical Setting.* Nashville: Abingdon Press, 1968 (D)

Leuba, James H. *A Study in the Psychology of Religious Phenomena.* Reprint from *The American Journal of Psychology*, April, 1896.

Lewis, C. S. *A Grief Observed.* HarperSanFrancisco, 1989 (D)

────. *Beyond Personality: The Christian Idea of* God. NY: The Macmillan Co., 1945 (D)

────. *Christian Behavior.* NY: The Macmillan Company, 1948 (D)

────. *God in the Dock: Essays on Theology and Ethics.* MI: Eerdmans, 1972 (D)

────. *Letters to Malcom Chiefly on Prayer.* London: Geoffrey Bles, 1964 (D)

────. *Mere Christianity.* NY: Macmillan, 1978 (D)

────. Miracles: A Preliminary Study. London: Geoffrey Bles, 1952 (D)

────. Surprised by Joy. The Shape of My Early Life. San Diego: A

Harvest Book, 1956 (D)

———. *The Case for Christianity*. NY: The Macmillan Company, 1944 (D)

———. *The Great Divorce*. NY: The Macmillan Company, 1946 (D)

———. *The Problem of Pain*. NY: The Macmillan Company, 1948 (D)

———. *The Screwtape Letters*. NJ: Barbour and Company, 1961 (D)

Liebman, Joshua Loth. *Hope for Man*. NY: Simon & Schuster, 1966 (D)

Ligon, Ernest M. *Their Future Is Now: The Growth and Development of Christian Personality*. New York: The MacMillan Company, 1945 (D).

———. *A Greater Generation*. NY: The MacMillan Company, 1948 (D).

Link, Henry C. *The Return to Religion*. New York: The Macmillan Company, 1937 (2) D1.

———. *The Way to Security*. New York: Doubleday & Company, 1951 (D).

Manderson, Rita. *The Awakening*. MD: Reese Press, 1968 (D)

Maugham, W. Somerset. *Of Human Bondage*. NY: Doubleday & Company, 1936 (D)

Merton, Thomas. *Life and Holiness*. NY: Herder and Herder, 1963 (D)

Miller, Keith. *The Taste of New Wine*. TX: Word Books, 1972 (D)

Morgan, Edward P. *This I Believe*. NY: Simon and Schuster, 1952 (D)

Murch, James DeForest. *Successful C.E. Prayer-Meetings*. Cincinnati: The Standard Publishing Company, 1930 (D)

Neibuhr, Reinhold. *Beyond Tragedy: Essays on the Christian Interpretation of History*. London: Nisbet and Co., 1947 (D)

———. *The Children of Light and The Children of Darkness*. NY: Charles Scribner's, 1945 (D)

Norberg, Sverre. *God-Controlled Lives*. Minneapolis: Augsburg Publishing House, 1938.

Ochs., William B. *This I Believe*. Washington, D.C. Review and Herald Publishing, 1951 (D)

Orr, J. Edwin. *Full Surrender*. London: Marshall, Morgan & Scott. 1951 (2) D1.

Ortlund, Anne. *The Disciplines of the Beautiful Woman*. TX: Word Books, 1983 (D)

Oursler, Fulton. *Greatest Book Ever Written, The*. NY: Doubleday & Co., 1951 (D)

———. *Lights Along the Shore*. NY: Hanover House, 1954 (2) (D2)

———. *Three Things We Can Believe In*. NY: Fleming H. Revell, 1952

(D)

———. *Why I Know There is a God.* NY: Doubleday & Co., 1950 (D)

Oursler, Fulton and April Oursler Armstrong. *The Greatest Faith Ever Known.* NY: Doubleday & Company, 1953 (D)

Oursler, Fulton and Will Oursler. *Father Flanagan of Boys Town.* NY: Doubleday & Co., 1959 (D)

Oursler, Will. *The Healing Power of Faith.* NY: Hawthorn Books, 1957 (D)

———. *The Road to Faith.* NY: Holt, Rinehart and Winston, 1960 (D)

Papini, Giovanni. *Life of Christ.* NY: Harcourt, Brace, 1925 (D)

Peabody, Richard. *The Common Sense of Drinking.* Boston: Little, Brown, 1935.

Peale, Norman Vincent. *The Art of Real Happiness.* NY: Prentice-Hall, 1950 (D).

———. and Smiley Blanton. *Faith is the Answer.* Rev. enl. NY: Guideposts Associates, 1955 (D)

Pietsch, William V. *The Serenity Prayer Book.* HarperSanFrancisco, 1990 (D)

———. *The Power of Positive Thinking.* NY: Prentice Hall, 1952 (D)

Rawson, F. L. *Man's Concept of God.* 2d ed. London: Society for Spreading the Knowledge of True Prayer, 1935 (D)

Savage, O. D. *F. L. Rawson: A Memoir.* London: Society for Spreading the Knowledge of True Prayer, 1933 (D)

Scott, John F. *The Religion of the Lord's Prayer.* NY: Abingdon-Cokesbury Press, 1956 (D)

Sheen, Fulton J. *Life is Worth Living.* NY: McGraw-Hill, 1953 (D)

———. *The Life of Christ.* NY: McGraw-Hill, 1958 (D)

Sheppard, H. R. L. *The Impatience of a Parson.* London: Hodder & Stoughton, 1927 (D)

Smith, Hannah Whitall. *The Christian's Secret of a Happy Life.* Reprint. Fleming H. Revell, 1952 (2).

Spencer, Herbert. *The Study of Sociology.* The University of Michigan Press 1961 (D)

Spreng, Samuel P. *History of the Evangelical Church: For the Use of Young People, Members of the Evangelical League of Christian Endeavor, Brotherhoods, and other Groups.* OH: Publishing House of the Evangelical Church, 1927 (D)

The Spiritual Maxims of Brother Lawrence. NJ: Fleming H. Revell, 1967 (D)

Spurgeon, C.H. *The Soul-Winner*. Wilmington, DE: Publishers Associates, n.d. (D)

St. Denis, Ruth. *An Unfinished Life*. NY: Harper & Brothers, 1939 (D)

Stalker, Rev. James. *The Atonement*. NY: Eaton and Mains, 1906 (D)

———. *Christian Psychology*. 2d ed. NY: Hodder & Stoughton, 1914 (D)

———. *Imago Christi: The Example of Christ*. London: Hodder and Stoughton, 1908 (D)

———. *The Ethic of Jesus: According to the Synoptic Gospels*. NY: George H. Doran Company, 1909 (D)

———. *The Life of St. Paul*. New York: Fleming H. Revell, n.d. (D)

———. *The Trial and Death of Jesus Christ*. Michigan: Zondervan, 1894 (D)

Tillich, Paul J., and others. *The Christian Answer*. NY: Charles Scribner's Sons, 1945 (D)

Trine, Ralph Waldo. *In the Fire of the Heart*. NY: McClure, Phillips & Co., 1906 (D)

———. *On the Open Road.*. NY: Thomas Y. Crowell, 1908 (D)

———. *What All The World's A-Seeking*. NY: Thomas Y. Trowell, 1896 (D)

Two Wayfarers. *The Christ of the English Road*. London: Hodder & Stoughton, 1929 (D)

Troward, *Thomas. Bible Mystery and Bible Meaning*. NY: Dodd, Mead, 1913 (D).

———. *The Creative Process in the Individual*. NY: McBride, Nast & Co., 1915 (2) D.

———. *The Dore Lectures*. NY: Dodd, Mead, 1909 (D)

———. *The Hidden Power. NY*: Dodd, Mead, 1958 (D)

———. *The Law and The Word*. NY: Dodd, Mead, 1953 (D)

Vanauken, Sheldon. *A Severe Mercy: C. S. Lewis Letters*. NY: Harper & Row, 1977 (D)

Verplough, Harry, ed.. *Oswald Chambers: The Best From All His Books, Vol 2*. Nashville: Oliver-Nelson Books, 1989 (D)

Vincent, John H. *The Inner Life: A Study in Christian Experience*. Boston: United Society of Christian Endeavor, 1900 (D)

Wallis, Charles L. *The Charles L. Allen Treasury*. NJ: Fleming H. Revell, 1970 (D)

Watson, Sydney. *"In the Twinkling of an Eye"* Fleming H. Revell Company, 1933 (D)

Wells, Amos R. *Expert Endeavor: A Text-book of Christian Endeavor*

Methods and Principles. Boston: International Society of Christian Endeavor, 1911 (2) D1.

Whyte, Alexander. *The Nature of Angels: Eight Addresses.* London: Hodder and Stoughton, 1930 [inscribed to Dr. Frank Buchman] (D)

Wooley, John G. *Civilization by Faith.* Chicago: The Church Press, 1899 (D)

Worcester, Elwood, Samuel McComb, and Isador H. Coriat. *Religion and Medicine: The Moral Control of Nervous Disorders.* New York: Moffat, Yard & Company, 1908 (2) D1.

Worcester, Elwood and Samuel McComb. *The Christian Religion as a Healing Power: A Defense and Exposition of the Emmanuel Movement.* NY: Moffat, Yard & Company, 1909 (D)

Young, Vash. *No Thank You.* Indianapolis, Bobbs-Merrill, 1934 (D)

Miscellaneous Books Used in Dick B.'s Research and Writings

Allen, Charles L. *All Things are Possible Through Prayer.* NJ: Fleming H. Revell, 1987 (D)

———. *Roads to Radiant Living.* NJ: Fleming H. Revell, 1968 (D)

———. *When You Lose a Loved One.* NJ: Fleming H. Revell, 1959 (D)

Allen, Hugh. *The Real-Life Story of Akron: Rubber's Home Town.* NY: Stratford House, 1949 (D)

Anonymous. *A Guide to True Peace, or The Excellency of Inward and Spiritual Prayer.* Compiled by Two Quakers in various editions from 1813 to 1877 from the writings of Fenelon, Guyon, and Molinos, and used as a devotional book by members of the Society of Friends.

Anonymous Press Edition of Alcoholics Anonymous, The: Study Edition. NY: The Anonymous Press, 1996. (Inscribed to Dick B.)

Bach, Marcus. *The Will to Believe.* Rev. ed. MN: T. S. Dennison Co., 1960 (D)

———. *Faith and My Friends.* NY: Bobbs-Merrill, 1951 (D)

Benson, Clarence H. *A Popular History of Christian Education.* Chicago: Moody Press, 1943. (D)

Best, Nolan Rice. *Two Y Men.* NY: Association Press, 1925 (D)

Bingham, Mitchell. *Psychic Adventure* [owned by T. Willard Hunter]

Bishop, Jim. *The Glass Crutch*. NY: Doubleday, Doran, 1945 (D)

Brandt, Johanna. *The Grape Cure*. NY: 1928 (D)

Brunner, Emil. *I Believe In The Living God*. Philadelphia: Westminster Press, 1961 (D)

Burns, Elizabeth. *The Late Liz*. NJ: Fleming H. Revell, 1957 (D)

Calvary Evangel fragment from Calvary Church Archives, December, 1954, regarding Sam Shoemaker, Sherwood Day, Redcap 42, Fulton Oursler, and Olive Jones.

Chappell, Clovis G. *Surprises in the Bible*. Nashville: Abingdon, 1967 (D)

———. *Sermons From The Psalms*. Nashville: Abingdon, 1961 (D)

———. *Chappell's Special Day Sermons*. NY: Abingdon-Cokesbury Press, 1936 (D)

———. *The Seven Words*. NY: Abingdon Press, 1952 (D)

———. *The Village Tragedy*. NY: Abingdon-Cokesbury, 1925 (D)

———. *The Sermon on the Mount*. NY: Abingdon-Cokesbury, 1930 (D)

———. *Sermons from Revelation*. NY: Abingdon-Cokesbury, 1953 (D)

———. *Living Zestfully*. NY: Abingdon-Cokesbury, 1954 (D)

———. *Meet These Men*. NY: Abingdon Press, 1956 (D)

Chicago Manual of Style, The: Thirteenth Edition, Revised and Expanded, for Authors, Editors, and Copywriters. Chicago: University of Chicago Press, 1982.

Christenson, Evelyn. *"Lord, Change Me."* IL: Victor Books, 1977 (D)

De Quincey, Thomas. *Confessions of an English Opium-Eater and Other Writings*. NY: Oxford University Press, 1985 (D)

Distler, Paul F. *Latin I. Beginning Reading*. Chicago: Loyola University Press, 1962.

Durant, Will. *The Story of Civilization: Caesar and Christ: A History of Roman Civilization and of Christianity from Their Beginnings to A.D. 325*. NY: Simon and Schuster, 1944.

Eagan, Joseph F. *Restoration and Renewal: The Church in the Third Millennium*.

Eister, Allan W., ed. *Changing Perspectives in the Scientific Study of Religion*. NY: John Wiley, 1974 (D)

Excerpt from the *1985 Guinness Book of World Records*, p. 325: Willard Hunter.

Faith at Work. *Christmas Greetings, 1966 (D)*.

Ferguson, Charles W. *Naked to Mine Enemies: The Life of Cardinal Wolsey*. NY: Time, 1958, Two Volumes (3) (D3)

Firestone, Harvey S. 1868-1938. Privately printed, 1938 (D).

5 Roman Catholic reprints pertaining to A.A. in an untitled, bound volume; Roman Catholic objections to Moral Re-Armament; and Roman Catholic viewpoints: (1) *Bill W.'s Address to the National Clergy Conference on on Alcoholism* (1960); (2) Robert E. Burns, *The Catholic Church and Alcoholics Anonymous*, 1952; (3) John J. Ford, *Moral Re-Armament and Alcoholics Anonymous*, 1960; (4) Clair M. Dinger, *Moral Re-Armament: A Study of Its Technical and Religious Nature in the Light of Catholic Teaching*, 1961; (5) Fulton J. Sheen, *The Love That Waits for You*, 1953.

Sharing Recovery through Gamblers Anonymous. Gamblers Anonymous Publishing, Inc.

Gray, James M. *Synthetic Bible Studies*. New. Rev. enl. ed. NY: Fleming H. Revell, 1923 (D)

Harnack, Adolph. *The Expansion of Christianity in the First Three Centuries* (Volumes I and II). Oregon: Wipf & Stock Publishers, 1998.

Henle, Robert J. *Latin Grammar for High Schools*. Rev. Ed. Chicago: Loyola University Press, 1945.

Hume, Robert Ernest. *The World's Living Religions*. NY: Charles Scribner's Sons, 1945 (D)

Kevane, Eugene. *The Lord of History*. MA: Daughters of St. Paul, 1980. (Excerpt.)

Koller, John M. *Oriental Philosophies*. 2d ed. NY: Charles Scribner's Sons, 1985.

Letters of the Scattered Brotherhood. NY: Harper & Brothers, 1948.

Lincoln on Alcoholism. From Lincoln's address to the Washingtonian Temperance Society, Springfield, Illinois, February 22, 1842.

London, Jack. *John Barley-Corn*. NY: Grosset & Dunlap, 1913 (D)

Lowndes, Marion. *Ghosts That Still Walk*. NY: Alfred A. Knopf, 1941 (D)

Mackinac: An Island Famous in These Regions. MI: Mackinac State Historic Parks, 1998 (D)

Mandino, Og. *The Greatest Secret in the World*. NY: Frederick Fell, 1965 (D)

McKenney, Ruth. *The Industrial Valley*. NY: Harcourt, Brace, 1939 (D)

McCurdy, Edward. *The Mind of Leonardo Da Vinci*. NY: Dodd, Mead & Co., 1928 (D)

Narcotics Anonymous. C.A.R.E.N.A. Publishing Co., 1982 (D)

New Guide and Almanac, A: Religions of America: Ferment and Faith in an Age of Crisis. Edited by Leo Rosten. New York: Simon & Schuster, 1975.

Physicians Desk Reference, 52 ed., 1998.

Pike, Thomas P. *Memoirs of Thomas P. Pike.* San Marino, CA: 1979

Schaff, Philip. *History of the Church*, Volumes I and II. Edinburgh: T. & T. Clark. 1891 (2) D2

Speir, F. Leslie. *Cleveland: Our Community and Its Government.* OH: Cleveland Public Schools, 1941 (D)

Roget's II, The New Thesaurus. Boston: Houghton Mifflin Company, 1980.

Roget's Thesaurus. NY: Garden City Publishing, 1940 (D)

70 books, booklets, pamphlets, and newsletters published by various branches of the United States Government on alcoholism, addiction, drugs, substance abuse, treatment centers, therapies, substance abuse faith communities, prevention, etc.: By such agencies as NIDA, COMSAT, SAMHSA, NIAAA, OAS.

Toner, Jules J. *A Commentary on St. Ignatius's Rules for Discernment of Spirits.* MO: The Institute of Jesuit Sources, 1995.

———. *Discerning God's Will: Ignatius of Loyola's Teaching on Christian Decision Making.*

28 binders and velo bound books containing copies of books in the collection. The copies were used by the author as working copies and also often were his only copies during the period they were used as writing resources.

The Way of Ignatius Loyola: Contemporary Approaches to the Spiritual Exercises. MO: The Institute of Jesuit Sources, 1991.

Webster's Encyclopedic Unabridged Dictionary of the English Language. New Rev. ed. NY: Portland House, 1996.

Webster's Illustrated Dictionary. NY: Books, Inc., 1957 (D)

Webster's Collegiate Dictionary. 5th ed. Mass: G & C. Merriam Co., 1940 (D)

Viereck, George Sylvester. *Roosevelt: A Study in Ambivalence.* NY: Jackson Press, 1919 (D)

Williams, Meade E. *Early Mackinac.* New and Rev. ed NY: Duffield & Co., 1912 (D)

Wright, G. Frederick. *Charles G. Finney: American Religious Leader.* Oregon: Schmul Publishing Co., 1996.

Zikmund, Barbara Brown, editor. *Hidden Histories in the United Church of Christ* (2) [owned by Willard Hunter].

Part 4
Temperance, Anti Saloon League, Prohibition, Abstinence, Alcohol Books and Pamphlets of an Earlier Time

Early Temperance, Alcoholism History Items

A Member of the Society. *The Foundation, Progress, and Principles of the Washington Temperance Society of Baltimore, etc.* Baltimore, 1842 (D)

An Address Delivered By Abraham Lincoln Before the Springfield Washingtonian Temperance Society. Springfield: O.H. Oldroyd Publisher, 1889 (D)

Arthur, Rev. T. S. *Strong Drink: The Curse and the Cure.* Philadelphia: Hubbard Brothers, 1877 (D)

———. *Ten Nights in a Bar-Room.* Chicago: W.B. Conkey Company, 1897. (3) D3

Blair, Senator Henry William. *The Temperance Movement: or, The Conflict Between Man and Alcohol.* Boston: William E. Smythe Company, 1888 (D)

Centennial Temperance Volume: A Memorial of the International Temperance Conference held in Philadelphia, June, 1876. NY: National Temperance Society and Publication House, 1877 (D)

Chapman, Ervin S. *Particeps Criminis: The Story of a California Rabbit Drive.* NY: Fleming H. Revell, 1910 (D)

Dacus, J. A. *Battling with The Demon: or, The Progress of Temperance.* St. Louis, Scammell & Company, 1878 (D)

Daniels, Rev. W. H. *The Temperance Reform and Its Great Reformers.* NY: Nelson & Phillips, 1878 (D)

Dickerson, O. C. *The Revel of t he Rum Fiend*. Brooklyn: Barbee & Sons, 1859 (D)

Doutney, Thomas N. *His Life Struggle, Fall, and Reformation*. Boston: Franklin Press, 1883 (D)

Finch, John B. *The People versus The Liquor Traffic: The Great Speeches of John B. Finch,* 6th ed. Chicago: Literature Com., R.W.G. Lodge, I.O. of G.T., 1883

Fisher, Irving and Eugene Lyman Fisk. Alcohol. OH: World League Against Alcoholism, 1925 (D).

Gough, John B. *Sunlight and Shadow, or Gleanings from My Life Work*. Hartford: Connecticut: A.D. Worthington And Company, 1882 (D).

Hargreaves, William. *Alcohol And Man, or The Scientific Basis, or Total Abstinence*. NY: The National Temperance Society and Publication Houses, 1881 (D)

Hewlett, Samuel Mudway. *The Cup and Its Conqueror: or, The Triumphs of Temperance*. Boston: Redding & Co., 1862 (D)

Johnson, William E. The South Carolina Liquor Dispensary. OH: American Issue Publishing, circa 1919 (D)

Palmer, Charles Follen. *Inebriety: Its Source, Prevention, and Cure*. Philadelphia: The Union Press, n.d. (D)

Shaw, Elton R., Editor. *The Curse of Drink: or, Stories of Hell's Commerce [Stories and Incidents related by John G. Wooley, John P. St. John, Eli Perkins, Charles M. Sheldon, Dwight L. Moody, Chauncey DePew, R.A. Torrey, Sam Jones, Henry Ward Beecher, John G. Gough, Theo. L. Cuyler, Ada Melville Shaw, T. DeWitt Talmage, L.A. Banks, Gen. Fred Grant, Gen Sheridan, Frank Beard, Rudyard Kipling, Ella Wheeler Wilcos, Wendell Phillips, and others*. Elton R. Shaw, 1909 (D).

The Anti-Saloon League Song Book. OH: American Issue Publishing Company, n.d. (D)

The National Temperance Quarterly, December, 1911. London: The National Temperance League (D).

The National Temperance Quarterly, March, 1912. London: The National Temperance League (D)

The Temperance Token. Auburn: Alden Beardsley, n.d. (D)

Wilson, Dick. *The Rumseller's Victim, or Humanity Pleading for the "Maine Law"* NY: C. M. Saxton, 1859 (D)

Booklets and Pamphlets

American Prohibition Year Book for 1904. Chicago: United Prohibition Press, 1903 (D)

American Prohibition Year Book for 1907. Chicago: Lincoln Temperance Press, 1907 (D)

American Prohibition Year Book for 1908. Chicago: Lincoln Temperance Press, 1908 (D)

American Prohibition Year Book for 1909. Chicago: Lincoln Temperance Press, 1909 (D)

American Prohibition Year Book for 1916. Chicago: The Prohibition National Committee (D)

Annual Report of the Commissioner of Internal Revenue for 1909. Washington, D.C.: 1909 (D)

Annual Report of the Commissioner of Internal Revenue for 1914. Washington, D.C.: 1914 (D)

Annual Report of the Commissioner of Internal Revenue for 1915. Washington, D. C.: 1915 (D)

Annual Report of the Commissioner of Internal Revenue for 1916. Washington, D.C.: 1916 (D)

Annual Report of the Commissioner of Internal Revenue for 1923. Washington, D.C." 1923 (D)

Annual Report of the Commissioner of Prohibition, 1929. Washington, D.C.: 1929 (D)

Anti-Saloon League Year Book, 1908. Chicago: The Anti-Saloon League of America (D)

Anti-Saloon League Year Book, 1909. OH: The Anti-Saloon League of America (2) D2

Anti-Saloon League Year Book, 1912. OH: The Anti-Saloon League of America (D)

Anti-Saloon League Year Book, 1913. OH: The Anti-Saloon League of America (D)

Anti-Saloon League Year Book, 1914. OH: The Anti-Saloon League of America (D)

Anti-Saloon League Year Book, 1915. OH: The Anti-Saloon League of America (D)

Anti-Saloon League Year Book, 1917. OH: The Anti-Saloon League of America (3) D3

Anti-Saloon League Year Book, 1918. OH: The Anti-Saloon League of America (2) D2

Anti-Saloon League Year Book, 1919. OH: The Anti-Saloon League of America (D)

Anti-Saloon League Year Book, 1920. OH: The Anti-Saloon League of America (D)

Anti-Saloon League Year Book, 1925. OH: The Anti-Saloon League of America (D)

Anti-Saloon League Year Book, 1926. OH: The Anti-Saloon League of America (D)

Anti-Saloon League Year Book, 1927. OH: The Anti-Saloon League of America (D)

Anti-Saloon League Year Book. 1928. OH: The Anti-Saloon League of America (2) D2

Anti-Saloon League Year Book, 1929. OH: The Anti-Saloon League of America (D)

Anti-Saloon League Year Book, 1930. OH: The Anti-Saloon League of America (D)

Anti-Saloon League Year Book, 1931. OH: The Anti-Saloon League of America (D)

Anti-Saloon League Year Book, 1932-33. OH: The Anti-Saloon League of America (D)

Cherington, Ernest H. *Report of the World League Against Alcoholism For Five Years Prior to January 1, 1925.* OH: World League Against Alcoholism (D)

———. *The Evolution of Prohibition in the United States of* America. OH: The American Issue Press, 1925 (D) lopton, Arner W. and Eli Ball. *Wisdom's Voice To The Rising Generation: A Selection of the Best Addresses and Sermons on Intemperance.* Philadelphia: The Compilers, n.d. (D)

Cutten, George B. *Should Prohibition Return?* Rev. ed. NY: Fleming H. Revell, 1946 (D)

Graham, Frances W. *Four Decades: A History of Forty Years' Work of the Women's Christian* Temperance Union of New York. NY: The Salvation Army Press, 1914 (D)

Gunder, Claude A. *Life of Claude A. Gunder: Saved By the Blood From A Drunkard's Hell.* Indiana, 1908 (D)

History, Pennsylvania Woman's Christian Temperance Union. PA: Quincy Orphanage Press, 1937 (D)

International Convention: The World League Against Alcoholism, 1922. Toronto (D)

Manual De Verdades Modernas Sobre El Alcohol. OH: American Issue Publishing, 1926 (D0

National German-American Alliance: Hearings Before the Subcommittee of the Committee on the Judiciary, United States Senate, 1918 (D).

Proceedings, '96 National Anti-Saloon Convention, 1896. Washington, DC: Published by the Secretary (2) D2

Proceedings, Third National Anti-Saloon Convention, 1898. Washington, D.C.: Published by the Secretary (2) D2

Proceedings, Fourth National Anti-Saloon Convention, 1898. Cleveland: Published by the Secretary (D)

Proceedings, Sixth National Anti Saloon Convention, 1901. MD: Published by the Secretary (D)

Proceedings, Seventh National Anti-Saloon Convention, 1902. MD: Published by the Secretary (2) D2

Proceedings, Eighth National Anti-Saloon Convention, 1903. PA: Published by the Secretary (2) D2

Proceedings, Ninth Anti-Saloon Convention, 1904. PA: Published by the Secretary (2) D2

Proceedings, Tenth Annual Convention of the Anti-Saloon League of America, 1905. PA: Published by the Secretary (2) D2

Proceedings, Thirteenth National Convention of the Anti-Saloon League of America, 1909. PA: Published by the Secretary (2) D2

Proceedings, Fourteenth National Convention of the Anti-Saloon League of America, 1911. Washington, D.C.: Published by the Secretary (2) D2

Proceedings, Fifteenth National Convention of the Anti-Saloon League of America, 1913. IND: Published by the Secretary (D)

Proceedings, Special Conference, Anti-Saloon League for Launching a Movement for World-wide Prohibition. Ohio: American Issue Publishing Company, 1918 (2) D2

Proceedings, Twentieth National Convention, Anti-Saloon League of America, 1921. Washington D.C.: Published by the Secretary (D)

Proceedings, Twenty-First Convention, Anti-Saloon League of America, 1924. OH: The America Issue Press (D)

Prohibition in U.S.A. and Canada, 1923. Official Report to Government of Western Australia. Published by Anti-Liquor League of

Western Australia (D)

Proceedings, International Conference against Alcoholism at Geneva. 1925. Switzerland: International Bureau Against Alcoholism (D)

Proceedings, Twentieth National Convention of the Anti-Saloon League of America, 1921. Washington , D.C.: Published by the Secretary (D)

Proceedings, Twenty-First Convention of the Anti-Saloon League of America, 1924. OH: The American Issue Press (D)

Proceedings, Twenty-Third Convention of the Anti-Saloon League of America, 1927. OH: The American Issue Press (4) D4.

Report of The Women's National Commission for Law Enforcement and Law Observance. Cambridge, MA: Woman's National Committee For Law Enforcement, 1931 (D)

Production and Conservation of Food Supplies. Hearing, Senate Committee on Agriculture and Forestry, 1917 (D)

Scientific Temperance Journal (Quarterly Issues from 1916 to 1939) Westerville, OH: The American Issue Publishing Company (134)D

Stoddard, Cora Frances and Amy Woods. *Fifteen Years of the Drink Question in Massachusetts.* Ohio: The American Issue Publishing Company, circa 1919 (D)

The Alliance Year Book: Temperance Reformer's Handbook For 1914. London: United Kingdom Alliance, 1914 (D)

The Alliance Year Book: Temperance Reformer's Handbook For 1916. London: United Kingdom Alliance, 1916 (D)

The Alliance Year Book: Temperance Reformer's Handbook For 1921. London: United Kingdom Alliance, 1921 (D)

The Alliance Year Book: Temperance Reformer's Handbook For 1922. London: United Kingdom Alliance, 1922 (D)

The Alliance Year Book: Temperance Reformer's Handbook For 1924. London: United Kingdom Alliance, 1924 (D)

The Alliance Year Book: Temperance Reformer's Handbook For 1925. London: United Kingdom Alliance, 1925 (D)

The Alliance Year Book: Temperance Reformer's Handbook For 1926. London: United Kingdom Alliance, 1926 (2) D2

The Alliance Year Book: Temperance Reformer's Handbook For 1927. London: United Kingdom Alliance, 1927 (D)

The Alliance Year Book: Temperance Reformer's Handbook For 1928. London: United Kingdom Alliance, 1928 (D)

The Alliance Year Book: Temperance Reformer's Handbook for 1929.
London: United Kingdom Alliance, 1929 (D)
The Alliance Year Book: Temperance Reformer's Handbook For 1930.
London: United Kingdom Alliance, 1930 (2) D2
The Alliance Year Book: Temperance Reformer's Handbook For 1931.
London: United Kingdom Alliance, 1931 (D)
The Alliance Year Book: Temperance Reformer's Handbook For 1933.
London: United Kingdom Alliance, 1933 (D)
The Alliance Year Book: Temperance Reformer's Handbook For 1934.
London: United Kingdom Alliance, 1934 (D)
The American Issue (1910) Pennsylvania Edition (D)
The American Issue (1911) New York Edition (D)
The American Issue (1916) Oklahoma Edition (D)
The Anti-Saloon League Y ear Book, 1911. OH: The American Issue
Publishing, 1911 (D)
*Publications from the Publishing House of the Anti-Saloon League of
America, 1929* (D)
Supplemental Catalog and Price List of the Literature Department of the
American Issue Publishing Company, 1929 (2) D2
The National Prohibition Law. Hearings Before the Subcommittee of the
Judiciary Committee, U.S. Senate, 1926 (2) D2
The National Temperance Quarterly, September, 1911. London: The
National Temperance League (D)
*The Foundation, Progress and Principles of the Washington Temperance
Society of Baltimore.* Baltimore: Printed by John D. Toy, 1842
(D)
The Value of Law Observance. Department of Justice, Bureau of
Prohibition, 1930 (D)

Part 5
Recent Books and Articles on Alcoholism, Addictions, and Dependency

Books and Pamphlets on Recovery Approaches

Alcoholic American, The. n.d.. (Blue Shield Pamphlet.)

Alcoholics Anonymous: Chaos or Christianity. CA: Dana Nova, n.d.

Alcoholics Anonymous: The Australian Experience. NY: Alcoholics Anonymous World Services, Inc., 1995.

Alcoholics Anonymous Workbook Edition. NY: IWS, 1995.

Alcoholism: Its Cause and Cure. CA: Science of Mind Publications, 1941.

Assorted A.A.-related publications in languages other than English, including: (a) 8 copies of "Blue Book: Alcoholics Anonymous" published in five languages other than English, (b) Ernie K. *90 Meetings in Ninety Days* in German, and (c) two other A.A. texts in German.

B. Dick. *Utilizing Early A.A.'s Roots for Recovery Today*, 1998. (Spiral bound.)

Beyond the Elementary. FL: LFC Bible Study, 1991.

Big Book Study Guide. AR: The Kelly Foundation, 1980.

Brother Andrew. *For the Love of My Brothers: Unforgettable Stories from God's Ambassador to the Suffering Church*. MN: Bethany House Publishers, 1998.

Codependency: A Christian Perspective. FL: Jean M. La Cour, 1994.

Counseling the Codependent. FL: Jean M. La Cour, 1996.

Cordeiro, Wayne. *Doing Church As a Team*. HI: New Hope Publishing, 1998.

Daily Moral Inventory. Fl: Dunklin Memorial Camp, n.d.

Daily Moral Inventory, The. FL: Dunklin Memorial Camp, n.d.

Dayton, Tian. *The Quiet Voice of Soul: How to Find Meaning in Ordinary Life.* FL: Health Communications, Inc., 1995.

——. *The Soul's Companion: Connecting with the Soul Through Daily Meditations.* FL: Health Communications, 1995.

Dunklin Memorial Church Christian Training Center. FL: Dunklin Memorial Church, n.d. (3).

Eleventh Step Retreat and Workshop Handbook. IA: Maya, 1999.

Else, J. David. *Life Is a Journey Back Home: The Stages of our Spiritual Journey.* PA: The Center for Spirituality in Twelve-Step Recovery, 1993.

Family Recovery Process, The. FL: Dunklin Memorial Camp, 1991.

First Edition [of *Alcoholics Anonymous*]. (A hardbound, small book, reprint). NY Works Publishing Company, 1939.

5 IWS small "first edition" paperback Big Books.

God and Alcohol Don't Mix. CA: Back to You Ministry, 1977.

God's Foolishness, Humanity's Freedom. An Anonymous Bond Servant, n.d. (Spiral bound.)

Hart, Stan. *Rehab.* NY: Harper & Row Publishers, 1988.

Hazelden: A Spiritual Odyssey. MN: Hazelden, 1987.

Hill, Harold. *How to Be a Winner.* NJ: Logos International, 1976.

Inner Healing. FL: Dunklin Memorial Camp, 1992.

Job Search Checkup. MI: Core Ministries, 1994.

Laos Institute Catalog. FL: Dunklin Memorial Camp, 1994.

Lechler, Walther H. *12 x 12* (in German.)

Little Big Book, The. (Reprint of the First Edition of *Alcoholics Anonymous.*) NY: AA Big Book Study Group, n.d.

Man's Checkup. MI: Core Ministries, 1994.

Naltrexone and Alcoholism Treatment. SAMHSA, 1998.

Narcotics Anonymous: CA: World Service Office, Inc., 1988 (2) D1.

Optimal Living Recipes. CA: Optimum Health Institute of San Diego, n.d.

Orientation Workbook. FL: Dunklin Memorial Camp, 1994.

Origins. CA: Origins Study Group, n.d.

Problems of Drug Dependence, 1997. NIDA Research Monograph Series.

Ray, Dave. *Inside Brother's Check-Up.* MI: Core Ministries, 1994.

Recovery Dynamics: Client Guidebook. AR: The Kelly Foundation, 1989.

Recovery Dynamics: Counselors Manual. AR: The Kelly Foundation, 1989.

Recovery Dynamics: Individual Evaluation Packet. AR: The Kelly Foundation, 1989.

Regeneration Contract. FL: Dunklin Memorial Camp, n.d.

Regeneration Workbook. FL: Dunklin Memorial Camp, 1992.

Response to the Twelve Steps in a Christian Setting, A. CA: Discernment Publications, n.d.

Roadmarks and Guideposts: An Epistle according to Anonymous, n.d. (Spiral bound.)

Rosemary. *One Day at a Time in Phobics Victorious.* MA: The Christopher Publishing House, 1995.

———. *The Twelve Steps of Phobics Victorious.* Palm Springs, CA: Phobics Victorious, 1993

Salomone, Gaetano, and Jack Trimpey. *Five Postulates of Pastoral Concern Regarding the 12-Step Recovery Movement.* CA: Rational Recovery Systems. (With letters to Dick B.)

SAMHSA National Survey on Drug Abuse, 1998. (Two copies.)

SAMHSA Uniform Facility Data Set, 1997.

Services Research Outcomes Study. SAMHSA, 1998.

Silent Sponsor, The. Calgary, Alberta, Canada, 1965.

Stoop, David. *Living with a Perfectionist.* NY: Thomas Nelson, 1987.

They Knew or Should Have Known. FL: Victory Over Addiction International, 1997.

Three Basic Text Study Aids. IN: Original Recipe Group, 1985.

Training Families to Do a Successful Intervention. MN: Johnston Institute, 1996.

Treatment Services: Directory of Alcohol and Other Drug Abuse Treatment Services in South Carolina: DAODAS, 1998.

Whatever Happened to Recovered. IN: Original Recipe Group, n.d. (Two copies.)

Wurtz, Vera. *Overcoming Negative Thoughts.* AL: Vera Wurtz, 1996.

Books and Pamphlets on Alcoholism and Other Addictions

A Member of Alcoholics Anonymous. *The Golden Book of Principles.* Indianapolis: SMT Publishing Company, 1954 (D)

——— *The Golden Book of Sponsorship.* Indianapolis: SMT Publishing Company, 1953 (D)

——. *The Book of Action*. Indianapolis: SMT Publishing Company, 1950 (D)

Abbey Press Pamphlets on Partnership and Acceptance. (2) D2

Abel, Ernest L. *"Alcohol" Wordlore and Folklore*. NY: Prometheus Books, 1987 (D)

Abrahamson, E. M. and A. W. Pezet. *Body, Mind & Sugar*. NY: Henry Holt, 1951 (D)

Ackerman, Robert J. ed. *Growing in the Shadow: Children of Alcoholics*. FL: Health Communications, Inc., 1986 (D)

ADA-M: Alcohol Drugs Anonymous Mormon: 12 Step Support Groups in the Victor Valley. A Program of LDS Social Services, n.d.

Adams, Carsbie C. *The Cure: The Story of an Alcoholic*. NY: Exposition Press, 1950 (D)

Adams, Leon D. *The Commonsense Book of Drinking*. NY: David McKay Co., 1960 (D)

Adler, Alfred. *What Life Should Mean to You*. NY: Grosset & Dunlap, 1931 (D)

Alcohol Education Digest, Jan-Mar, 1958. Washington, D.C. National Temperance League (D)

Alcohol Education Digest, Third Quarter, 1960. Washington, D.C., National Temperance League (2) D2

Alcohol Education Digest, Fourth Quarter, 1960. Washington, D.C., National Temperance League (4) D4 (14)

Alcohol, Science and Society: Twenty-nine Lectures with Discussions as given at the Yale Summer School of Alcohol Studies. New Haven: Quarterly Journal of Studies on Alcohol, 1945 (D)

An Alcoholic. *The Life of An Alcoholic: The Answer to Anyone's Liquor Problem*. CA: Northern California Publishers, 1948 (D)

Alcoholism In Industry. NY: Christopher D. Smithers Foundation, 1974 (D)

Anderson, Daniel J. *The Psychopathology of Denial*. MN: Hazelden, 1991 (D)

Anderson, Dwight. *The Other Side of the Bottle*. NY: A.A. Wynn, 1950 (D)

Anthony, Norman, and O. Soglow. *The Drunk's Blue Book*. Rev. ed. PA: J. B. Lippincott, 1933 (D)

Anthony, Susan B. *The Ghost In My Life*. NY: Chosen Books, 1971 (D)

Ashley, Herbert. *The Great Illusion: An Informal History of Prohibition*. NY: Doubleday, 1950 (D)

Aspects of Alcoholism. Philadelphia: J. B. Lippincott Company, 1963 (D)

Aspects of Alcoholism Volume II. Philadelphia: J. B. Lippincott Company, 1966 (D)

Atkinson, Jim. *The View From Nowhere*. NY: Harper & Row, 1987 (D)

B., Mel *Pride*. MN: Hazelden, 1985 (D)

Beasley, Joseph B. *How to Defeat Alcoholism*. NY: Times Books, 1989 (D)

Beattie, Melody. *Beyond Codependency: And Getting Better All the Time*. MN: Hazelden, 1989 (D)

Bell, R. Gordon. *Escape from Addiction*. NY: McGraw-Hill, 1970 (D)

Bellwood, Lester Raymond. *Alcoholism: The Common Neurosis of Our Time*. CO: Bell-Hart, 1973 (D)

Bishop, George. *The Booze Reader: A Soggy Saga of Man in His Cups*. CA: Sherbourne Press, 1965 (D)

Block, Marvin A. *Alcoholism: Its Facets and Phases*. NY: The John Day Company, 1973 (D)

Blum, Eva Maria and Richard H. Alcoholism: *Modern Psychological Approaches to Treatment*. San Francisco: Jossey-Bass Inc., 1967 (D)

Booth, Father Leo. *When God Becomes a Drug: Breaking the Chains of Religious Addiction & Abuse*. Los Angeles: Jeremy P. Tharcher, Inc., 1991 (D)

Brean, Herbert. *How to Stop Drinking: Science Looks at Your Drinking Habits*. NY: Henry Holt and Company, 1958 (D)

Birsolara, Ashton. *The Alcoholic Employee: A Handbook of Helpful Guidelines*. NY: Human Sciences Press, 1979 (D)

Burridge, S. *Alcohol and Anesthesia*. London: Williams and Norgate, 1934 (D)

Cary, Sylvia. *The Alcoholic Man*. Los Angeles: Lowell House, 1990 (D)

Catanzaro, Ronald J. *Alcoholism: The Total Treatment Approach*. IL: Charles C. Thomas, 1968 (D)

Chafetz, Morris E. Liquor: *The Servant of Man*. Boston: Little, Brown, 1965 (D)

Chafetz, Morris E. and Harold W. Demone, Jr. *Alcoholism & Society*. NY: Oxford University Press, 1962 (D)

Cherrington, Ernest Hurst. *History of the Anti-Saloon League*. OH: The American Issue Publishing Company, 1913 (D)

———. *The New Crusade: A Handbook of Facts about Prohibition and Law Enforcement*. IL: David C. Cook, 1928 (D)

Chidsey, Donald Barr. *On And Off the Wagon: A Sober Analysis of the Temperance Movement from the Pilgrims through Prohibition*. NY: Cowles Book *Company, 1969 (D)*

Christopher, James. *How* To Stay Sober: Recovery Without Religion. NY: Prometheus Books, 1988 (D)

——. *SOS Sobriety: The Proven Alternative to 12-Step Programs*. NY: Prometheus Books, 1992 (D)

Clancy, Jay. *Clancy Got Well*. Iowa: McGrevey Book Store, 1951 (D)

Classics of the Alcohol Literature, edited by Jellinek. New Haven: Quarterly Journal of Studies of Alcohol, 1945 (D)

Cleveland, Martha. *Twelve Step Response To Chronic Illness and Disability: Recovering Joy in Life*. MN: Hazelden, 1988 (D)

Clinebell, Howard J., Jr. *Understanding and Counseling The Alcoholic: Through Religion and Psychology*. Rev. enl. NY: Abingdon Press, 1968 (D)

Colclough, Beauchamp. *Tomorrow I'll Be Different*. NY: The Overlook Press, 1994 (D)

Conan, Mrs. M. *Staggering Feet: Or This Drunken America*. Los Angeles: 1941 (D)

Coppolino, Carl A. and Carmela M. Coppolino. *The Billion Dollar Hangover: Alcoholism in America*. NY: A.A. Barnes, 1965 (D)

Dannenbaum, Jed. *Drink and Disorder: Temperance Reform in Cincinnati from the Washingtonian Revival to the WCTU*. Chicago: University of Illinois Press, 1984 (D)

Dardis, Tom. *Thirsty Muse: Alcohol and the American Writer*. NY: Tiknor & Fields, 1989 (D)

De Quicy, Thomas. *Confessions of an English Opium Eater*. NY: Halcyon House, n.d. (D)

De Voto, Bernard. *The Hour*. Boston: Houghton Mifflin, 1951 (D)

DeWitt, William A. *Drinking And What To Do About It*. NY: Grosset & Dunlap, 1952 (D)

Drews, Toby Rice. *Getting Them Sober: A Guide for Those Who Live with an Alcoholic*. NJ: Bridge Publishing, 1984 (D)

Dobyns, Fletcher. *The Amazing Story of Repeal: An Expose of the Power of Propaganda*. Chicago: Willett, Clark & Co., 1940 (2) D2

du Blanc. *Relief in Recovery*. CA: Visual Books, 1996 (D)

Doe, Father John. *Sobriety Without End*. Indianapolis: SMT Guild, 1983 (D)

——. *The Golden Book of Excuses*. Indianapolis: SMT Guild, 1952 (D)

————. *The Golden Book of Decisions*. Indianapolis: SMT Guild, 1957 (D)

————. *The Golden Book of Passion*. Indianapolis: SMT Guild, 1960 (D)

————. *The Golden Book of Resentments*. Indianapolis: SMT Guild, 1955 (D)

Dorr, Rheta Childe. *Drink: Coercion or Control?* NY: Frederick A. Stokes, 1929 (D)

Durfee, Charles H. *Should You Drink*. NY: The Macmillan Company, 1954 (D)

————. *To Drink or Not to Drink* NY: Longmans, Green and Co., 1938 (D)

Earle, Clifford J. *How to Help an Alcoholic*. Philadelphia: The Westminster Press, 1952 (D)

Elbert, Joyce. *Murder At A.A.* NY: New American Library, 1980 (D)

Elkin, Michael. *Families Under the Influence: Changing Alcoholic Patterns*. NY: W.W. Norton, 1984 (D)

Emerson, Haven. *Alcohol and Man: The Effects of Alcohol in Health and Disease*. NY: The Macmillan Company, 1932 (D)

Engelmann, Larry. Intemperance: The Lost War Against Liquor. NY: The Free Press, 1979 (D)

Evans, David G. *A Practitioner's Guide to Alcoholism and the Law*. MN: Hazelden, 1983 (D)

Everett, Chad. *A Toast to Shelby*. The Original Company, 1971 (D)

Ewing, John A. *Drinking to Your Health*. VA: Reston Publishing Co., 1981 (D)

Experimentation: The Fallacy of "Controlled Drinking" Where Alcoholism Exists. NY: The Christopher D. Smithers Foundation, 1971 (D)

Fairchild, Daniel and Thomas N. Fairchild, David Starr, Ed Woolums. *Everything You Always Wanted to Know about Drinking Problems: And then a few things you didn't want to know*. FL: Health Communications, Inc., 1978 (D)

Fein, Rashi. *Alcohol in America: The Price We Pay*. CA: Care Institute, 1984 (D)

Fisher, Irving. *Prohibition At Its Worst*. NY: The Macmillan Company, 1925 (2) D2

————.*The "Noble Experiment."* NY: Alcohol Information Committee, 1930 (D

Fisk, Eugene Lyman. *Alcohol: Its Relation To Human Efficiency and*

Longevity. NY: Funk & Wagnalls, 1917 (D)

FitzGibbon, Constantine. *Drink: A Self-help Book on Alcoholism*. NY: Doubleday & Co., 1979 (D)

Fletcher, Geoffrey. *Down Among The Meths Men*. London: Hutchinson of London, 1966 (D)

Forbes, John Girtin. *The Mourning After*. CA: McClellan Publishing, 1948 (D)

Ford, Betty. *Betty: A Glad Awakening*. NY: Doubleday, 1987 (D)

———. *The Times of My Life*. NY: Harper & Row, 1978 (D)

Ford, John C. *What About Your Drinking?* NJ: Paulist Press, 1955 (D)

———. *Man Takes A Drink*. NY: P. J. Kennedy, 1955 (D)

Fort, Joel. *Alcohol: Our Biggest Drug Problem*. NY: McGraw-Hill, 1973 (D)

Fosdick, Raymond B. and Albert L. Scott. *Toward Liquor Control*. NY: Harper & Brothers, 1933 (D)

Fowler, Gene. *Good Night, Sweet Prince: The Life & Times of John Barrymore*. Philadelphia: The Blakiston Company, 1944 (D)

Franklin, Jimmie Lewis. *Born Sober: Prohibition in Oklahoma, 1907-1959*. Norman: University of Oklahoma Press, 1971 (D)

Fredericks, Carlton & Herman Goodman. *Low Blood Sugar And You*. NY: Constellation International, 1972 (D)

Funk, Wilfred. *If You Drink*. NY: Wilfred Fund, Inc., 1940 (D)

Furnas, J. C. *The Life and Times of The Late Demon Rum*. London: W.H. Allen, 1965 (D)

Gary, Sylvia. Jolted Sober: *Getting to the Moment of Clarity in the Recovery from Addiction*. Los Angeles: Lowell House, 1989 (D)

Gerber, Samuel R. *Alcohol and Accidents*. Rev. ed. OH: School and College Service, 1956 (D)

Gleason, William F. *The Liquid Cross of Skid Row*. WI: The Bruce Publishing Co., 1966 (D)

Goodwin, Donald W. *Alcohol and the Writer*. NY: Penguin Books, 1988 (D)

Gordon, C. M. and Gifford Gordon. *35,000 Miles of Prohibition*. Australia: The Victorian Anti-Liquor League, circa 1923 (D)

Gordon, Ernest. *The Maine Law: Studies and Documents of the Anti-Alcohol Movement*. NY: Fleming H. Revell, 1919 (D)

Gravitz, Herbert L. and Julie D. Bowden. *Recovery: A Guide for Adult Children of Alcoholics*. NY: Simon & Schuster, 1985 (D)

Griffith, H. Winter. *Complete Guide to Prescription and Non-*

Prescription Drugs. Los Angeles: The Body Press, 1990 (D)

Gross, Leonard. *How Much is Too Much?: The Effects of Social Drinking*. NY: Random House, 1983 (D)

Haggard, H.W. & E. M. Jellinek. *Alcohol Explored*. NY: Doubleday & Co., 1942 (D)

Harkness, Kenneth M. and Lyman M. Fort. *Youth Studies Alcohol*. Chicago: Benj. H. Sanborn, 1938 (D)

Harris, Sara. *Skid Row U.S.A.* NY: Doubleday & Company, 1956 (D)

Harrison, Earl. *Boozlebane on Alcoholism and Work*. MN: Hazelden, 1984 (D)

Hazelden Pamphlets on Surrender, Reaching Out, Meditation, Relationships, Principles, Inadequacy, Humility, Gratitude, Forgiveness, Accepting Criticism. 1985-86 (10) D10

Hearn, C. Aubrey. *Alcohol The Destroyer*. Nashville: Broadman Press, 1952 (D)

——. *Alcoholism or Abstinence*. Ohio: The Standard Publishing Company, 1951 (D)

Hernon, Peter & Terry Ganey. *Under The Influence: The Unauthorized Story of the Anheuser-Busch Dynasty*. NY: Simon & Schuster, 1991 (d)

Hill, Harold. *How to Live Like a King's Kid*. NJ: Bridge Publishing, 1974 (D)

——. *How Did It All Begin?:* A revolutionary look at evolution. NJ: Logos International, 1976 (2)D

——. *Power To Change*. NJ: Bridge Publishing, 1987 (D)

——. *How To Be a Winner*. NJ: Logos International, 1986 (D)

——. *How To Live in High Victory*. NJ: Bridge Publishing, 1977 (D)

——. *How to Flip Your Flab Forever*. NJ: Logos International, 1979 (D)

——. *How To Live The Bible*. NY: Fleming H. Revell, 1980 (D)

——. *The Money Book for King's Kids*. NJ: Fleming H. Revell, 1984 (D)

Hirsh, Joseph. *The Problem Drinker*. NY: Duell, Sloan & Pearce, 1940 (D)

Hirschfield, Jerry. *My Ego, My Higher Power, And I*. NY: Coleman, 1985 (D)

Hoffman, Frederick G. *A Handbook on Drug and Alcohol Abuse: The Biomedical Aspects*. NY: Oxford University Press, 1975 (D)

Hoffer, Abram & Humphrey Osmond. *New Hope for Alcoholics. NY*: University Books, 1968 (D) ooton, Caradine R. *What Shall We Say About Alcohol?* NY: Abingdon Press, 1960 (D) ough, Henry

Beetle. *An Alcoholic to His Sons*. NY: Simon and Schuster, 1954 (D)

Johnson, Vernon E. *I'll Quit Tomorrow*. NY: Harper & Row, 1973 (D)

Jones, Kenneth L. and Louis W. Shainberg and Curtis O. Byer. *Drugs, Alcohol & Tobacco*. San Francisco: Canfield Press, 1970 (D)

Jorgensen, Donald G., Jr. and June A. Jorgensen. *Secrets Told by Children of Alcoholics*. Summit, PA: Tab Books, 1990 (D)

Karpman, Benjamin: *The Alcoholic Woman: Case Studies in the Psychodynamics of Alcoholism*. Washington, D.C.: The Linacre Press, 1956 (D)

Kellermann, Joseph L. *Alcoholism: A Guide for the Clergy*. NY: National Council on Alcoholism, n.d. (D)

Kellner, Esther. Moonshine: *Its History and Folklore*. NY: Weathervane Books, 1971 (D)

Kendall, Elizabeth. *The Phantom Prince: My Life With Ted Bundy*. Seattle: Madrona, 1981 (D)

Kent, J. David. *The Ring on the Bar is Mine*. NY: Carlton Press, 1971 (D)

Kent, Patricia. *An American Woman & Alcohol*. NY: Holt, Rinehart and Winston, 1974 (D)

Kerr, K. Austin. *Organized For Prohibition: A New History of the Anti-Saloon League*. New Haven: Yale University Press, 1985 (D)

Kessel, Neil and Henry Walton. *Alcoholism*. MD: Penguin Books, 1969 (D)

Kettlehack, Guy. *Third-Year Sobriety*. HarperSanFrancisco, 1992 (D)

King, Arthur. *Seven Sinners*. NY: Harcourt, Brace, 1961 (D)

King, Elspeth. Scotland: *Sober and Free: The Temperance Movement 1829-1979*. Glasgow: Glasgow Museums and Art Galleries, 1979 (D)

Larson, Earnie. *Stage II Relationships: Love Beyond Addiction*. San Francisco: Harper & Row, 1987 (D)

Lawson, Gary W. and Dan C. Ellis, P. Clayton Rivers. *Essentials of Chemical Dependency Counseling*. Maryland: Aspen Publishers, Inc., 1984 (D)

Leiner, Katherine. *Something's Wrong in My House*. NY: Franklin Watts, 1988 (D)

Lichtman, Gail. *Alcohol: Facts for Decisions*. NY: New Readers Press, 1964 (D)

Lindbeck, Vera. *The Woman Alcoholic*. NY: Public Affairs Committee,

Inc., 1980 (D)

Luks, Allan, *Will America Sober Up?* Boston: Beacon Press, 1983 (D)

Mackenzie, Compton. *Whiskey Galore.* London: Chattow & Windus, 1950 (D)

Manual on Alcoholism of the American Medical Association. IL: 1968 (2) D1

Manual on Alcoholism of the American Medical Association. Rev. ed. IL: 1973 (D)

Martin, Sara Hines. *Healing for Adult Children of Alcoholics.* Nashville: Broadman Press, 1988 (D)

Maxwell, Milton A. *Alcohol, Man, and Science.* TX: Hogg Foundation for Mental Health, 1966 (D)

Maxwell, Ruth. *The Booze Battle.* NY: Praeger Publishers, 1976 (D)

McCarthy, Raymond G. and Edgar M. Douglass. *Alcohol and Social Responsibility.* NY: Thomas Y. Crowell, 1949 (D)

McCarthy, Raymond G., ed. *Alcohol Education for Classroom and Community.* NY: McGraw-Hill, 1964 (D)

———, ed. *Drinking and Intoxication.* New Haven, CT: College and University Press, 1959 (D)

McDougall, M. T. *The Daiquiri Tree.* San Diego: Joseph Tabler Books, 1993 (D)

McGovern, George. *Terry.* NY: Villard, 1996 (D)

Meyer, Lewis. *Off the Sauce.* NY: Doubleday, 1967 (D)

Molloy, Paul. *Where Did Everybody Go?* NY: Warner Books, 1981 (D)

Moody, Jess. *A Drink at Joel's Place.* Waco, TX: Word Books, 1967 (D)

Mortlock, Geoffrey and Stephen Williams. *The Flowing Bowl.* London: Hutchinson, n.d. (D)

Nace, Edgar P. *The Treatment of Alcoholism.* NY: Brunner/Mazel, 1987 (D)

Newlove, Donald. *The Drunks.* NY: E. P. Dutton & Co., 1974 (D)

Newman, Peter C. *King of the Castle: The Making of a Dynasty: Seagram's and the Bronfman Empire.* NY: Atheneum, 1979 (D)

Oates, Wayne E. Alcohol - *In and Out of the Church.* TN: Broadman Press, 1966 (D)

Pastor Paul. *The 13th American.* IL: David C. Cook, 1973 (2) D2

Peale, Norman Vincent. *The Tough-Minded Optimist.* NJ: Prentice-Hall, Inc., 1961 (D)

Peel, Norman Lemon. *The Power of Positive Drinking.* NY: Pyramid Books, 1963 (D)

Pfau, Father Ralph and Al Hirshberg. *Prodigal Shepherd.* Indiana: The SMT Guild, 1958 (D)

Pinkham, Mary Ellen. *How To Stop The One You Love From Drinking.* NY: G. P. Putnam's Sons, 1986 (D)

Pittman, David J. and Charles R. Snyder, eds. *Society, Culture, and Drinking Patterns.* NY: John Wiley & Sons, 1962 (D)

Poley, Wayne, Gary Lea, and Dale Vide. *Alcoholism: A Treatment Manual.* NY: Gardner Press, 1979 (D)

Poling, Daniel A. *John Barleycorn: His Life and Letters.* Chicago: The John C. Winston Co., 1933 (D)

Prescription Drugs. IL: Home Health Handbook, 1991 (D)

Plaut, Thomas F. A. *Alcohol Problems: A Report to the Nation.* NY: Oxford University Press, 1967 (D)

Presnall, Lewis F. *The Search For Serenity and how to achieve* it. Utah: U.A.F., 1959 (D)

Proceedings of the First Annual Alcoholism Conference of the National Institute on Alcohol Abuse and Alcoholism. MD: National Institute of Health, 1971 (D)

Prohibition: A National Experiment. The Annals of The American Academy of Political and Social Science, September, 1932 (D)

Que Se Puede Hacer Respecto Al Consuma De Drogas En America. US Dept Health, NCAD, 1991 (D)

Reeves, Ira L. *'Ol Rum River: Revelations of a Prohibition Administrator.* Chicago: Thomas S. Rockwell Company, 1931 (D)

Reilly, Hugh. *Easy Does It: The Story of Mac.* NY: P.J. Kennedy & Sons, 1950 (D)

Reilly, Richard L. *I'm not an alcoholic because . . .* MO: Liguori, 1978 (D)

Rice, Thurman B. and Rolla N. Harger. *Effects of Alcoholic Drinks Tobacco Sedatives Narcotics.* Chicago: Wheeler Publishing Company, 1952 (D)

Richardson, Eudora Ramsay and Josiah Pitts Woolfolk. *Drink And Stay Sober.* NY: Bridgehead Books, 1954 (D)

Robertson, James D. *The Great American Beer Book.* NY: Warner Books, 1978 (D)

Rorabaugh, W. J. *The Alcohol Republic: An American Tradition.* NY: Oxford University Press, 1979 (D)

Rosenfield, Joe, Jr. *The Happiest Man in the World.* NY: Doubleday &

Company, 1955 (D)

Roth, Lillian. *I'll Cry Tomorrow*. NY: Frederick Fell, 1954 (D)

———. *Beyond My Worth*. London: Arthur Barker, 1958 (D)

Royce, James E. *Alcohol Problems and Alcoholism: A Comprehensive Survey*. NY: The Free Press, 1981 (D)

Sandimaier, Marian. *The Invisible Alcoholics: Women and Alcohol Abuse in America*. NY: McGraw Hill, 1980 (D)

Sands, Bill. *My Shadow Ran Fast*. NJ: Prentice-Hall, 1964 (D)

———. *The Seventh Step*. NY: The New American Library, 1967 (D)

Scott, Natalie Anderson. *The Story of Mrs. Murphy*. NY: E. P. Dutton, 1947 (D)

Seabrook, William. *Asylum*. NY: Harcourt, Brace, 1935 (D)

Seliger, Robert V. *Alcoholics are Sick People*. Baltimore: Alcoholism Publications, 1945 (D)

Sherman, Harold. *Anyone Can Stop Drinking (Even You)*. NY: C & R. Anthony, 1959 (D)

Sinclair, Upton. *The Cup of Fury*. NJ: Fleming H. Revell, 1956 (D)

Singer, Jefferson A. *Message in a Bottle: Stories of Men and Addiction*. NY: The Free Press, 1969 (D)

Smith, Fred B., ed. *Law vs. Lawlessness: Addresses Delivered at the Citizenship Conference*, Washington, D.C., October 13, 14, 15, 1923. NY: Fleming H. Revell, 1924 (D)

Smith, Randolph Wellford. *The Sober World*. Boston: Marshall Jones, 1919 (D)

Smith, Walton Hall and Ferdinand C. Helwig. *Liquor: The Servant of Man*. Boston: Little, Brown, 1940 (D)

Snyder, Solomon H., ed. *The Encyclopedia of Psychoactive Drugs: Alcohol and Alcoholism*. New Haven, Chelsea Press, 1986 (D)

Spickard, Anderson and Barbara R. Thompson. *Dying for a Drink: What You Should Know about Alcoholism*. Waco, TX: Word Books, 1985 (D)

Stairway to Serenity: The Eleventh Step. MN: Hazelden, 1988 (D)

Starr, John. *The Purveyor: The Shocking Story of Today's Illicit Liquor Empire*. NY: Holt, Rinehart & Winston, 1961 (D)

Steiner, Claude. *Games Alcoholics Play: The Analysis of Life Scripts*. NY: Grove Press, 1971 (D)

Stewart, David A. *Thirst For Freedom*. MN: Hazelden, 1960 (D)

Strachan, J. George. *Alcoholism: Treatable Illness*. Vancouver: Mitchell Press, Ltd., circa 1967 (D)

Strecker, Edward A. *One Man's Meat.* NY: The Macmillan Company, 1938 (D)

Taylor, Robert Lewis. *Vessel of Wrath: The Life and Times of Carry Nation.* NY: The New American Library, 1966 (D)

The Alcoholic American. Chicago: Blue Shield Association, 1978 (D)

The Blue Book of Happiness. Indianapolis: SMT Publishing Company, 1951 (D)

The Book of Excuses. Indianapolis: SMT Publishing Company, 1952 (D)

The Golden Book of the Spiritual Side. Indianapolis: SMT Guild, 1949 (D)

The Key Role of Labor in Employee Alcoholism Programs. NY: The Christopher D. Smithers Foundations, 1971 (D)

The International Student, 1940 - 1964 (6) D6

The Problem: Alcohol-Narcotics. Teacher's Handbook, 4th rev. ed. TX: TANE Press, 1991 (D)

The Silver Book of Attitudes. Indianapolis: SMT Publishing Company, 1949 (D)

The Social History of Alcohol Review Spring/1992. NY: Journal of Alcohol and Temperance History Group (D)

The Social History of Alcohol Review Spring/Fall 1993. NY: Journal of Alcohol and Temperance History Group (D).

The Social History of Alcohol Review Fall1993/Spring, 1994. NY: Journal of Alcohol and Temperance History Group (D).

The Thirtieth Anniversary Reader's Digest Reader. NY: Pleasantville, 1951 (D)

The Twelve Steps of Alcoholics Anonymous Interpreted By The Hazelden Foundation. NY: Harper/Hazelden, 1987 (D)

Tiebout, Harry M. *Direct Treatment of a Symptom.* MN: Hazelden, n.d. (D)

———. *Surrender Versus Compliance in Therapy.* MN: Hazelden, 1953 (2) D2

———. *The Ego Factors in Surrender in Alcoholism.* MN: Hazelden, 1954 (D)

———. *The Act of Surrender in the Therapeutic Process.* MN: Hazelden, 1990 (D)

Thomson, George. *Science Speaks to Young Men: On Liquor, Tobacco, Narcotics, and Marijuana.* Mountain View, CA: Pacific Press Publishing Association, 1938 (D)

Thompson, Vance. *Drink and Be Sober.* NY: Moffat, Yard, 1916 (D)

Tietsort, Francis J., ed. *Temperance or Prohibition: The Hearst Temperance Contest Committee*, NY: New York American, 1929 (D)

TimeCapsule/1939

Treat, Roger. *The Endless Road*. NY: A.S. Barnes, 1959 (D)

Trice, Harrison M. *Alcoholism in America*. NY: McGraw-Hill, 1966 (D)

Turnbull, Grace. *Fruit of the Vine: As Seen By Many Witnesses of All Times*. Baltimore: The Lord Baltimore Press, 1950 (D)

Twerski, Abraham J. *Caution: "Kindness" Can Be Dangerous To the Alcoholic*. NJ: Prentice-Hall, 1981 (D)

Tyrrell, Ian R. *Sobering Up: From Temperance to Prohibition in Antebellum America, 1800-1860*. Westport, CT: Greenwood Press, 1979 (D)

Valles, Jorge. *From Social Drinking to Alcoholism*. Dallas, TX: TANE Press, 1969 (D)

Vaughn, Clark. *Addictive Drinking: The Road to Recovery for Problem Drinkers and Those Who Love Them*. NY: The Viking Press, 1982 (D)

Van Blair, Bruce. *A Year To Remember*. WA: Glen Abbey Books, 1988 (D)

Van Impe, Jack. *Alcohol: The Beloved Enemy*. Nashville: Thomas Nelson Publishers, 1980 (D)

Wallace, John. Alcoholism: *New Light on the Disease*. RI: Edgehill Publications, 1985 (D)

Wallerstein, Robert S., and others. *Hospital Treatment of Alcoholism*. NY: Basic Books, 1957 (D)

Ware, Harlan. *Come, Fill the Cup*. NY: Random House, 1952 (D)

Warner, Harry S. Prohibition, *An Adventure in Freedom*. Ohio: The *World League Against* Alcoholism, 1928 (D)

Washton, Arnold & Donna Bundy. *Willpower's Not Enough: Understanding and Recovering From Addictions of Every Kind*. NY: Harper & Row, 1989 (D)

Watson, Donald E. *Surviving Your Crises: Reviving Your Dreams*. MA: Mills & Sanderson, 1994 (D)

Weeks, Courtenay C.. *Alcohol and Human Life*. London: H. K. Lewis, 1929 (D)

Weinstock, Matt. *Mascatel at Noon*. NY: William Morrow, 1951 (D)

Welch, Bob and George Vecsey. *Five O'Clock Comes Early: A Young Man's Battle with Alcoholism*. NY: William Morrow, 1982 (D)

Weldon, Robert S. *From Boxcar to Pulpit: The Autobiography of an Alcoholic.* NY: Exposition Press, 1968 (D)

What everyone should know About Alcohol. MA: Channing L. Bete Co., 1993 (D)

Wheeler, Wayne B., comp. *Federal and State Laws Relating to Intoxicating Liquor.* OH: The American Issue, 1916 (D)

White, John. *Ward N-1.* NY: A.A. Wynn, 1955 (D)

Whitney, Elizabeth D. *The Lonely Sickness.* Boston: Beacon Press, 1965 (D)

———, ed. *World Dialogue on Alcohol and Drug Dependence.* Boston: Beacon Press, 1976 (D)

Willis, Aubrey. *I Was an Alcoholic.* NY: Vantage Press, 1956 (D)

Wilson, Donald Powell. *My Six Convicts: A Psychologist's Three Years in Fort Leavenworth.* NY: Rinehart, n. d. (D)

Yablonsky, Lewis. *The Tunnel Back: Synanon.* NY: The Macmillan Company, 1965 (D)

Whitlock, Brand. *The Little Green Shutter.* NY: D. Appleton And Company, 1931 (D)

Williams, Edward Huntington. *Alcohol Hygiene and Legislation.* NY: The Goodhue Co., 1915 (D)

Williams, Jerry. *Deadly Dilemma (the "Periodic").* CA: Star Lodge Hospital, 1979 (D)

Williams, Roger J. *Alcoholism: The Nutritional Approach.* TX: University of Texas Press, 1959 (2)D

Willis, Aubrey. *Our Greatest Enemy: Beveraged Alcohol.* NY: Exposition Press, 1958 (D)

Willis, George W. *The Bottle Fighters.* NY: Random House, 1963 (D)

Woititz, Janet Geringer. *Adult Children of Alcoholics.* FL: Health Communications, Inc., 1983 (D)

Part 6
Details on Our Contributors and Their Collections

Importance of the Materials

The research notes, books, pamphlets, articles, correspondence, photos, tapes, and papers are not merely a collection of historical items. All bear directly on Dick B.'s quest to find, detail, and disseminate the facts about the all-but-forgotten biblical roots of early A.A. The materials fed into Dick's research, writing, footnotes, and bibliographies. They provide the raw materials that document the points he has made. For the most part, they have been ignored, overlooked, or just plain rejected by those who seek to make of A.A. today an all-inclusive fellowship with all faiths and creeds and nationalities and races with no particular belief system. In fact, scores of A.A. factual presentations today assert that you need not believe in God to recover; that you can make the group or a chair your "higher power;" or that you need not believe in anything at all. This shift has been and important contributor to the totally abysmal success rate in today's fellowships, treatment programs, and therapies (a rate something like one to five percent at best). This presents a clear contrast between what one professional characterized as today's "seventy-five percent failure rate" and the early success rate of seventy-five to ninety three percent. Knowing the early history will not change A.A. or Twelve Step Fellowships or programs or treatments or therapy. It can, however, insure that those, who want to recover by the power of our Creator, to establish their relationship with Him through Jesus Christ, and to know and understand the spiritual matters, will be able to do so with a knowledge that just such reliance was the foundation stone of early A.A. On the other hand, today's meetings, writings, and pronouncements so critical of religion, church, Bible, God, and Jesus Christ seem almost certain to obliterate the real power from the scene, the power of God that was sought and produced true recovery. And to render far less effective or even nullify the widely commendable, applauded, and continuing efforts of unselfish present-day AAs to help others still suffering and to and to carry a real and vital life-or-death message of hope and deliverance through the power of the Creator Who is so frequently mentioned (even today) in A.A.'s basic textbook..

The Intended Purpose of This Body of Materials Today

AAs, churches, clergy, seminaries, physicians, therapists, treatment centers, and public officials are, in general, completely uninformed about where A.A.'s program and practices came from. Many are intimidated at the prospect of mentioning the Creator, Jesus Christ, the Bible, the gift of Holy Spirit, religion, or church. And they tend to buy the idea that A.A. today is about some "higher power" of one's own conception and fashioning. The writers and scholars and historians who have studied A.A., and the staff of A.A. itself who publish A.A.'s materials, continue to ignore the biblical roots and Christian fellowship that were the A.A. of yesteryear. The books of Dick B. are just part of the picture. They can be placed on a shelf, or criticized, or ignored. But they rest on solid factual, historical evidence gathered over ten years and embodied in Dick B.'s books. Hence the integrity, veracity, and usefulness of the research and writings is founded on the materials from which they were drawn. And these foundational evidentiary materials have not been accessible, nor much sought after, nor understood, nor explained, nor frequently mentioned. The vast body of collected materials here described will be placed in an accessible location, with no charge for viewing, with usable copy facilities, with easy viewing, and with actual opportunity in the nearby Wilson House to reside next to the materials and/or to copy, to study, to analyze, and to evaluate. And stewarded by active, 12 Step people who have sought these materials, who understand their importance, and who will preserve their integrity and make certain the very continuance of their existence.

It is hoped and in fact planned that many of these materials-piece-by-piece-will be made available on the internet once they have been housed, catalogued, and funded for that particular purpose too. Their host facility is a recognized non-profit, charitable entity and will own the collections outright once they are funded, acquired, shipped, and placed..

General Summary

The eight collections are in process of being purchased, acquired, assembled, and specifically described at this time. They consisted of seven shelves of books, booklets, pamphlets, articles, video tapes, and audio tapes. In addition, Dick's own notes and papers were being assembled in four containers (13" x 22" each), segregated into files organized and categorized in terms of their particular relationship to some aspect of A.A.'s spiritual history.

Funds were sought in the amount of $325,000.00 to cover the cost incurred over the past ten years and still being disbursed at the present time for acquisition of these materials. Tax-deductible gifts, in cash or in kind (such as appreciated securities, land, or other items) can be made to one of three different 501(c) three charitable entities, with the choice of the entity being dependent upon the nature and size and origin of the particular gift. All gifts will be acknowledged by the charitable entity (church, school, or foundation) receiving the gift. The funds will be turned over to Dick B. to cover the costs of buying, collecting, assembling, analyzing, packing, and shipping the items. A letter of acknowledgment suitable for the IRS will be sent by the charitable entity to the donor. A report will be made to the charitable and entity by Dick B. when the collections have been paid for. And the body of materials will then be shipped to the host facility (a tax exempt, non-profit charity such as The Wilson House), accepted by agreement of the facility, and become the sole property of that charity and be held in accordance with its agreement and mission statement.

Should the host charity become unable to continue its stewardship or become defunct, the materials will be given free to a permanent tax-exempt host, preferably the University of Akron, which is located where A.A.'s founders day activities are held, and in the city where A.A. was founded. Arrangements for such ultimate transfer will be made with such a university at the same time the collection agreement is executed with the host facility.

To insure that the collections are properly housed, described, and used as intended, Dick B. will personally travel to the host facility and assist in the receipt, description, and placement of the items.

And now, in the following pages, the exact items comprising the historical materials and collections will be described, category-by-category, with each major section of this volume of descriptive material being devoted to those materials provided by each particular specified donor or collector.

Dick B.'s Personal Research and Writing Collection

Where Dick B. Acquired His Research Materials and Books

Throughout the period beginning in 1990 and continuing to the present date in the year 2000, author Dick B. has visited the places specified and/or has acquired notes, papers, journals, correspondence, manuscripts, articles, and memos from the following places:

1. The Archives at Stepping Stones (Bill Wilson's home at Bedford Hills, New York); at A.A. General Services in New York; at Dr. Bob's Home in Akron, Ohio; at archives or Ray Grumney, archivist for Dr. Bob's Home (Newton Falls, Ohio); at the home and exhibits of Gail LaCroix, archivist for Founders' Day in Akron (Cuyahoga Falls, Ohio); at Hartford Seminary where Frank Buchman taught (Hartford, Connecticut); at Princeton University Alumni Archives, Princeton being the University attended by, and where Dr. Sam Shoemaker was Secretary of the Philadelphian Society); at Frank Buchman Home (where the Oxford Group Founder's own library and papers are housed), Allentown Pennsylvania; at Calvary Episcopal Church in New York (where Dr. Shoemaker was rector in A.A.'s formative years); at Calvary Episcopal Church in Pittsburgh (where Dr. Shoemaker was rector); at The Pittsburgh Experiment (founded by Dr. Shoemaker); at The Wilson House (where Bill Wilson was born) at East Dorset, Vermont; at Episcopal Church Archives at Austin, Texas (where the great body of Sam Shoemaker's correspondence and personal papers are lodged); at Tirley Garth (British archives of the Oxford Group); at Moral Re-Armament Headquarters in Washington D.C.; and the personal archives of Bill Pittman, when he was with Glenn Abbey Books in Seattle, Washington; of Mitchell Klein, Washingtonville, New York: of Earl Husband, Oklahoma City, Oklahoma; of Clancy Uterhardt, Wainae,

Hawaii; of Charles Bishop, Jr., Wheeling West Virginia; of Nell Wing, A.A.'s first Archivist, Manhattan, New York: of Frank Mauser, A.A.'s second Archivist, Manhattan, New York; of Ray Mews, Oahu, Hawaii; of Grace Snyder (widow of pioneer Clarence Snyder), Jacksonville, Florida; of Danny Whitmore, Palmdale, California; of T. Willard Hunter, Claremont, California; of Dale Morfitt, Amery, Wisconsin; and also historical data of A.A. historians: Ernest Kurtz, Ph.D., Ann Arbor, Michigan; Charles Knippel, Ph.D., Missouri; Bill Pittman, Center City, Minnesota; Dennis Cassidy, New Britain, Connecticut; Ray Washburn, Florida; Father Paul Blaes, Florida; Ron Ray, Florida; George Trotter, Illinois; Bob Perko, Arizona; Mel Barger of Toledo, Ohio; Mary Darrah, Ohio; Wally Paton, Arizona; Bob Roeder, Maryland., Berry Wild, Idaho; Bill Ragin, Maryland; John Gillen, Hawaii; Charles Sigler, Pennsylvania; Mary T. Webb, Ph.D., and David Sacks, Ph.D., Princeton, New Jersey.

2. Libraries at Princeton, New Jersey; Baltimore, Maryland; San Francisco Theological Seminary, San Anselmo, California; Golden Gate Baptist Seminary at Mill Valley, California; Graduate Theological Union, Berkeley, California; Substance Abuse Library, Berkeley, California; Hawaii State Library, Honolulu, Hawaii; Makawao Public Library, Makawao, Hawaii; Wailuku Public Library, Wailuku, Hawaii; Kahului Public Library, Kahului, Hawaii; Kihei Public Library, Kihei, Hawaii; and Ed Andy's "A.A.'s First Library" at Lorrain, Ohio.

3. Interviews, correspondence, phone and fax communications, email correspondence and personal visits with (1) Oxford Group activists and leaders Dr. Morris Martin (Dr. Buchman's personal secretary), Arizona; Michael Hutchinson, Great Britain; Garth Lean, Great Britain; Kenneth Belden, Great Britain; Frederick Watt, Canada; Dr. Robin Mowat, Great Britain; Eleanor Forde Newton and James Draper Newton, Florida; Charles Haines, Pennsylvania; Harry Almond, Massachusetts; Richard Ruffin, Washington, D.C.; Michael Henderson, Portland, Oregon; Richard Hadden, Michigan; Mrs. W. Irving Harris, New Jersey; Rev. Howard Blake, California; James Houck, Maryland; George Vondermuhll, Jr., Connecticut; L. Parks Shipley, Sr., New Jersey: D. Morgan Firestone, Canada. (2) Sam Shoemaker's family, colleagues, and friends: Mrs. Helen Shoemaker, Maryland; Sally Shoemaker Robinson, Maryland; Nickie Shoemaker Haggart, Florida; Sinclair Hart, Kentucky; Rev. Paul Everett, Pittsburgh; "The Golf Club Crowd" at Pittsburgh; Dr.

Norman Vincent Peale, New York; Leonard Firestone, California; Bill Cohea, New England. (3) Families of A.A. Founders: Robert and Betty Smith, Texas; Sue Smith Windows, Ohio; John F. Seiberling, Ohio; Dorothy Seiberling, Ohio; Mary Seiberling Huhn, Pennsylvania; Dorothy Williams Culver, California. (4) A.A. Pioneers and survivors: Larry Bauer, Ohio; Geraldine O. Delaney, New Jersey; Grace Snyder, Florida; Steve and Sue Foreman, Florida; John Slater, Canada; Dick Stutz, Florida; Dick Snyder, California; Micky Snyder, California; Cebra Graves, internet. (5) A.A. Big Book Seminar Leaders: Joe McQuany and Charles Parmley, Arkansas. (6) Recovery field leaders and writers: Betty Ford, Dr. Paul Wood, Joseph Califiano, Jr.; Leonard Firestone, Dennis Wholey; R. Brinkley Smithers; Senator Harold E. Hughes. (7) Managers of The Wilson House (Bonnie and Ozzie Lepper); Stepping Stones (Paul Lang); Dr. Bob's Home (Rosalie Povich); Dr. Bob's Birthplace at Founders Hall, St. Johnsbury, Vermont.

4. Conferences, seminars, and panels at (1) The Wilson House, East Dorset, Vermont; (2) A.A. International Convention, Seattle; A.A. International Convention, San Diego; (3) Big Book Seminars at Sacramento, California; (4) Founders Day Conventions at Akron, Ohio; (5) A.A. Area Conventions at Monterey, Fresno, Sacramento, and Oakland, California; Maui, Hawaii; Honolulu, Hawaii; (6) A.A. Rule 62 Convention in Kentucky; (7) A Day in Marin Conferences in Mill Valley, California; (8) A.A. Historian and Archivist Conferences in West Virginia and at Center City, Minnesota; (9) Clarence Snyder Retreats at (a) Amery, Wisconsin, (b) Palmdale, California, (c) Orlando, Florida; (10) Alcoholics Victorious Conventions in New Jersey and California; (11) Overcomers Meetings in Florida and Minnesota; (12) NET Ministry Conference in Florida; (13) World Addiction and Recovery Conference, Florida; (14) Overcomers Outreach Convention in California; (15) Shepherding the Shepherds Recovery Training Conference in California; (16) Brown University Conference in Rhode Island; (17) Bill Wilson Celebration in Pittsburgh; (18) CLEAR Conferences of Pittsburgh Leadership Foundation in Pittsburgh; (19) A.A. and Treatment Center Seminars in Nashville, Tennessee.

5. Regular Alcoholics Anonymous meetings in California, Hawaii, Washington, Arkansas, Florida, New York, Vermont, Minnesota,

Kentucky, Rhode Island, West Virginia, Ohio, New Jersey.

6. Internet web sites and email messages containing historical data, biblical data, recovery data, Oxford Group data, recovery discussions, Christian materials, and book lists. Dick has had internet capability from 1995. He has regularly searched the net and regularly exchanged emails with scholars, historians, archivists, recovery workers, religious ministries, publishers, writers, physicians, psychologists, teachers, therapists, AAs and many other Twelve Step leaders and fellowship members.

7. Historical, recovery, and biblical books and materials purchased from and/ or donated by almost every one of the foregoing people and sources. These items have also been purchased and sometimes been received free from general, used, Christian, recovery, government, university, religious, medical, and treatment bookstores and also internet outlets. Stores have been searched in California, Hawaii, New England, Michigan, Minnesota. Wisconsin, Florida, Tennessee, and Maryland. Dick B.'s son has conducted a continuing world-wide search for necessary books and research materials over a period of several years.

Dick B.'s Personal Historical Resources

Books, Pamphlets, and Articles

These items number more than 940 books, pamphlets, and articles, and they are described with particularity at pages 31 to 65 inclusive of the red prospectus mailed in March, 2000. Again, these items will not be detailed here and are, of course, included in the foregoing master inventory.

Video and Audio Cassette Tapes of Dick B.'s Talks

These video and audio cassette tapes are currently being inventoried. They include talks Dick has given on public television, and at The Wilson House annual seminars, at Archives 2000 in Minneapolis, at The University of Nations, at Clarence Snyder retreats, and at various conventions and conferences and seminars of Overcomers Outreach, Inc., Overcomers of Brevard, Overcomers, Alcoholics Victorious, The Net

Ministries, the ISAAC conference in Florida, the Shepherding the Shepherds Conference in California, the Lutheran Seminary in Wisconsin, and various other 12 Step meetings and fellowships.

Video and Audio Cassette Tapes of Others

These items are also currently being inventoried. In the course of his ten years of research, Dick has collected and used video cassette tapes of Oxford Group events, Clarence Snyder talks and retreats, The Bill Wilson Story, Dawn of Hope, and other historical events. In addition, he has collected audio cassette tapes of Bill Wilson, Dr. Bob, Clarence Snyder, Henrietta Seiberling, Samuel M. Shoemaker, Helen Shoemaker, Dr. Bob's son, and many other A.A. oldtimers and speakers.

Other Research Materials (especially papers)

These are currently housed in four (4) plastic storage bins. Each bin is 22 inches in length, 13 inches in width, and 10 inches in height. They are described with particularity at pages 7 through 30 inclusive of the red prospectus that was prepared and mailed in March, 2000. The detailed itemization will not be repeated here.

The James D. and Eleanor F. Newton Collection

[126 books and 50 pamphlets]

About James D. and Eleanor F. Newton

Jim and Ellie, as they like to call themselves, are possibly the best known and oldest living survivors of Dr. Frank N. D. Buchman's Oxford Group. Jim survived into his late nineties, and Ellie died at 103 years of age. They livedin Fort Myers Beach, Florida, near the area where Jim developed Edison Park many many decades ago and became the close friend of Henry Ford, Harvey Firestone, and Thomas A. Edison.

Eleanor Napier Forde hailed from Canada. She heard Sam Shoemaker preach in a New York church in the early 1920's and soon went to work for Sam during his stint as Rector of Calvary Episcopal Church in New York. Sam recommended that she join Frank Buchman in his Oxford Group work; and Eleanor became a close Oxford Group associate of both Sam Shoemaker, a prominent American leader, and

Frank Buchman, the founder. Buchman sent Eleanor Forde to many places abroad to work as an Oxford Group volunteer. And Ellie is frequently mentioned in Sam Shoemaker's correspondence and personal journals. In 1927, Eleanor wrote an early manuscript on The Guidance of God. By 1930, it was printed by The Oxford Group itself, and is still in circulation today. In short, Eleanor Napier Forde has been an Oxford Group activist since the early 1920's and has contributed much information and material to Dick B. in his research and writing on the Oxford Group and Alcoholics Anonymous. Though Eleanor met Jim Newton in the 1920's, they did not marry for more than a decade. Eleanor's ideas are quoted in the journal kept by Dr. Bob's wife Anne Ripley Smith; and Bill Wilson's wife Lois Burnham Wilson mentions in her diary that she and Bill met both Jim Newton and Eleanor Forde at Oxford Group houseparty functions.

James Draper Newton wandered into an Oxford Group meeting in the early 1920's and soon became sold on the Oxford Group fellowship and its principles. Jim became a good friend of Dr. Frank Buchman and of The Rev. Sam Shoemaker. Because of his friendship with Harvey Firestone, Sr., Newton was brought to Akron to become Firestone's secretary. Newton met Harvey's son Russell, discovered Russell was an alcoholic, and arranged to have Sam Shoemaker come to Akron and take Russell to an Oxford Group meeting in Denver to help Russell be delivered from alcoholism. This was in 1931. Shoemaker brought Russell to a decision for Christ in a train compartment on their return from Denver. Russell was miraculously cured of alcoholism and began witnessing, often in company with Jim Newton, in Great Britain and elsewhere, on Oxford Group principles and practices. In 1933, Newton arranged with the Firestones to have Dr. Frank Buchman and a team of thirty come to Akron and conduct huge meetings in the churches, schools, and a dinner meeting attesting to Oxford Group victories. From these, Dr. Bob's wife, Henrietta Seiberling, and others became enthused over the Oxford Group. They induced Dr. Bob to join, eventually to pray for deliverance, and finally to become the sober leader of the Oxford Group meetings at T. Henry Williams's home which constituted the first group of Alcoholics Anonymous, Akron Number One.

Meanwhile, Newton left the employ of Firestone Tire and Rubber and became a full-time Oxford Group volunteer for many years. He married Eleanor Forde, and the two continued their affiliation with the Group and later with Moral Re-Armament; and that affiliation continues to this very day.

In the course of their Oxford Group work, the Newtons became thoroughly conversant with Oxford Group literature, principles, and practices. They attended Oxford Group meetings and Oxford Group house-parties. They worked in Oxford Group teams. And they have known an endless number of Oxford Group leaders and volunteers throughout the world. They have each supplied A.A.'s "unofficial historian" Dick B. with Oxford Group books, videos, pamphlets, tapes, diaries, news articles, and correspondence that would enable a full understanding of Oxford Group ideas and how they have related to A.A.'s own spiritual program of recovery. They have kept in touch with Sam Shoemaker and his daughters. And they have endorsed Dick B.'s books on the Oxford Group and on Sam Shoemaker and have provided financial assistance for the research, writing, printing, publishing, and distribution of those books. Ellie's story is told in part in her book, *I Always Wanted Adventure*. Jim's is told in his book *Uncommon Friends: Life with Thomas Edison, Henry Ford, Harvey Firestone, Alexis Carrel, & Charles Lindbergh*. Newton's part in the A.A. story is told in Dick B.'s *The Akron Genesis of Alcoholics Anonymous*.

The Newtons remained active in, and supportive of, Buchman's Christian movement and its offspring from almost its beginning about 1918. They belonged to the Group when it became known as A First Century Christian Fellowship, then as the Oxford Group, and then as Moral Re-Armament. They often participated in recent Moral Re-Armament work, including attendance at its center at Caux, Switzerland. They gave much counsel to Dick B. in his search for accurate resources and a full understanding of the precise Oxford Group ideas that became a part of early A.A.'s fellowship, basic text, and ultimately Twelve Steps. Many of Dick B.'s contacts, interviews, archival materials, and books have come by or through his close association over a decade with Jim and Eleanor Newton and their good friend T. Willard Hunter.

The Newton's library on Oxford Group, MRA, and A.A. materials was turned over for inclusion in our Center to the Dick B. Historical Collections in July, 1999. The summary of the books and pamphlets follows. There are one hundred twenty-six books and fifty pamphlets.

Books from James D. and Eleanor F. Newton

The Oxford Group

TITLE	AUTHOR
Conversion of the Church	Sam Shoemaker
Faith to Move Nations	Dr. J. B. Belk
For Sinners Only	A. J. Russell
God Who Speaks	Burnett Hillman Streeter
Guidance of God	Eleanor Napier Forde (Newton)
I Always Wanted Adventure	Eleanor Napier Forde (Newton)
Life Began Yesterday	Stephen Foot
Life Changers	Harold Begbie
Philosophy of Courage	Philip Leon
Remaking the World	Frank Buchman
Soul Surgery	H. A. Walter
Victorious Life	Howard Blake
What is the Oxford Group?	L. W. Grensted (sic)
World that Works	George West

Moral Re-Armament

TITLE	AUTHOR
All the Paths Are Peace	Michael Henderson
All Things Are Possible	Kay Linburg
America Needs an Ideology	Campbell & Howard
American Proposition	Francis Bradley
Best of Friends	Alan Thornhill
Beyond Violence	Agnes Leakey Hofmyer
Cast Out Your Nets	Garth Lean
Chou En Lai	John McCook Roots
Climbing Turns	Patrick Foss
Columbia	Juliet Boobyer
Crowning Experience	James Hardiman
Design for Dedication	Peter Howard
Discovering Moral Re-Armament	Rex Dilly
Dose of My Own Medicine	Paul Campbell

Experiencing Pasadena	Denise Woods
Experiment with God	Gosta Ekmar
Flying Norsemen	Leif Hovelsen
Footprints	Michael Barrett
For God Alone	John Tyndale-Biscoe
For Tomorrow, Yes	David Blair
Forgiving Factor	Michael Henderson
Forty Five years with Philips	Frederick Philips
Frank Buchman As I Knew Him	Bunny Austin
Frank Buchman By his friends	
Frank Buchman's Secret	Peter Howard
Free Woman	Claire Evans
God Calling	A. J. Russell (sic)
God Can be Real	Edward Perry
Good God it Works	Garth Lean
Hit Hard and Enjoy It	Dickie Dodds
Hope for Today	Marsh & Elliott
Horizons of Hope	John G. Pibram
Hour of the Helicopter	K. D. Belden
Hurdles & Jumping	Frances McCall
I Am Not Alone	John Hogan
I Choose Sarah	Lawrence Slattery
Innocent Men	Peter Howard
Iraqui Statesman	Harry Almond
Japan's Deciding Decade	Basil Entwistle
John Riffe of the Steelworkers	William Grogan
Life & Times of G. Cecil Morrison	G. Cecil Morrison
Lionheart	Dennis Foss
Listen for a Change	Anjenet Campbell
Listening Ear	Paul Tornier
Making Cities Work	Basil Entwistle
Man & Structures	Jens J. Wilhelmsen
Man of Many Loves	Paul Petrocokino
Mission Dimension of Statecraft	Six Scholars
Modern Prophetic Voices	R. C. Mowat
Modernizing America	Belk/Howard et. al.
Moving the Mountain	Ronald Mann
MRA Vital to the Future Publication	
MRA What is It?	Entwistle/McCook Roots

Muslim Mind	Chris Waddy
My Search for Faith	Lucille Tretheway Libby
Mystery of Human Experience	Rodney Usher-Wilson
Never Lose my Vision	Claire Jaeger
New Man for the New World	Paul Petrocokino
Niels' Legacy	Ely
Now I Call Him Brother	Alec Smith
On History's Coat Tails	Michael Henderson
One Fight More	Alan Thornhill
Out Every Night	Leif Hovalsen
Pamphlets (Various about 50)	(Various)
Paul Hogue	Meta Hogue
Personal Story	David Carey
Peter Howard-Life & Letters	Anne Wolrige Gordon
Philadelphia Rebel	Clare Jaeger
Poems	Hanford Twitchell
Preview of the New World 1939-1946	
Reaching the Millions	New World News
Rediscovering Freedom	John Lester & Pierre Spoerri
Reflections of M.R.A.	K. D. Belden
Return of the Indian Spirit	The Johnsons
Shoot a Line	Dennis Foss, with Basil Entwistle
Spin a Good Yarn	W. Farra Vickers
Spiritual Forces International Politics	R. C. Mowat
Step Ahead of Disaster	Von Teuber, with Basil Entwistle
Streams	Mark Guldseth
Suicide of Adoration	R. N. Usher-Wilson
Thankful at Every Turns	Paul Gundersen
To Phyl with Love	Bunny Austin
Unbeatable Breed	Bob Lowery
Way to Go	Howard Blake
Which Way Cambodia	Friends of MRA
Who Dare to Live	Frederick Watt
Window	Signe Lund Strong
World at the Turning	Charles Piguet Michel Sentis
World My Country	Marjorie Proctor

Alcoholics Anonymous

TITLE	AUTHOR
A.A. and M.R.A.	T. Willard Hunter
Alcoholics Anonymous [Basic Text]	
Anne Smith's Spiritual Workbook	Dick B.
Dr. Bob and His Library	Dick B.
Dr. Bob's Library	Dick B.
Lois Remembers	Lois Wilson
New Wine	Mel B.
Anne Smith's Journal	Dick B.
Pass It On Story of Bill Wilson (sic)	
Stairway to Serenity/11th Step	Homer P.
Turning it Over	Homer P.
Twelve Steps to A.A.	Hazelden
Understanding Alcoholism	LeClair Bissell
The Akron Genesis of A.A.	Dick B.
Back to Basics	Wally P.
Courage to Change Sam Shoemaker	[Dick B. & Bill P.]
Design for Living	Dick B.
Good Morning!	Dick B.
The Good Book and The Big Book	Dick B.
Is There Life after Sobriety	Mel B.
New Light on Alcoholism	Dick B.
One Day at a Time	Al-Anon
The Oxford Group and A.A.	Dick B.
Turning Point	Dick B. (audiobook and softcover)

The Willard Hunter Collection

[Total number of books: 141]

About T. Willard Hunter

Willard Hunter has been an Oxford Group activist since the late 1930's. He has also been a friend of Alcoholics Anonymous. Hunter knew Sam Shoemaker, Frank Buchman, and many of the Oxford Group personalities in Dick B.'s books. He has written a pamphlet on the Oxford Group and Alcoholics Anonymous, with A.A. history writer Mel B., that has been a handout at A.A.'s GSO offices in New York for many years. Hunter is quoted extensively in A.A.'s own biography of Bill Wilson (Pass It On). He has collaborated with Mel B. on A.A. history research. He has assisted Dick B. for several years in obtaining Oxford Group-Shoemaker materials and names and addresses. He has spoken on the platform of an A.A. Seminar with Dick B., Mel B., and Dr. Bob's son Robert Smith. He is author of the Foreword to The Oxford Group & Alcoholics Anonymous by Dick B. He is a news columnist, orator, and writer. He recently authored for Moral Re-Armament its pamphlet on the early A.A. Connection. He is a law school graduate, an ordained minister, and former assistant to the President at Claremont School of Theology. He will shortly add his collection of important Oxford Group books to the foregoing collections of Dick B., James Newton, and Eleanor Forde Newton.

The Willard Hunter Books and Pamphlets

Oxford Group

Adam, Karl. *Extracts from Moral Re-Armament and Christianity in the West*
Almond, Harry J. *Foundations for Faith*

Begbie, Harold. *Life Changers*
Begbie, Harold. *More Twice-Born Men*
Begbie, Harold. *Twice-Born Men*
Belk, J. B. *A Faith to Move Nations* (2 copies)
Bochmuehl, Klaus. *Listening to the God Who Speaks* (2 copies)
Brodersen, Paul. *The Church and the Destiny of Nations*
Brown, J. C. *The Oxford Group Movement: Is It of God or of Satan?*
Buchman, Frank N. D. *The Making of a Miracle*

Campbell, Paul. *A Dose of My Own Medicine*
Campbell, Paul, and Peter Howard. *America Needs an Ideology*
Campbell, Paul, and Peter Howard. *A Story of Effective Statesmanship*
Campbell, Paul, and Peter Howard. *Remaking Men*
Church Information Board of the Church Assembly: *Moral Re-Armament: A Study of the Movement*
Clark, Walter Houston. *The Oxford Group: Its History and Significance*
Cook, Sydney and Lean, Garth. *The Black and White Book*

Crowley, Patrice. *Pickle Bill of Pickle Hill (Town & Gown Magazine, February, 1978)*

Drakeford, John W. *People to People Therapy: Self Help Groups: Roots, Principles, and Processes*
Driberg, Tom. *The Mystery of Moral Re-Armament: A Study of Frank Buchman and His Movement*
Du Maurier, Daphne. *Come Wind, Come Weather*

Eister, Allan W. *Drawing Room Conversion* (2 copies)
Ekman, Gosta. *Experiment with God: Frank Buchman Reconsidered*
Entwistle, Basil. *Japan's Decisive Decade*

Foot, Stephen. *Life Begins Today*
Frank Buchman: 80. Compiled by His Friends

Gandhi, Rajmohan. *A Writer's Duty*
Gordon, Anne Wolrige. *Peter Howard Life and Letters (2)*
Grogan, William. *John Riffe of the Steelworkers*

Hagedorn, Hermann. *The Bomb That Fell on America*
Hagedorn, Hermann. *While There Is Time*
Hamlin, Bryan T. *Moral Re-Armament and Forgiveness in International Affairs*
Hanna, David. *"Come Up and See Me Some Time": An Uncensored Biography of Mae West*
Hannen & Cameron. *Where Do We Go from Here?*
Hannon, Peter. *Who's Side Is God On?*
Henderson, Michael. *A Different Accent*
Henderson, Michael. *From India with Hope*
Hicks, Roger. *The Endless Adventure*
Hofmeyer, Bremer. *How to Listen*
Howard, Peter. *Design for Dedication*
Howard, Peter. *The Ladder*
Howard, Peter. *Pickle, Bill*
Howard, Peter. *Happy Deathday*
Howard, Peter. *Ideas Have Legs*
Howard, Peter. *Britain and the Beast*
Howard, Peter. *A Renaissance That Unites East and West*

Howard, Peter. *Beyond Communism to Revolution*

Howard, Peter. *Tomorrow Will Be Too Late*

Howard, Peter. *The World Rebuilt: Men and Women of Moral Re-Armament*

Howard, Peter. *Innocent Men*

Howard, Peter. *Fighters Ever*

Howard, Peter. *That Man Frank Buchman*

Howard, Peter, and Alan Thornhill. *Music at Midnight*

Howard, Peter, and Alan Thornhill. *The Hurricane*

Howard, Peter, and Cecil Broadhurst. *The Vanishing Island*

Howell, Edward. *Escape to Live*

Jaeger, Annie. *Annie*

Jaeger, William. *The World Struggle of Ideologies*

Lean, Garth. *Cast Out Your Nets: Sharing Your Faith with Others*

Lean, Garth. *Frank Buchman a Life: Notes for Study*

Lean, Garth. *Good God, It Works!*

Lean, Garth. *Strangely Warmed: The Amazing Life of John Wesley*

Leon, Philip. *The Philosophy of Courage*

Lunn, Arnold and Lean, Garth. *The New Morality*

Magor, Cliff and Edna. *The Song of a Merry Man*: Ivan Menzies of the D'Oyly Cart Gilbert & Sullivan Operas

Marcel, Gabriel. Ed. *Fresh Hope for the World: Moral Re-Armament in Action (2)*

Martin, Morris. *Up with People: Born to Live in the Future*

McCassey, Sir Lynden. *The Oxford Group and Its Work of Moral Re-Armament*

Moral Re-Armament. *An Idea Takes Wings*

Moral Re-Armament. *The Fight to Serve: Moral Re-Armament and the War*

Morrison, J. M. *Honesty and God*

Morrison, John. *The Statesman's Dream and Other Poems*

Mottu, Philippe. *The Story of Caux: From La Belle Epoque to Moral Re-Armament*

Mowat, Robin. *An Approach to "Remaking the World"*

Mowat, R.C. *Moral Re-Armament*

Mowat, R.C. Spiritual Forces in International Politics

161

Niel's Legacy: The Story of an American Boy Who Lived at the Heart of a World Family

Pershing, General of the Armies John J. *You Can Defend America*
Phillimore, Miles G. *Just for Today*
Prestwich, Irene. *Irene Prestwich of Tirley Garth: A Personal Memoir*
Proctor, Marjorie. *The World My Country: The Story of Daw Nyein Tha of Burma*

Rodzinski, Halina. *Our Two Lives*
Roots, John McCook. *An Apostle to Youth*
Roots, John McCook. *Modernizing America: Action Papers of National Purpose*
Rose, Cecil. *When Man Listens*

Schollgen, Werner. *The Basic Problem of Education in Morals* (2 copies)
Spoerri, Theophil. *Basic Forces in European History*
Spoerri, Theophil. *Dynamic out of Silence: Frank Buchman's Relevance Today*
Spoerri, Theophil. *Who Are the True Europeans?*
Streeter, B.H., *The God Who Speaks (An abridgement of.)*

The Layman with a Notebook. *What Is The Oxford Group?*
The Oxford Group. *Live Wires*
Thornhill, Alan. *Best of Friends: A Life of Enriching Friendships*
Thornhill, Alan. *Bishops Move*
Thornhill, Alan. *Hide Out*
Thornhill, Alan. *Mr. Wilberforce, MP*
Thornhill, Alan. *The Significance of the Life of Frank Buchman (2)*
Thornton-Duesbery, J. P. *The Open Secret of MRA*
Thornton-Duesbery, J. P. *The Oxford Group: A Brief Account of Its Principles and Growth*
Twitchell, Kenaston. *Frank Buchman: Twentieth Century Catalyst*
Twitchell, Kenaston, *How Do You Make Up Your Mind?*
Twitchell, Kenaston, *Supposing You Were Absolutely Honest*

Viney, Hallen. *How Do I Begin?*
Viney, Hallen, *Which Way is Right?*

West, George. *The World That Works*
Williamson, Geoffrey. *Inside Buchmanism*

Oxford Group Sources

Smith, George Adam. *The Life of Henry Drummond*
Stewart, George. *Life of Henry B. Wright*
Stewart, George. *The Letters of Maxwell Chaplin*

Wright, Henry B. *The Will of God and a Man's Life Work*

Frank Buchman Alma Mater

Perkiomen School. *Perkiomen: Here's to You: A Centennial History of Perkiomen School*
Tappert, Theodore G. *History of the Lutheran Theological Seminary at Philadelphia: 1864-1964*

Samuel M. Shoemaker, Jr.

Shoemaker, Helen Smith. *I Stand by the Door: The Life of Sam Shoemaker*
Shoemaker, Samuel M. *How to Become a Christian*
Shoemaker, Samuel M. *If I Be Lifted Up*
Shoemaker, Samuel M. *The Church Can Save the World*
Shoemaker, Samuel M. *The Experiment of Faith*
Shoemaker, Samuel M. *The Gospel According to You*
Shoemaker, Samuel M. *With the Holy Spirit and with Fire*

Books on Recovery

B., Dick. [Set of ten (10) books by Dick B. on the biblical origins of Alcoholics Anonymous.]
B., Mel. *Is There Life after Sobriety?*
B., Mel. *The Slogans.*
Gamblers Anonymous Publishing, Inc. *Sharing Recovery through Gamblers Anonymous.*
Hazelden. *The Twelve Steps of Alcoholics Anonymous.*
Hazelden. *Twenty-Four Hours a Day.*
Rudy, David R. *Becoming Alcoholic: Alcoholics Anonymous and the Reality of Alcoholism.*
Thomsen, Robert. *Bill W.*
W., Bill. *Why Alcoholics Anonymous Is Anonymous.*

Miscellaneous

Bingham, Mitchell. *Psychic Adventure*
Excerpt from the *1985 Guinness Book of World Records*, p. 325: Willard Hunter
Two Listeners. *God Calling*
Zikmund, Barbara Brown, editor. *Hidden Histories in the United Church of Christ 2*

The Frederick Robert Johnston Collection

[Total number of books: 78]

About Frederick Robert Johnston

Bob Johnston is an active, recovered A.A., and Bible student who lives in the State of Hawaii and has sponsored a number of people in A.A. He is currently active as secretary and treasurer of regular A.A. meetings. He has attended A.A. Conferences in Hawaii and elsewhere; and he has also attended spiritual retreats for AA s and the Dick B. Seminars at The Wilson House. Recently, he began purchasing for this group of collections the hard-to-find books that had been part of Dick B.'s research and/or A.A.'s spiritual roots but were not part of any of the included collections. These items included particularly books on and about Dwight Moody, Horace Bushnell, John R. Mott, F.B. Meyer, Henry Drummond, and others who figured in the spiritual ideas and practices that early AAs adopted. He also helped to collect books on Christian Endeavor, which was the group to which Dr. Bob belonged in his youth and which involved many of the activities in which Dr. Bob was later to engage in early A.A.: Bible Study, the Quiet Hour, Prayer, Fellowship, and witness, as well as support of the local church. Bob has been with Dick recently in connection with efforts to assemble and fund the acquisition and placement of the historical collections.

Books from Frederick Robert Johnston

Allen, James. *The Heavenly Life*

Barton, George A. *Jesus of Nazareth*
Begbie, Harold. *Souls in Action*
Bennett, John C. *Social Salvation*

Cantril, Hadley. The Psychology of Social Movements
Chapman, J. Wilbur. *The Life and Work of Dwight L. Moody*
Cheney, Mary Bushnell. *Life and Letters of Horace Bushnell*
Clark, Glenn. *Fishers of Men*
Clark, Glenn. *How to Find Health through Prayer*
Clark, Glenn. *Two or Three Gathered Together*

Driberg, Tom. *The Mystery of Moral Re-Armament*
Drummond, Henry. *The Changed Life*
Drummond, Henry. *The New Evangelism* (2 copies)

Eddy, Sherwood. *A Pilgrimage of Ideas*

Ferguson, Charles. *The Confusion of Tongues*
Fillmore, Charles. *Christian Healing*

165

Fillmore, Charles. *Teach Us to Pray*
Finney, Charles. *Memoirs*
Fitt, Emma Moody, editor. *Day by Day with D. L. Moody*
Fosdick, Harry Emerson. *A Great Time to Be Alive*
Fox, Emmet. *Alter Your Life*
Fox, Emmet. *Find and Use Your Inner Power*
Fox, Emmet. *Getting Results by Prayer*; *You Must Be Born Again*; *The Great Adventure*. (3 articles in one booklet.)
Fox, Emmet. *Make Your Life Worth While*

Gilkey, Charles Whitney. *Jesus and Our Generation*
Glimm, Francis X. (trans.). *The Fathers of the Church* (Vol. 1)
Goodspeed, Edgar J. *Strange New Gospels.*
Grensted, L. W. *The Person of Christ*

Harnack, Adolf. *The Expansion of Christianity in the First Three Centuries* (2 vols.)
Harrison, Marjorie. *Saints Run Mad*
Henson, Herbert Hensley. *The Oxford Groups.*
Hopkins, C. Howard. *John R. Mott, 1865-1955: A Biography*

Jones, E. Stanley. *Along the Indian Road.*
Jones, E. Stanley. *Christ and Human Suffering*
Jones, E. Stanley. *The Choice before Us*

Landau, Rom. *God Is My Adventure*
Laymon, Charles M. *A Primer of Prayer*
Ligon, Ernest M. *The Psychology of Christian Personality.*
Lupton,, Dilworth. *Religion Says You Can*

Mann, A. Chester. *F. B. Meyer*
Meyer, F. B. *"Five Musts" of the Christian Life*
Meyer, F. B. *The Secret of Guidance*
Moody, D. L. *Heaven*
Moody, Dwight L. *Secret Power*
Moody, Emma Fitt. *Day by Day with D. L. Moody.*
Moody, Paul D. *My Father: An Intimate Portrait*
Moody, William R. *The Life of Dwight L. Moody*
Mott, John R., ed. *Evangelism for the World Today*

166

Mott, John R., *Five Decades and a Forward View*
Mott, John R. *The Evangelization of the World in This Generation.*
Mott, John R. The Larger Evangelism.
Mott, John R. The Pastor and Modern Missions.

Niebuhr, Reinhold. Christianity and Power Politics.
Norborg, Sverre. God-Controlled Lives.

Pollock, J. C. *Moody: A Biographical Portrait*

Raynor, Frank. *The Finger of God*
Redwood, Hugh. *Kingdom Come.*
Rosell, Garth M., and Richard A. G. Dupuis. *The Memoirs of Charles G. Finney.*

Sheean, Vincent. *Lead Kindly Light*
Strachey, Ray. *Group Movements of the Past and Experiments in Guidance.*
Streeter, Burnett Hillman. *Reality: A New Correlation of Science & Religion.*

Trine, Ralph Waldo. *The Man Who Knew.*
Trumbull, H. Clay. *Individual Work for Individuals.*
Trumbull, H. Clay. *The Evangelization of the World.*

Wells, Amos R. *Expert Endeavor*
Werber, Eva Bell. *Quiet Talks with the Master*
Williams, R. Llewelyn. *God's Great Plan*
Wilson, Jan R., and Judith A. Wilson. *Addictionary*

The Original Manuscript [of *Alcoholics Anonymous*], 1938.

[A set of Dick B.'s books is also included]

The George Vondermuhll, Jr., Collection

[Total number of books: 569]

About George Vondermuhll, Jr.

George Albert Vondermuhll, Jr. was born in New York City on August 14, 1912. He attended St. Mark's School in Southboro, Massachusetts, graduating in 1931 and received an AB degree from Princeton University in 1935. He was with the Postgraduate Institute of International Studies at Geneva from 1935-1936. He was Research Assistant at the International Labor Office in Geneva from 1936-1937, and was then on the editorial staff of Business Week Magazine until 1939.

He became a field representative of Moral Re-Armament, Inc. in 1940. He served in Germany from 1947 to 1950, Europe and Asia from 1955-1956 and 1961 to 1965. He was corporate secretary of MRA from 1969 to 1977, and a director from 1975 to 1981.

He is a member of the First Congregational Church of Litchfield, Connecticut, and served as a deacon from 1979 to 1984.

Mrs. W. Irving Harris, wife of Sam Shoemaker's assistant minister suggested about ten years ago that I get in touch with George. She said he kept the Shoemaker faction informed of activities in MRA after the Buchman/Shoemaker split. T. Willard Hunter described George as a Moral Re-Armament "pack rat" who kept in touch with everybody and kept everything he found that pertained to MRA work. When the request came for Oxford Group/MRA books and materials, George responded with hundreds of items he made available for this project.

Throughout the last ten fifteen years of my research, George has supplied names, addresses, contacts, books, and resources pertaining to MRA and the Oxford Group. He has spent time with me and communicated by mail, phone, and internet. He has endorsed my books and continually encouraged my research work.

Books, Pamphlets, and Periodicals from George Vondermuhll, Jr.
Books

Arnold, Minister President Karl (Foreword), ROAD FROM RUIN. Dusseldorf, 1949, paper, pp.86. Graphic photos and text of post-war Germany and the impact of the MRA plays The Good Road and The Forgotten Factor. (11 copies)

Begbie, Harold, LIFE CHANGERS. New York and London, Putnam, 1927, cloth, pp. 142. First US edition of the first book about Frank Buchman and his work, published in England in 1923. Individual chapters about FB and half a dozen of his early recruits at Oxford. (one copy)
Ibid. 11th Edition, London, Mills & Boon, 1932, cloth, pp.188, including article "The Groups" by John McCook Roots. (one copy)

Belk, (The Rev. Dr.) J. B. (Sr.), A FAITH TO MOVE NATIONS. New York, Moral Re-Armament, Inc., paper, pp. 126. Sermons, selected by him for publication as a challenge to other ministers. (57 copies)

Bradley, Francis, THE AMERICAN PROPOSITION--A New Type of Man. New York, Moral Re-Armament, Inc., cloth, pp.178, index. The role of faith in the founding and history of the US. (4 copies)

Buchman, Frank N. D., REMAKING THE WORLD. Abridged preliminary editions of his speeches. (1) London, Wm. Heinemann, 1941, paper, pp.64. Forewords by Arthur Baker & J.P. Thornton-Duesbery (one copy) (2) Washington, DC, Moral Re-Armament, 1945, paper, pp.32. Memorable foreword by Hon. C.J. Hambro, president of the Norwegian Parliament. (one copy)

Buchman, Frank N. D., REMAKING THE WORLD. London, Blandford Press, various editions 1953-1961, pp. 142, with settings and contemporary comment, appendices, index. (9 cloth, 2 paper)

Campbell, Paul, and Howard, Peter, AMERICA NEEDS AN IDEOLOGY. London, Frederick Muller, 1957, pp. 184. Update on MRA around the world. (9 cloth, 16 paper)

Campbell, Paul and Howard, Peter, REMAKING MEN. New York, Arrowhead Books, 1954, cloth, pp. 128. The why and the how. (2 copies)

Campbell, Paul, and Howard, Peter, A STORY OF EFFECTIVE STATESMANSHIP. London, Blandford Press, 1956, cloth, pp. 86. The life, achievements, challenges, example of St. Paul. (55 copies)

Channer, Maj. Gen. George O. DeR., IDEOLOGICAL OFFENSIVE. London, 1961, paper, pp.76. Report on MRA in the armed forces. (1 copy)

Christensen, Ane, & Rasmussen, HOW TO CREATE A SING-OUT. Los Angeles, Pace Publications, 1968 (6th edition), paper, pp. 120 (12 copies)

Copeman, Fred, REASON IN REVOLT. London, Blandford Press, 1948, cloth, pp. 236. Autobiography of a revolutionary British worker. (1 copy)

Dennison,Les, THE MAN FROM NO PLACE. South Wales Voice, undated, paper, pp. 32. Biography of a union shop steward in search of a revolution, who found one on his own building site. (13 copies)

DuMaurier, Daphne, COME WIND, COME WEATHER. New York, Doubleday Doran, 1941, paper, pp. 80. The famous novelist reports about ordinary citizens on Britain's WW II home front. With introductory letter to American readers. (19 copies)

Entwistle, Basil, and Roots, John McCook, MRA -- WHAT IS IT? Los Angeles, Pace Publications, 1967, pp. 243. Authoritative history, documents, photographs. (150 copies)

Evans, Trevor,(illustrator), THE PRODIGAL SON. London, Blandford Press, undated. Child's painting book. (3 copies)

Foss, Hannen, Ed., THE RICHES OF CHRISTMAS. London, Blandford Press, 1951, cloth, pp. 204. Lovely anthology, illustrated. (1 copy)

"Hannen & Cameron" -- Foss, Hannen, & Cameron-Johnson, William, WHERE DO WE GO FROM HERE? London, undated, pp.64. Cartoon guide to "the world we live in , and what to do about it." (hardback 42 copies, paper 16, large-format paper 3)

Gain, Geoffrey, A BASINFUL OF REVOLUTION -- Tod Sloan's Story. London, Moral Re-Armament, 1957, paper, pp. 64."Watchmaker by trade, agitator by nature." (6 copies)

Up to Gain, Geoffrey, GV has print-out. From Hansford, Robert on, everything was lost by accident 6/7/00. So here goes again:

Hansford, Robert, author, and Cameron-Johnson, William, illustrator, WHO SAYS WE'RE BUFFALOED? Mackinac Island, Mich., Moral Re-Armament, 1964, paper, pp .32. Hilarious words and drawings challenge reader to be a world-remaker. (15 copies)

Hardiman, James W.,Ed. THE CROWNING EXPERIENCE -- Book of the Film. New York, Random House, 1960, boards, pp.40, stills in full color, notes on actors, contemporary comment. Based on the life of African-American educator and presidential adviser Mary McLeod Bethune, and starring opera mezzo-soprano Muriel Smith, dramatizes the wear of ideas in the hearts of individuals and nations. (24 copies)

Hicks, Roger, LETTERS TO PARSI. London, Blandford Press, 1950, cloth, pp.84. Answering a young Indonesian prince's questions about Christianity. (4 copies)

Howard, Peter., BRITAIN AND THE BEAST. London, Heinemann, 1967, pp.128. Pungent pictures of the assaults on national character, and a call for an uprising of the country's best. (20 cloth, 5 paper)

Howard, Peter, BEAVERBROOK. London, ... 196...., pp. .... A close friend's evaluation of, and challenge to, the Canadian-born British press lord and WW II head of aircraft production. (20 copies)

Howard, Peter, DESIGN FOR DEDICATION. Chicago, Henry Regnery, 1964, pp.192. World-ranging speeches delivered across US and Canada Dec.-Mar. 1963-4. (40 cloth, 104 paper)

Howard, Peter, FIGHTERS EVER. London, Wm. Heinemnn, 1941, pp. 96. This sequel to "Innocent Men" tells th inside story of the Oxford Group's God and freedom -- an of the opposition. (3 copies)

Howard, Peter, FRANK BUCHMAN'S SECRET. Garden City, NY, Doubleday, 1961, cloth, pp.95. Assessment of his life and influence, written right after his death. (93 copies)

Howard, Peter, AN IDEA TO WIN THE WORLD. London, Blandford Press, 1958, paper, pp. 128. Account of the Statesmen's Mission around the world with the musical "The Vanishing Island." (2 copies)

Howard, Peter. IDEAS HAVE LEGS. London, Frederick Muller, 1945, cloth, pp. 190. In the perspective of his own eventful life, Howard illuminates the world struggle of ideas and the side which must win. (1 copy)

Ibid., New York, Coward-McCann, 1946. (1 copy)

Howard, Peter, INNOCENT MEN. London, Wm. Heinemann, 1941.Cloth, pp.164. Assigned to expose a supposed subversive group, reporter discovers the opposite. (9 copies)

Howard, Peter, MEN ON TRIAL. London, Blandford Press, 1945, cloth, pp. 108. Candid sketches of British political leaders, 1939-45, and their post-war potential. (8 copies)

Howard, Peter, THAT MAN FRANK BUCHMAN. London, Blandford Press, 1946. Cloth, pp.110, photos, two portraits in color. "The best-known, unknown man of the age, and the force for inspired democracy he mobilized. (7 copies)

Howard, Peter, TOMORROW WILL BE TOO LATE. Los Angeles, 1965, paper, pp.64. His speeches at 17 U.S. universities, Nov.-Dec. 1964. (140 copies)

Howard, Peter, THE WORLD REBUILT. New York, Duell, Sloan & Pearce, 1951, paper, pp.250. The true story of Frank Buchman and the achievements of Moral Re-Armament. (6 copies)

Howard, Peter, & Broadhurst, Cecil, THE VANISHING ISLAND. 1955. Text of the musical play dramatizing the struggle between disciplined dictatorship and indulgent democracy. Went around world with Statesmen's Mission. (Regular edition, 13 copies; special edition to accompany Phlips LP Recording, 7 copies)

Howard, Peter & Anthony, SPACE IS SO STARTLING. London, 1962, paper, pp.22, with photographs. . Lyrics of the musical play, dramatizing a boy's nightmare of his divided family and the divided world, with a spaceman bringing the solution.

Howell, Edward, ESCAPE TO LIVE. London, Longmans, Green, 1947/50, paper, pp.178, maps. Shot down over Crete, a British pilot finds new direction for his life, starting with a miraculous escape from prison hospital in German-occupied Greece. (6 copies)

Langcroft, Peggy, THEIRS BY RIGHT. London, Blandford Press, undated, paper, pp.80. Heartening change in a once-heartless home for homeless children. (2 copies)

Lean, Garth, BRAVE MEN CHOOSE. London, Blandford Press, 1961, cloth, pp. 210. The "real revolutionaries" of 19th Century Britain's political, industrial, and social life. (12 copies)

Lean, Garth, JOHN WESLEY, ANGLICAN. London, Blandford Press, 1964, paper, pp. 130. Life of the man whose work is credited with saving Britain from a French-style revolution. (5 copies)

Lunn, Sir Arnold, & Lean, Garth, THE NEW MORALITY. London, Blandford Press, 1964, pp. 154, indexed. Chronicles the concerted attack, especially in the mass media, upon the moral foundations of Britain, and the appeasing response of too many Christians. (Cloth, 2 copies; paper, 36 copies)

Lunn, Sir Arnold, & Lean, Garth, THE CULT OF SOFTNESS. London, Blandford Press, 1965, pp.164, with index. The fight to capture the mind and culture of Britain for secularism. (1 copy)

Maccassey, Sir Lyndon, Q.C. (Foreword), THE OXFORD GROUP AND ITS WORK OF MORAL RE-ARMAMENT. London, 1954, paper, pp. 86. Concise chapters on history, structure, activities , criticisms.

Statements by public figures. (2 copies)

Morrison, John (M.), THE STATESMAN'S DREAM and Other Poems. Edinburgh, Collins, 1957, cloth, pp.198. Poems, profound to whimsical, of and for individuals and issues in the battle for change in men and nations. (one copy)

Mowat, R. C., (Editor), REPORT ON MORAL RE-ARMAMENT. London, Blandford Press, 1955, paper, pp. ?, photos. With statements by world-wide civic, and especially religious, leaders. (5 copies)

Mowat, R.C., CLIMAX OF HISTORY. London, Blandford Press, 1951, cloth, pp. ? . Civilizations in history, an the crucial choices facing ours. (6copies)

Mowat, R. C., THE MESSAGE OF FRANK BUCHMAN. London, Blandford Press 1951, paper, pp. ? . A study guide to "Remaking the World." (3 copies)

Orglmeister, Peter, AN IDEOLOGY FOR TODAY. Brazil, 1962, paper, pp. 24. Dilemmas facing Catholics and the Church, and the contribution of MRA. (60 copies)

Perry, Edward T., GOD CAN BE REAL. New York, Moral Re-Armament, Inc., 1969, paper, pp.38. Simple, practical steps to that reality, offered by an experienced international educator. (130 copies -- plus 40 seconds)

Phillimore, Miles, JUST FOR TODAY. USA, 1940, paper, pp. 72 (many purposefully blank). Favorite sentences, hymns, poems of Frank Buchman,
quoted by him at Tahoe retreat. (3 copies)

Reader's Digest, May 1967 issue complete. Includes article by Hall, Clarence W., SING OUT, AMERICA! (1 COPY)

Reader's Digest, January 1968 issue complete. Includes article by Hall, Clarence W., THEY'RE OUT TO REMAKE THE WORLD. (1 copy)

Roote, John McCook, Ed., MODERNIZING AMERICA - Action Papers of National Purpose (by MRA spokesmen from around the world). Los Angeles, Pace Publications 1965, paper, pp.160. (25 copies)

Skard, Oyvind, IDEOLOGICAL STRATEGY. London, Blandford Press, 1954, paper, pp.80. Norwegian industrial and military psychologist asks whether democracy can take offensive and win people subject to totalitarian governments. (2 copies)

Slattery, Sarah Lawrence, I CHOOSE. Winchester, Mass., University Press, 1969.; Cloth, pp. 180. Daughter, sister, and widow of Episcopal bishops--and first woman in Massachusetts to drive an automobile -- emerges into a fascinating life as part of a worldwide Christian revolution. (41 copies)

Thornhill, Alan, GIVE A DOG A BONE. Coloring book, illustrated by Wm. Cameron-Johnson, of the pantomime that played for many London holiday seasons. Paper, pp. ? . (17 copies)

Thornhill, Alan, ONE FIGHT MORE. London, Frederick Muller, 1943, cloth, pp. 64, illustrated. The last eventful years of Prof. B.H. Streeter, renowned Oxford biblical scholar. (one copy)

Twitchell, Kenaston, FRANK BUCHMAN - Twentieth Century Catalyst. Allentown, Lehigh County Historical Society. Reprint of Society Proceedings, 1974, pp. 16. Speech vividly sketching FB's origins, life, and legacy, by one of his closest colleagues. (3 copies)

Twitchell, Kenaston, REGENERATION IN THE RUHR. Princeton, NJ, 1981, paper, pp. 88. Behind-the-scenes account of how in the industrial heart of post-WW II Germany the forces of inspired democracy routed those of Moscow-directed communism. (167 copies)

Usher-Wilson, Rodney N., NO HUMAN AFFAIR. Princeton, NJ, 1984, pp. 202, with maps, indices. Detailed study of the dramatic life and message of a fanatical foe of Christianity who became its all-time most effective proponent -- St. Paul. (19 copies)

Usher-Wilson, Rodney N., SUICIDE OR ADORATION. New York,

Vantage Press, 1971. Cloth, pp.67. In a technological age, the search for supreme reality and its survival in individuals and society. (ca. 200 copies)

Usher-Wilson, Rodney N., WORSHIP IS A MODERN NECESSITY. New York, Moral Re-Armament, Inc., 1975., paper, pp.32. In our fragmented, secular society, the search for meaning and harmony. (200 copies)

Valentine, Denys, illustrator, JESUS & ZACCHAEUS. London, Blandford Press, undated. A Blandford Very First Bible Painting Book. (7 copies)

Wilson, Mary, GOD'S PLAN IN HISTORY. London, Grosvenor Books, 1960-1983. Vols. 1 through 5 - from the creation to the late Middle Ages. (1 set of 5 volumes)

Wolridge-Gordon, Anne, PETER HOWARD LIFE AND LETTERS. London, The Oxford Group, 1969, pp. 318. The dramatic life, private and public, of the cynical political columnist turned winning practicer and propagator of revolutionary Christianity. (7 cloth, 1 paper)

Anonymous, ASSEMBLY OF THE AMERICAS for the Moral Re-Armament of the Hemisphere. Petropolis, Brazil, 1961, paper, pp. 24. (5 copies)

Anon., DEMOCRACY'S INSPIRED IDEOLOGY. Undated, but obviously published in USA 1946 or 1947. Spiral bound, pp. 40. Largely photos and newspaper reports and editorials of MRA in the USA before and through WW II. (6 copies)

Anon., THE FIGHT TO SERVE. Moral Re-Armament, Inc., 1943, paper, pp.96. MRA and WW II, with special reference to MRA's full time volunteer workers. (2 copies)

Anon., FRANK BUCHMAN EIGHTY. London, 1958, cloth, pp. 214. Messages, photos, events celebrating the birthday. (5 copies)

Anon., AN IDEA TAKES WINGS. Miami, Florida, 1951,paper, pp.72, illustrated. The Miami-based airlines experience MRA and take it to the world. Exhilarating. (Also made into a movie.) (15 copies)

Anon., MIAMI ASSEMBLY REPORT. 1950, paper, pp. ? .Focus on Latin America, in ? framework of labor and management in the Miami-based airlines and other industries.

Anon., SONGS FOR MORAL RE-ARMAMENT. Words only. OG and MRA songs plus favorite hymns. 1944, paper, pp.40. (2 copies)

Ibid., Mackinac Edition, including US and Canadian patriotic songs. 1946.
paper, pp. 64. (One copy)

Anon., SONGS OF THE RISING TIDE. London, The Oxford Group, 1938. paper, pp.50. Full-size , words and music. (12 copies)

Anon., A SUMMIT CONFERENCE FOR THE MORAL RE-ARMAMENT OF THE WORLD. Caux, 1958, paper, pp. 50. A summary report. (2 copies)

Anon., YOU CAN DEFEND AMERICA, foreword by Gen. John J. Pershing. Washington, Judd & Detwiler, 1941,paper, pp. 16. Handbook for the home front. (15 copies)

Periodicals

A. Moral Re-Armament--in chronological order

NEW WORLD NEWS, Los Angeles
1947: 1 each for Jan., Apr., Dec.; 2 for Oct.; 3 each for May, June

1948: 5 for each month
1949: 5 each Jan, Feb, Mar, May, June, July; 4 Apr; 3 Aug; 1 Oct
1950: 3 June, July, Aug.

MRA INFORMATION SERVICE, Los Angeles
Published twice a month. Bound and indexed.
Vol. I   June 1952-May 1953   (2 copies)
Vol. II June 1953-May 1954   (2 copies)
Vol. III June 1954-May 1955   (2 copies)
Vol. IV June 1955-May 1956   (2 copies)
Vol. VI June 1957-May 1958   (3 copies)
Vol. VII June 1958-May 1959   (2 copies)
Vol. VIII June 1959-May 1960   (2 copies)
Vol. XII June 1963-Aug.1964   (2 copies)

MRA INFORMATION SERVICE, London
Weekly
(1) Scattered issues, 1965,1967-69, 1972
(2) Complete, Jan 1968-Dec 1970 (in spring binder)
(3) Complete, Jan 1971-Dec 1973   "   "   "
(4) Complete, Jan 1974-Dec 1976   "   "   "

TOMORROW'S AMERICAN, Los Angeles Weekly
Vol. 1, various issues, 1964-5, also complete in spring binder
Vol. 2,   "   "   1965-6,   "   "   " "   "
Vol. 3, 1966-7, complete in spring binder
==name changed to
TOMORROW'S AMERICAN NEWS, Los Angeles
Vol.4, 1967
Vol.5, 1968
Vol.6, 1969

PERSPECTIVE, Up With People, Los Angeles
Newsletter, every two weeks, 1967-71

UP WITH PEOPLE NEWS, Los Angeles
April 1971 - May 1974
September 1974-Fall 1976

Pamphlets, Programs, Articles, Single Speeches (from 2 to 20 copies each) by the following:

Buchman, Frank N.D.
Campbell, Paul
Howard, Peter
Jaeger, Bill
Martin, Morris
Oberlander, Theodor
Pinsent, Roy
Thornton-Duesbery, J.P.
Wilson, Mary
Wood, Lawson
Up With People
Anonymous

Books and/or Pamphlets in Languages other than English

Larger selections: French, German

Others: Arabic, Danish, Dutch, Finnish, Greek, Iranian, Norwegian, Portuguese, Russian, Spanish, Swedish, Turkish

Books from the Moral Re-Armament (MRA) Headquarters

[Total number of books: 52]

About Moral Re-Armament

The Moral Re-Armament of today is not the First Century Christian Fellowship, the Oxford Group, or even the Moral Re-Armament of the 1920's and 1930's, or of its founder Dr. Frank N. D. Buchman, or of his chief American lieutenant, The Rev. Canon Samuel M. Shoemaker, Jr., D.D., S.T.D. The structure is different. The objectives are different. The present-day leaders are mostly different. And its techniques are different, as are its areas of outreach.

For one thing, there are several different legal entities. One is The Oxford Group in Great Britain. Another is the governing entity at Caux in Switzerland. And there is Moral Re-Armament, Inc. in the United States. All, however, are in close touch and are mutually supportive. The M.R.A. of "God Control," of "guidance," of "life-changing," of "sharing," of a "second birth," of "Christian Fellowship," and of "God-consciousness" that so marked the work of the 1920's and 1930's, that earned the criticism of the Roman Catholic Church, and that caused Bill Wilson to be less than candid about A.A.'s Oxford Group origins are gone. The Four Absolutes are mentioned, but seldom in the context of Jesus Christ. Restitution is important, but has given way to the phrase "reconciliation and forgiveness." And the Protestant flavor of the Groups that caused the Roman Church to condemn them as "Buchmanism" has been replaced with convocations involving a Roman Catholic Cardinal, the Jewish Rabbi of London, the Dali Lama, and many in Japan and elsewhere who have no allegiance to Christianity.

But the loyalty to, interest in, and approbation of the leadership of Dr. Frank Buchman are still very much present. Also, though the earliest activists are now in their late 80's and 90's, many are still active voices for MRA and for the work of Frank Buchman. Many attend MRA functions in the United States and Switzerland and are in a first-name, frequent-contact situation. Furthermore, many have written books about their own lives, about Buchman, and about the work of Moral Re-Armament. And the author Dick B. has found almost all to be intensely interested in the original relationship between Alcoholics Anonymous and the Oxford Group.

Fortunately, the author Dick B. was able to meet personally with, speak by telephone with, or frequently correspond with almost every early Oxford Group leader still alive and competent in the early 1990's when Dick began his work. These included the British contingent (Garth D. Lean, of Oxford, Frank Buchman's biographer; Garth's colleague at Oxford, Michael Hutchinson; Kenneth Belden of England, a prolific Oxford Group writer; Dr. Robin Mowat, professor and writer; Sidney Cook, writer). They included the early American activists (Eleanor Forde Newton, who wrote The Guidance of God; James Draper Newton, who wrote Uncommon Friends; Harry Almond, who wrote Foundations for Faith; George Vondermuhll, Jr., long the corporate secretary of Moral Re-Armament; T. Willard Hunter, Oxford Group activist, writer, and orator; Charles Haines who was one of the earliest American workers; L. Parks Shipley, Sr., who was active around the world in Oxford Group causes; Mrs. W. Irving Harris, wife of Sam Shoemaker's assistant minister; Howard Blake, who wrote Way to Go; and several others such as Leonard Firestone). It also included the group currently active in leadership: Richard Ruffin in Washington, D.C.; James Houck of Maryland, who knew Bill Wilson; Michael Henderson of Oregon, a very active writer of today; Bryan Hamlin of New England; and Mary Lean in London,

Our collections now include all of the basic Oxford Group books and pamphlets in use by or directly impacting on A.A.'s developmental people and years. These are Soul Surgery (laying out the "Five C.'s" which are the heart of the Twelve Steps); The God Who Speaks (the work of the distinguished biblical scholar B. H. Streeter); The Guidance of God by Eleanor Forde; When Man Listens by Cecil Rose; Quiet Time by Howard Rose; Sharing by J.P. Thornton-Duesbury; Remaking the World (a collection of Frank Buchman's speeches); The Principles of the Group by Sherwood Day; Life-Changers and Twice-Born Men by Harold Begbie; For Sinners Only by A. J. Russell; Life Began Yesterday by Stephen Foot; I Was A Pagan by Victor Kitchen, the Venture of Belief by Philip Marshall Brown; the many books of Roger Hicks; the basic summary by Miles G. W. Phillimore in 1940; and, of course, the many books of the Rev. Sam Shoemaker, and ideological summaries by "Bunny" Austin, Theophil Spoerri, and Peter Howard.

In March of 2000, Moral Re-Armament Headquarters in Washington, D.C., provided the following additional Oxford Group books which make the study of the ideas and movement a much easier task by the addition of some new books and the addition of several vital duplicates..

Books from the MRA Headquarters

Almond, Harry. *Foundations for Faith*. Ohio: Barbour, 1997. Part of *The Little Library*.

Austin, H. W. "Bunny." *Frank Buchman As I Knew Him*. London: Grosvenor Books, 1975.

——. *Moral Rearmament: The Battle for Peace*. London William Heinemann, 1938.

Barnes, Stanley. *200 Million Hungry Children*. London: Grosvenor, 1990.

Belden, K. D. *Meeting Moral Re-Armament*. London: Grosvenor Books, 1979.

Bradley, Francis. *The American Proposition: A New Type of Man*. New York: Moral Re-Armament, Inc., 1977.

Buchman, Frank N. D. *Remaking the World*. New and rev. ed. London: Blandford Press, 1961. (2 copies.)

Buchman, Frank N. D. *Remaking* the World. New and rev. ed. London: Blandford Press. 1953.

Campbell, Paul. *The Art of Remaking Men*. Bombay: Himmat Publications Trust, 1970.

——. *Modernising Man*. London: Grosvenor Books, 1968.

——, and Peter Howard. *America Needs an Ideology*. London: Frederic Muller, 1957.

——, and Peter Howard. *The Strategy of Saint Paul*. London: Grosvenor Books, 1956.

——, and Peter Howard. *Remaking Men*. New York: Arrowhead Books, 1954.

Du Maurier, Daphne. *Come Wind, Come Weather*. New York: Doubleday, Doran, 1941.

Ekman, Gosta. *Experiment with God: Frank Buchman Reconsidered*. London: Hodder and Stoughton, 1971.

Entwistle, Basil. *Japan's Decisive Decade: How a Determined Minority Changed the Nation's Course in the 1950's*. London: Grosvenor

Books, 1985.

——. *Making Cities Work: How Two People Mobilized a Community to Meet Its Needs*. Pasadena, CA: Hope Publishing, 1990.

Evans, Claire. *Freewoman*. Oxford: Becket Publications, 1979.

Frank Buchman 80 by His Friends. London: Blandford Press, 1958.

Grogan, William. *John Riffe of the Steelworkers: American Labor Statesman*. New York: Coward-McCann, 1959.

Guldseth, Mark O. *Streams: The Flow of Inspiration from Dwight Moody to Frank Buchman*. Alaska: Fritz Creek Studios, 1982. (2 copies.)

Hagedorn, Hermann. *The Bomb That Fell on America*. New York: Association Press, 1948.

Hicks, Roger. *Letters to Parsi from Roger Hicks*. London: Blandford Press, 1950.

——. *The Lord's Prayer and Modern Man: A Contemporary Approach*. London: Blandford Press, 1967.

——. *The Endless Adventure*. London: Blandford Press, 1964. (2 copies.)

Howard, Peter. *An Idea to Win the World*. London: Blandford Press, 1955.

——. *Britain and the Beast*. London: Heinemann, 1963.

——. *Design for Dedication*. Chicago: Henry Regnery, 1964.

——. *Frank Buchman's Secret*. New York: Doubleday, 1961. (2 copies.)

——. *Fighters Ever*. London: William Heinemann, 1941.

——. *Ideas Have Legs*. London: Frederick Muller, 1945.

——. *That Man Frank Buchman*. London: Blandford Press, 1946.

——. *The World Rebuilt: The True Story of Frank Buchman and the Achievements of Moral Re-Armament*. New York: Duell, Sloan, and Pearce, 1951.

Lean, Garth. *Brave Men Choose*. London: Blandford Press, 1961.

——. *Frank Buchman: A Life*. London: Constable, 1985.

——. *God's Politician: William Wilberforce's Struggle*. London: Darton, Longmann & Todd, 1980.

——. *On the Tail of a Comet: The Life of Frank Buchman*. Colorado Springs: Helmers & Howard, 1988.

Lunn, Arnold, and Garth Lean. *Christian Counter-Attack*. London:

Blandford Press, 1969.

——. *The New Morality*. London: Blandford Press, 1964.

Morrison, J. M. *Honesty and God*. Edinburgh: The Saint Andrew Press, 1966.

Mottu, Philippe. The Story of Caux: From La Belle Epoque to Moral Re-Armament. London: Grosvenor Books, 1969.

Philips, Frederik. *15 Years with Philips: An Industrialist's Life*. London: Blandford Press, 1978.

Piguet, Charles, and Michel Sentis. *The World at the Turning: Experiments with Moral Re-Armament*. London: Grosvenor, 1982.

Slattery, Sarah Lawrence. *I Choose*. Winchester, MA.: The University Press, 1969.

Spoerri, Theophil. *Dynamic out of Silence: Frank Buchman's Relevance Today*. London: Grosvenor Books, 1976.

Thornton-Duesbery, J. P. *The Open Secret of MRA: An Examination of Mr. Driberg's "Critical Examination" of Moral Re-Armament*. London: Blandford Press, 1964.

Vrooman, Lee. *The Faith That Built America*. New York: Arrowhead Books, 1955.

Walter, H. A. *Soul-Surgery: Some Thoughts on Incisive Personal Work*. 4th Ed. Oxford: The Oxford Group, 1932.

West, George. *The World That Works*. London: Blandford Press, n.d.

Where Do We Go from Here. N.p.: Duell, Sloan & Pearce, n.d.

The Dennis C. Collection

(49 Books)

About Dennis C.

Dennis C. is a recovered alcoholic who lives in Connecticut, is an active member of the fellowship of Alcoholics Anonymous, and has been sober for more than twenty-years. He has spent many years collecting items pertaining to the early history of Alcoholics Anonymous. His materials have come from a number of persons close to A.A. co-founder Bill Wilson, to Lois Burnham Wilson (co-founder of Al-Anon and wife of Bill Wilson), to A.A. co-founder Dr. Bob Smith, and to Dr. Bob's wife Anne Ripley Smith. These sources have made available to him more than one hundred audio tapes of speeches by Bill Wilson and a number of original manuscripts containing drafts of A.A. and Al-Anon literature. He has attended A.A. historian, A.A. archivist, and A.A. conference panels and discussions and spoken at several of them. He has accompanied Dick B. on a research trip to the Hartford Seminary Archives and has visited the home of Oxford Group founder Frank Buchman in Allentown, Pennsylvania, where many of Buchman's books and memoirs are on display. He gathered there an inventory of all of Frank Buchman's library located there. Recently, Dennis has been acquiring many of the Oxford Group books, Shoemaker books, and Christian books cited in Dick B.'s bibliographies. Dennis has visited A.A. archives at Bill Wilson's birthplace in East Dorset, Vermont; the Stepping Stones home of Bill and Lois Wilson at Bedford Hills, New York; and Dr. Bob's Home in Akron, Ohio. Also, the A.A. General Service Office archives in New York City. He counts Dr. Bob's daughter Sue Smith Windows and Ray G., the archivist at Dr. Bob's Home, as good friends and has spent substantial time and traveled with both to A.A. meetings and conferences.

Dennis has turned over forty-nine books to our Center as part of the Dick B. Historical Collections. The books in Dennis's collection supplement the materials in Dick B.'s own collections in the following ways: (1) They contain a number of books *about* the Oxford Group by commentators, critics, and scholars. (2) They contain some rare books by or about the early Oxford Group mentors such as Horace Bushnell, Henry Drummond, Dwight L. Moody, F.B. Meyer, John R. Mott, Robert E. Speer, and Henry B. Wright. (3) They contain a number of significant Christian books studied and recommended by A.A. founder Dr. Bob on Christian healing, Jesus Christ, prayer, love, the Church Fathers, and also on "new thought" ideas. The authors of books in this third group include George Barton, Charles Fillmore, Harry Emerson Fosdick, Gerald Heard,

James Moore Hickson, E. Stanley Jones, Toyohiko Kagawa, Frank Laubach, Charles M. Layman, Dilworth Lupton, F. L. Rawson, James Stalker, Thomas Troward, and Ethel R. Willitts. These books give excellent flavor to the non-Oxford Group Christian and religious literature that contributed to A.A. ideas.

The Dennis Cassidy Books

A.A. Sponsorship: Its Opportunities and Its Responsibilities. Cleveland, Ohio, 1944.

Barton, George A. *Jesus of Nazareth*
Bennett, John C. *Social Salvation.*
Braden, Charles Samuel. *These Also Believe.*
Browne, Lewis. *This Believing World.*
Bushnell, Horace. *The New Life.*

Cantrill, Hadley. *The Psychology of Social Movements.*
Chapman, J. Wilbur. *Life and Work of Dwight L. Moody.*
Cheney, Mary B. *Life and Letters of Horace Bushnell.*
Clapp, Charles. *Drinking's Not the Problem.*
Clapp, Charles, Jr. *The Big Bender.*
Clark, Walter Houston. *The Oxford Group: Its History and Significance.*
Crossman, R. H. S. *Oxford and The Groups.*
Crothers, Susan. *Susan and God.*

Driberg, Tom. *The Mystery of Moral Re-Armament.*
Drummond, Henry. *Essays and Addresses.*
Drummond, Henry. *The Changed Life.*
Drummond, Henry. *The Ideal Life.*

Eister, Allan W. *Drawing Room Conversion.*

Ferguson, Charles W. *The Confusion of Tongues.*
Fillmore, Charles. *Christian Healing.*
Findlay, James F., Jr. *Dwight L. Moody: American Evangelist.*
Fosdick, Harry Emerson. *A Great Time to Be Alive.*
Fosdick, Harry Emerson. *As I See Religion.*
Fosdick, Harry Emerson. *The Manhood of the Master.*

186

Gordon, S.D. *The Quiet Time*.
Grensted, L. W. *The Person of Christ*.
Grey, Jerry. *The Third Strike*.

Harnack, Adolph. *The Expansion of Christianity in the First Three Centuries*.
Heard, Gerald. A *Preface to Prayer*.
Henson, Herbert Hensley. *The Oxford Group Movement*.
Hickson, James Moore. *Heal the Sick*.
Hopkins, C. Howard. *John R. Mott*.
Howard, Peter. *Frank Buchman's Secret*.
Howard, Peter. *Fighters Ever*.
Howard, Peter. *Innocent Men*.
Howard, Peter. *Ideas Have Legs*.
Howard, Peter. *That Man Frank Buchman*.

Jones, E. Stanley. *Abundant Living*.
Jones, E. Stanley. *Christ at the Round Table*.
Jones, E. Stanley. *The Christ of the American Road*.
Jones, E. Stanley. *The Christ of the Mount*.

Kessell, Joseph. *The Road Back: A Report on Alcoholics Anonymous*.
Kagawa, Toyohiko. *Love: The Law of Life*.

Laubach, Frank. *Prayer (Mightiest Force in the World)*.
Layman, Charles M. *A Primer of Prayer*.
Lupton, Dilworth. *Religion Says You Can*.

Macintosh, Douglas C. *Personal Religion*.
Meyer, F. B. *Five Musts*.
Meyer, F. B. *The Secret of Guidance*.
Moody, William R. *The Life of D.L. Moody*.
Mott, John R. *The Evangelization of the World in This Generation*.
Mott, John R. *Five Decades and a Forward View*.

Nichols, Beverley. *The Fool Hath Said*.

Rawson, F. L. *The Nature of True Prayer*.

Raynor, Frank C. *The Finger of God.*
Russell, Arthur J. *One Thing I Know.*

Sangster, W. E. *God Does Guide Us.*
Smith, George Adam. *The Life of Henry Drummond.*
Speer, Robert E. *Studies of the Man Christ Jesus.*
Stalker, James. *The Life of Jesus Christ.*
Stewart, George, Jr. *Life of Henry B. Wright.*

The Fathers of the Church.
Troward, Thomas. *The Edinburgh Lectures on Mental Science.*

Uspenskii, Peter. *Tertium Organum.*

Weatherhead, Leslie D. *Discipleship.*
Weatherhead, Leslie D. *How Can I Find God?*
Weatherhead, Leslie D. *Psychology and Life.*
Willitts, Ethel R. *Healing in Jesus Name.*
Wilson, Jan R., and Judith A. Wilson. *Addictionary.*
Winslow, Jack C. *Church in Action.*

The Danny W. Collection

About Danny W.

Danny is a Christian, a recovered alcoholic, and a member of the film industry. He regularly attends a Christian church. And he is a hands-on member of Alcoholics Anonymous and an ardent pursuer of its spiritual history. He has spent long hours working with wet drunks and new AAs, recruiting the newcomers from detox centers, treatment facilities, and halfway houses.

Clean and sober for about a decade, this man has sponsored hundreds of AAs. His A.A. sponsor was Grace Moore Snyder, widow of AA pioneer Clarence Snyder, and leader of the Clarence Snyder retreats until her recent death. Danny was the leader of a Snyder retreat for AAs and their families in Southern California. He has been leading the A.A. Roots Revival Group for a number of years. He donated his home for the use of recovering AAs, who wanted to learn the Big Book, Twelve Steps, Bible, and early A.A. spiritual history and reside together.

Danny truly caught the history bug several years ago. He began traveling all over the United States for the purpose of knowing and interviewing families of the founders, AAs who were historians and writers and collectors. He has worked closely with Dick B. and a number of other historians and archivists over the years. He began developing an enormous library (without equal) in his home. And he roamed the United States, bookstores, and the internet to obtain first-rate historical materials, not only on the spiritual roots of the Twelve Step movement, but on its founders, participants, and the physical evidence about them. He traveled thousands of miles and spent tens of thousands of dollars out of his own income in order to collect books, booklets, pamphlets, papers, documents, correspondence, video tapes, audio tapes, pictures, photos, newspaper and magazine articles and then checked their importance and integrity with A.A. pioneers, founding families, archivists, collectors, historians and writers (including Dick).

There is little doubt that if his total collected materials were placed on the market for sale, their fair market value would be appraised at an amount in excess of one million dollars. And Danny made it possible for Dick to acquire almost all of this collection and make it a part of this project.

The Items Included in Danny's Collection

Every item that has come from Danny's collection is marked with a "D" in the foregoing inventory. It has been impossible to list and specifically describe each item in time for the placement of the inventory items. However, all of the materials have been assembled, shipped to Maui, and temporarily place in our Maui Historical Recovery Resource Center for eventual allocation to the various libraries. And Danny will probably be present to assist in identifying the items for the principal recipient libraries and centers.

In summary, the items we have in our possession from Danny's collection and library are:

40 historical binders, each of which is 4 inches wide, with the individual items carefully preserved in acetate folders, and including historical materials on A.A., Al-Anon, alcoholism, religion, medicine, the Bible, Quiet Time, Rev. Sam Shoemaker, the Oxford Group, the Oxford Group's mentors, Anne Smith (Dr. Bob's wife), Henrietta Seiberling, T. Henry and Clarace Williams, Clarence Snyder, Grace Snyder, and a host of early A.A. personalities and events. In addition, he assembled several bookshelves of material on temperance, WCTU, the Washingtonians, Emanuel Movement, anti-saloon league, prohibition, and writings of early temperance and prohibition speakers and activists. There is much "official" A.A. historical material include Conference Approved books, financial reports, Grapevine Articles, and the like. **These number approximately 8,800 items** (not pages, but items which often are pamphlets)

2,171 Books, Pamphlets and Articles

6 Boxes of Audio and Video Cassette Tapes containing A.A. speeches and historical matters.

2 Large Boxes of Pictures and Photographs.

Part 7
Our Advisory Council Supporting Members

Paul Wood, Ph.D., Honorary Chair: Former Pres. National Council on Alcoholism and Drug Dependence, Inc.; presently with Salvation Army (Ohio)

Hon. John F. Seiberling, Honorary Vice-Chair: Attorney, Former Congressman from Ohio; Director of University of Akron Peace Center; son of A.A. co-founder Henrietta Seiberling (Ohio).

Dick B., J.D., Chair: Retired Attorney, Author, active, recovered A.A. (Hawaii)

Jeffrey Boyd, M.D., M.Div., M.P.H., Vice Chair: Psychiatrist, ordained Episcopal Priest, President of New England Theological Association (Connecticut)

Dennis C. Archivist, A.A. historian, active, recovered, A.A. (Connecticut)

The Rev. Michael Liimatta; Education Director, Association of Gospel Missions (Missouri).

Robert J.: Leader, Good Book/Big Book Study Group; active, recovered A.A. (Hawaii)

Ozzie L.: President/Manager, The Wilson House; active, recovered A.A. (Vermont)

Jean La Cour, Ph. D., Dean, The NET Training Institute (Florida)

Clifford M., President, Alpha Omega Foundation; active, recovered alcoholic (Florida)

Dale M.: Leader, Spiritual Retreat for AAs and their Families; active, recovered A.A. (Wisconsin)

Karen Plavan, Ph.D., Asst. Professor of Counselor-Education-Chemical Dependency, The Penn State University; consultant to The Pittsburgh Leadership Foundation. (Pennsylvania)

The Rev. Charles Puskas, Jr., Ph. D., Former instructor, minister; author of Introduction to the New Testament (Minnesota).

Chris R.: Alumni Representative, La Hacienda Treatment Center; active, recovered A.A. (Texas)

Col. Mel Schulstad, USAF Retired; NCACII, Author, Co-Founder and Past President of National Association of Alcoholism and Drug Abuse Counselors; Co-founder of SOAR   (Washington)

Darvin Smith, M.D., Specialist in Addiction Medicine, Vice President of ISAAC, Director of Behavior Counseling Ministries, International, University of Nations, YWAM (Colorado)

Danny W., Leader A.A. Roots Revival Group, active, recovered A.A. (California).

Addenda

There is always a flow of new books coming my way. Also manuscripts. Some are recent recovery works. Some are recent A.A. history works. And some are by Christian writers who put their particular interpretations on the Steps, on A.A., and on recovery. These I have not included here because they have not directly been used in my own work. But you will never cease to see new information, new approaches, and new opinions. They keep us mentally alert, and they keep me busy.

However, there are three particular types of materials that have figured heavily in my recent thinking and writing. I'm going to suggest that you look elsewhere for the bibliographies because my research is still in progress and any list provided here would be incomplete in a year or so, if not already. Nonetheless, you ought to know some directions in which you might go to learn more about the Biblical history, cures, and potential of A.A. as it was, and as it could be.

The Healing Books

Of late, I have been very much interested in, and pursuing materials about healing. In several works–*God and Alcoholism, Cured, Why Early A.A. Succeeded, When Early Aas Were Cured and Why,* I've touched heavily on the first decade of A.A. where almost every one of the pioneers and the Akron group claimed their alcoholism had been cured.

This caused me to look at many religious books on the history of Divine healing from Old Testament Times, Apostlic Times, the New Testament, and church writings. They certainly fell into several categories: (1) the records of healings and miracles in the Old Testament. (2) the records of healings by Jesus. (3) the records of healing in the Book of Acts. (4) healings in the ante-nicene church period. (5) healings through the centuries of Christian church records to the 19th century. (5) the work of healers from 1800 to the founding of A.A. (6) the healing literature in Dr. Bob's Library and that he read and circulated. (7) present-day miracles and healings. A little time on the internet will lead you to some excellent sources, and the bibliographies in some of the leading writings on the subject will provide further study items.

You will find lots of these books covered in my recent titles, and you will see more as I continue my work.

Richard K.'s Work

Richard K.'s Research and Writing on the Pioneers, early cures in A.A., and the First Forty bring new life to A.A. history pursuits.

Richard is a young (36) cured A.A., a Christian, and a Bible student. He lives in Mass., and our publishing company has published the first three of what I hope will be his continuing work.

Check them out in Books in Print and through the internet. He may have stopped writing and publishing, but these are the important volumes he provided to me and which I use in talks and in my own work:

K., Richard. A *New Light: The First Forty: A Chronological Survey of th Early A.A. Pioneers (December 1934-April 1939)*. Now Appendix One of New Freedom (below).
_____. *New Freedom: Reclaiming Alcoholics Anonymous*. Self-published, 2005.
_____. *So You Think Drunks Can't Be Cured: Press Releases by Witnesses to the Cure*. Haverhill, MA: Golden Text Publishing Company, 2003.

United Christian Endeavor Society

There are many important works on Christian Endeavor. Dr. Francis Clark, its founder, wrote copiously and provides lots of the answers we sought on what Christian Endeavor was all about. Amos Wells was editor of CE publications and wrote some excellent materials on meetings and principles. The evangelist Dwight L. Moody had a number of pieces published by CE. The English clergyman F. B. Meyer held some important posts and made some important contributions. We were surprised to see that the famous book *In His Steps* by Sheldon was much read and very useful in providing information about CE.

There is a huge archives collection I very much want to see, acquire, and have contributed to the Griffith House Library, and there are many newspapers and local church logs that will provide a fine picture of what Dr. Bob was learning and doing in his Christian Endeavor days in Vermont.

You will find some of the preliminary references in my new title, *The James Club and The Original A.A. Program's Absolute Essentials*.

Biblical Research

To understand the Bible better, there is an enormous amount of work to be done on manuscripts, versions, and commentaries. My son Ken is an ordained minister and has been researching the Word of God and teaching about it for several decades. He helps me with my A.A. history books and writings; and I hope to work with him on the Bible materials. As he does and I do this work, you'll find the results posted on the web and hopefully in titles and articles by my son.

New Biographies

There is a constant flow of new biographies of A.A. personalities now being published, but two I have found very useful are these:

Borchert, William G. *The Lois Wilson Story: When Love Is Not Enough.* Center City, MN: Hazelden, 2005.
Brown, Sally and David R. *Mrs Marty Mann: The First Lady of Alcoholics Anonymous.* Center City, MN: Hazelden, 2001.
Hunter, T. Willard. *Busdrivers Never Get Anywhere: A Rendezvous with the Twentieth Century.* Claremont, CA: Regina Books, n.d.
Mitchel, Dale. Silkworth: *The Little Doctor Who Loved Drunks.* Center City, MN: Hazelden, 2002.

About the Author

Dick B. writes books on the spiritual roots of Alcoholics Anonymous. They show how the basic and highly successful biblical ideas used by early AAs can be valuable tools for success in today's A.A. His research can also help the religious and recovery communities work more effectively with alcoholics, addicts, and others involved in Twelve Step programs.

The author is an active, recovered member of A.A.; a retired attorney; and a Bible student. He has sponsored more than one hundred men in their recovery from alcoholism. Consistent with A.A.'s traditions of anonymity, he uses the pseudonym "Dick B."

He has had twenty-eight titles published including: *Dr. Bob and His Library*; *Anne Smith's Journal, 1933-1939*; *The Oxford Group & Alcoholics Anonymous*; *The Akron Genesis of Alcoholics Anonymous*; *The Books Early AAs Read for Spiritual Growth*; *New Light on Alcoholism: God, Sam Shoemaker, and A.A.*; *Courage to Change* (with Bill Pittman); *Cured: Proven Help for Alcoholics and Addicts*; *The Good Book and The Big Book: A.A.'s Roots in the Bible*; *That Amazing Grace: The Role of Clarence and Grace S. in Alcoholics Anonymous*; *Good Morning!: Quiet Time, Morning Watch, Meditation, and Early A.A.*; *Turning Point: A History of Early A.A.'s Spiritual Roots and Successes*, *Hope!: The Story of Geraldine D., Alina Lodge & Recovery; Utilizing Early A.A.'s Spiritual Roots for Recovery Today; The Golden Text of A.A.; By the Power of God; God and Alcoholism; Making Known the Biblical History of A.A.; Why Early A.A. Succeeded*; *Comments of Dick B. at The First Nationwide A.A. History Conference; Henrietta Seiberling: Ohio's Lady with a Cause;* and *The James Club*. The books have been the subject of newspaper articles and reviews in *Library Journal*, *Bookstore Journal*, *The Living Church*, *Faith at Work*, *Sober Times*, *Episcopal Life*, *Recovery News*, *Ohioana Quarterly*, *The PHOENIX*, and *The Saint Louis University Theology Digest.* They are listed in the biographies of major addiction center, religion, and religious history sites. He has published over 150 articles on his subject, most posted on the internet.

Dick is the father of two sons (Ken and Don) and has two granddaughters. As a young man, he did a stint as a newspaper reporter. He attended the University of California, Berkeley, where he received his A.A. degree with Honorable Mention, majored in economics, and was elected to Phi Beta Kappa in his Junior year. In the United States Army, he was an Information-Education Specialist. He received his A.B. and J.D. degrees from Stanford University, and was Case Editor of the Stanford Law Review. Dick became interested in Bible study in his childhood Sunday School and was much inspired by his mother's almost daily study of Scripture. He joined, and was president of, a Community Church affiliated with the United Church of Christ. By 1972, he was studying the origins of the Bible and began traveling abroad in pursuit of that subject. In 1979, he became much involved in a Biblical research, teaching, and fellowship ministry. In his community life, he was president of a merchants' council, Chamber of Commerce, church retirement center, and homeowners' association. He served on a public district board and has held offices in a service club.

In 1986, he was felled by alcoholism, gave up his law practice, and began recovery as a member of the Fellowship of Alcoholics Anonymous. In 1990, his interest in A.A.'s Biblical/Christian roots was sparked by his attendance at A.A.'s International Convention in Seattle. He has traveled widely; researched at archives, and at public and seminary libraries; interviewed scholars, historians, clergy, A.A. "old-timers" and survivors; and participated in programs and conferences on A.A.'s roots.

The author is the owner of Good Book Publishing Company and has several works in progress. Much of his research and writing is done in collaboration with his older son, Ken, an ordained minister, who holds B.A., B.Th., and M.A. degrees. Ken has been a lecturer in New Testament Greek at a Bible college and a lecturer in Fundamentals of Oral Communication at San Francisco State University. Ken is a computer specialist and director of marketing and research in Hawaii ethanol projects.

Dick is a member of the American Historical Association, Research Society on Alcoholism, Alcohol and Drugs History Society, Organization of American Historians, The Association for Medical Education and Research in Substance Abuse, Coalition of Prison Evangelists, Christian Association for Psychological Studies, and International Substance Abuse and Addictions Coalition. He is available for conferences, panels, seminars, and interviews.

Good Book Publishing Company Order Form

(Use this form to order Dick B.'s titles on early A.A.'s roots and successes)

Qty.	Titles by Dick B.	Price
____	*A New Way In*	$19.95 ea. $ _____
____	*A New Way Out*	$19.95 ea. $ _____
____	*Anne Smith's Journal, 1933-1939*	$22.95 ea. $ _____
____	*By the Power of God: A Guide to Early A.A. Groups and Forming Similar Groups Today*	$23.95 ea. $ _____
____	*Cured! Proven Help for Alcoholics and Addicts*	$23.95 ea. $ _____
____	*Dr. Bob and His Library*	$22.95 ea. $ _____
____	*Dr. Bob of Alcoholics Anonymous*	$24.95 ea. $ _____
____	*God and Alcoholism*	$21.95 ea. $ _____
____	*Good Morning! Quiet Time, Morning Watch, Meditation, and Early A.A.*	$22.95 ea. $ _____
____	*Henrietta B. Seiberling*	$20.95 ea. $ _____
____	*Introduction to the Sources and Founding of A.A.*	$22.95 ea. $ _____
____	*Making Known the Biblical History and Roots of Alcoholics Anonymous*	$24.95 ea. $ _____
____	*New Light on Alcoholism: God, Sam Shoemaker, and A.A.*	$24.95 ea. $ _____
____	*Real Twelve Step Fellowship History*	$23.95 ea. $ _____
____	*That Amazing Grace: The Role of Clarence and Grace S. in Alcoholics Anonymous*	$22.95 ea. $ _____
____	*The Akron Genesis of Alcoholics Anonymous*	$23.95 ea. $ _____
____	*The Books Early AAs Read for Spiritual Growth*	$21.95 ea. $ _____
____	*The Conversion of Bill W.*	$23.95 ea. $ _____
____	*The First Nationwide A.A. History Conference*	$22.95 ea. $ _____
____	*The Golden Text of A.A.*	$20.95 ea. $ _____
____	*The Good Book and the Big Book: A.A.'s Roots in the Bible*	$23.95 ea. $ _____
____	*The Good Book-Big Book Guidebook*	$22.95 ea. $ _____
____	*The James Club and the Original A.A. Program's Absolute Essentials*	$23.95 ea. $ _____
____	*The Oxford Group and Alcoholics Anonymous*	$23.95 ea. $ _____
____	*Turning Point: A History of Early A.A.'s Spiritual Roots and Successes*	$29.95 ea. $ _____
____	*Twelve Steps for You*	$21.95 ea. $ _____
____	*Utilizing Early A.A.'s Spiritual Roots for Recovery Today*	$20.95 ea. $ _____
____	*When Early AAs Were Cured and Why*	$23.95 ea. $ _____
____	*Why Early A.A. Succeeded*	$23.95 ea. $ _____

(Order Form continued on the next page)

Good Book Publishing Company Order Form
(continued from the previous page)

Order Subtotal: $ _____

Shipping and Handling (S&H) **: $ _____

(** For Shipping and Handling, please add 10% of the Order Subtotal for U.S. orders or 15% of the Order Subtotal for international orders. The minimum U.S. S&H is $5.60. The minimum S&H for Canada and Mexico is US$ 9.95. The minimum S&H for other countries is US$ 11.95.)

Order Total: $ _____

Credit card: VISA   MasterCard   American Express   Discover   (circle one)

Account number: _____   Exp.: _____

Name: _____ (as it is on your credit card, if using one)

(Company: _____)

Address Line 1: _____

Address Line 2: _____

City: _____ State/Prov.: _____

Zip/Postal Code: _____ Country: _____

Signature: _____ Telephone: _____

Email: _____

No returns accepted. Please mail this Order Form, along with your check or money order (if sending one), to: Dick B., c/o Good Book Publishing Company, PO Box 837, Kihei, HI 96753-0837. Please make your check or money order (if sending one) payable to "Dick B." in U.S. dollars drawn on a U.S. bank. If you have any questions, please phone: 1-808-874-4876 or send an email message to: dickb@dickb.com. Dick B.'s web site: www.DickB.com.

If you would like to purchase Dick B.'s entire 29-volume reference set on early A.A.'s roots and successes (and how those successes may be replicated today) at a substantial discount, please send Dick B. an email message or give him a call.

Paradise Research Publications, Inc.
PO Box 837
Kihei, HI 96753-0837
(808) 874-4876
Email: dickb@dickb.com
URL: http://www.dickb.com/index.shtml
http://www.dickb-blog.com

3100383

Made in the USA